...God's
Still Calling...

...finding
GOD'S FINGERPRINTS

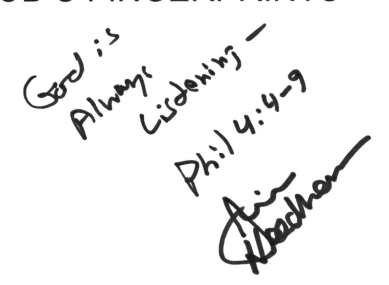

God is
Always
Listening —
Phil 4:4-9

James R Needham

ISBN 979-8-88685-934-8 (paperback)
ISBN 979-8-89130-357-7 (hardcover)
ISBN 979-8-88685-935-5 (digital)

Christian Faith Publishing
832 Park Avenue
Meadville, PA 16335
www.christianfaithpublishing.com

Printed in the United States of America

The Celtic cross on the cover is from the tiny island of Iona, just west of the Isle of Mull in the Outer Hebrides, across a narrow neck of ocean that connects with Edinburgh, Scotland. In 563 AD, St. Columba and a dozen of his Christian brothers established their first Celtic church and monastic community there. This cross on Iona is the symbol of the early community that ultimately spread Christianity to Scotland, England, and mainland Europe.

Contents

Preface ix

Acknowledgments xi

Chapter 1: The Beginning.. 1

Chapter 2: Beginnings 4

Chapter 3: Grandpa's Early Days................................... 12

Chapter 4: Trying to Get Noticed.................................. 18

Chapter 5: Cedar Lake, Indiana: Living on a
"Real Farm"... 23

Chapter 6: Time to Be a City Boy 28

Chapter 7: You Got Trouble, My Friend—Right Here 39

Chapter 8: Turning a Corner.. 44

Chapter 9: The Biggest Step So Far 48

Chapter 10: Trippin' in Israel: Unforgettable 50

Chapter 11: My Job Now, Going Forward....................... 53

Chapter 12: Music Is My Life... 55

Chapter 13: Flunking a Physical and My Master's 59

Chapter 14: I Made It Through the Rain 67

Chapter 15: TV Producer at Last.................................... 69

Chapter 16: TV Changes Lives for the Better.................. 74

Chapter 17: Indianapolis, Here I Come 82

Chapter 18: Young Life: Getting Ready for What Is Next ... 86

Chapter 19: The Climb of a Lifetime................................ 90

Chapter 20: God's Surprise: Who Is Corrie TenBoom?.... 94

Chapter 21: How Do I Grow My Faith?........................... 103

Chapter 22: A New General Manager at WIPB-TV 116

Chapter 23: Who Is This Woman? 121

Chapter 24: The Approval Tour...................................... 128

Chapter 25: Vacations 134

Chapter 26: Missionaries to Utila.................................. 138

Chapter 27: My Parents and Their Last Days 144

Chapter 28: Bob Ross and the *Joy of Painting*.............. 154

Chapter 29: Other Notable Prayer Life Events and
Our Accident 159

Chapter 30: God Prepares a Place for Me in Korea....... 169

Chapter 31: Nazareth to Jerusalem: God Is My Witness... 181

Chapter 32: Mother, Wife, Boss (My Gift from God)....... 190

Chapter 33: How God Prepared Me for Teaching 200

Chapter 34: Some Final Stories That Must Be Shared 209

Chapter 35: Burglarized—God or Fear?........................ 222

Chapter 36: A Hobby in My Spare Time, After All That... 227

Chapter 37: Leaving WIPB-TV for Good 234

Chapter 38: Other Children Who Have Chosen Us........ 238

Chapter 39: Other Life Lessons and What I Truly
Believe 245

Chapter 40: Just a Few More Stories 257

Chapter 41: Other Strange and Unforgettable
Experiences 262

Chapter 42: An Out-of-This-World Adventure................. 269

Chapter 43: So How Does God Grow Faith in Him
in Me? 273

Chapter 44: My Family's Encounter with God and
Prayer 276

Chapter 45: Life After Life—You're Kidding, of Course? ...286

Chapter 46: The Incredible Woman Who Had
Ninety-Nine Kids—What Could I Learn? 289

Chapter 47: Crutches, Wheelchairs, Canes—
Everywhere.. 293

Chapter 48: Bible Roulette 295

Chapter 49: You Scream; I Scream—We All Scream.....300
Chapter 50: Spiritual Gifts 302
Chapter 51: Dieting—Do We Know What We're Doing?...306
Chapter 52: Leading Me Through My Shadow of
                        Death: Cancer...309
Chapter 53: Truth Is Stranger Than Fiction: Where
                        Are You Now, God?....................................315
Chapter 54: THE BEST FOR LAST 319
My FINAL Thoughts and My Blessing for You 325
Epilogue..329

Preface

This book is dedicated to the grandchildren who asked the question: Addison, Aubrey, Steve, and Ben, and to the other five who weren't there but who are loved just as much and who were not able to participate in the "birthing" of this lengthy, familial tome. My hope is you will all benefit generously from what I have shared.

So for Arianna, Elliott, Sofia, Nathan, and Caroline, thanks for being a part of our family and also for being willing to jump in and see the humor in some of this and the love that permeates everything that is related here. All of it is true from my perspective, though as I talk with each of you, your memories of some of these things may differ from mine. I have had a wonderful life with all of you, and as always, when you love someone, you never do get enough time with them. Let's keep working at that, and maybe over the next period of years, we'll be able to add something to these stories that will be a benefit to you and additional joy for Grandma and me. We love each and every one of you, are proud of you, and we love it when we can be with you.

Finally, I want to include the most important person in my life—my partner, confidante, and the love of my life who has carefully made her way through this "screenplay," corrected some of what could be corrected, and marveled that I lived through the rest of it. Writing this book for you has been an adventure of a lifetime, and for that, I am grateful to God that it was the path He laid out for me.

I do believe that God is sovereign and that nothing that happens to us is a surprise to Him. I also believe that He goes before us every step of the way and never leaves us or forsakes us, and in the midst of our triumphs and tragedies, He is there waiting to help and nurture us through these passages, and never leaves us alone, without hope. There is always a way. That is true for me and Grandma, and it is equally true for you.

Finally, I thank God I was born when and where I was in New Albany, Indiana, and for the parents who raised me and tolerated my growing up and nurtured me until I was able to stand on my own two feet and move out on my own. It was a bumpy journey, but a good one, and unforgettable. Most of all, I learned to love other people, to love God, and to recognize His fingerprints all around me, almost all of the time. That is one of the greatest gifts my parents helped me discover.

One other thought as you begin: I don't know where I heard it or learned it, but I do believe it to be true in my own life and in the lives of others who recognize that God is Love. "Love is the only thing that exists that, the more you give away, the more you have." It mirrors Jesus' second great commandment—to love your neighbor as yourself.

Acknowledgments

Thank you for picking up this book to join me in the journey of finding out who I am and Whose I am. Whoever you are, whether we know each other or are just being introduced here, I want you to have this. That means my desire and prayer for YOU is for you to become the very best version of you that you can possibly be for as long as you can, and that you will have peace, fulfillment, and joy and a close relationship with God throughout all your life. When that happens for you, I will feel like I have done my job and that my time on earth accomplished much of what God intended for me.

It is impossible to take credit for who I am because I am the result of countless gifts and instances of unmerited favor from God Who numbered my days while I was being formed in my mother's womb (see Psalm 139:16), gifts from my parents whom I knew well, my grandparents—most of whom I never knew well, from my sisters and brother, my children, my grandchildren, our six "grafted-in kids" we have added over the years, and from my exceptional wife, who still teaches me daily and has improved this labor of love with her insightful comments and questions before it could be published.

I could not have begun this work or project that is now in its sixth year of quiet time in front of our laptop, often in the Yorktown Library, without the respites from our day-to-day life at home. In that sense, the energy I've dedicated over the last five winters has been well-invested because I can finally see the light at the end of the tunnel. If I had realized it would take almost six years to complete, I might not have begun this project. But for the prompting of my grandchildren, I still might not have completed it. But they have mercilessly prompted me without hesitation. And to their credit, here it is.

Linda is not only my generous, long-suffering wife, but the principal partner in all that I do and the encourager and audience for my successes and detours that regularly crowd our lives with peaks and valleys. Over the years, they have continued to bring joy and tears in times of celebration and a deepening commitment to the things that must be addressed now, and in some instances, are mercifully, back-burnered forever.

This work is also a testimony to Linda's patience and her ability to find her own rhythm and allow me to find mine and to focus on what I believe is important when others might think I am on a fool's errand in trying to recover so many stories, allegories, and wise sayings, diving into situations where we are invited but unaware of where we are being led.

Most of all, I cherish Linda because we share a conviction that the most important person in our lives is Jesus Christ. Without that shared Central Presence, we never would have gotten together in the first place. To that end, we are most grateful to Dr. Alan Habanski, who counseled Linda, in the midst of her questioning after the death of her husband Steve—the father of our three children, that she should go home and fix the hottest bath she could tolerate, pour herself a glass of wine, and then get in the tub, sip the wine, and read the book of James.

When she met me, she told me the story, and I remember saying, "I'm glad Alan gave you a prescription for taking care of your backache. Here I am." And she laughed.

Did that really happen? It did…the kind and insightful friend and doctor, the wine, the book of James, and me.

What follows is what happened before she read the book of James and drank the wine and soaked in the tub. It transformed Linda's life, and Linda and our three children, in turn, have transformed mine in a wonderful and fulfilling way that only someone responding to the nudging of the Holy Spirit could embrace a person like me—a man wanting to find a woman who loved God first and that would invite me to make a home with her and our three children where, together, we would nurture, inspire, protect, and guide each other in the paths that led to a fulfilling life and a happy home for themselves and their children as they meandered and sometimes, "charged" through the seasons of their lives.

Finally, I want to thank our children, who have lived through much of my life (now forty-five years and counting), and the other important persons who have become part of our family, sometimes through no fault of their own. Occasionally, some have asked if they could be "adopted in" because they too wanted to be beneficiaries of "the promise" that God gives to all of us who call each other, for those who choose to believe, "brothers and sisters in Christ." We love each of them, and they are welcome in our family.

These others, now six in all (five married and one wanting to be), and counting spouses—ten in all, with seven additional "grandchildren"—they make up quite a crowd of witnesses to many of the events recounted here. In other situations, they have been the audiences for some of these stories (though sometimes told differently by Linda or Steve or Kirsten or Brian), depending on the year, the day, or the hour and the company where the storytelling happened. In the midst of this narrative, they will surely recognize much of what I have recounted below.

These stories are true to the best of my recollections and are intended to be shared here with those to whom this is addressed and honored and those who get to observe from a distance, this tale of intimacy in its loose chronology that mirrors my peripatetic life. These witnesses also have been

able occasionally, to eavesdrop on the exciting and dangerous adventures that have, on and off again, depended partly
or wholly on God's grace or on His hand to make it possible
for me to survive and tell these tales at last.

I am grateful that some of my memories are incomplete,
such that they will not frighten you the way they frightened
me or overwhelm you the way my visit from the angel of the
Lord amazed and confounded me in a very early morning
dream in 2007.

Linda's practical approach counseled me to recognize
that unless I judiciously reduced the tonnage of this book
to manageable dimensions—from what she characterized
as "too long" to its present length, most of you would be
fast asleep before you could absorb the myriad details and
minutia that led you astray. As it is, there are many adventures and misadventures included. Some will amuse you or
shock you—some will make you cry with me, and I suppose,
some could bore you out of your mind or, at best, given so
much to chew on, relegate Grandma and me to a status
where we might never be invited to visit you again for fear
that I would pick up where I left off.

Having said all that, I want to thank our grandchildren
for your love and support through this project and for periodically urging me to finish what I started. I do claim to have
some expertise in writing, though it was passing, and comes
initially from interviewing twenty-four mystery writers from
Ball State's Midwest Writers' Workshop when the interviewer turned up sick and I got to step in with no notice and
do twenty-four half-hour interviews. It was energizing, and
it enabled me to learn how these authors wrote, what motivated them, what form their writing took, how they developed plots and subplots, and what their writing habits were
like. Unfortunately, it appears I did NOT learn how to write
really terse, tight, short sentences, did I?

At High Street Methodist Church, I also taught the
elderly classes for twenty-six years and, every week, wrote

the discussion notes for what we spent an hour pondering and celebrating. As I look back, I have had a bit of practice saying what I want to say. I would be remiss if I didn't mention that in my six years as an undergraduate and graduate student, I successfully completed the required assignments for my BS in Psychology and Theater and MS in Radio-TV at Indiana State University.

Okay, I promise—no more long sentences. So I've done a lot of writing—different kinds of writing—enjoyed much of it, and have not proofed all of it as carefully as my secretary, Patti Foster, proofed each of our Grant Applications. Over the years, we were successful in obtaining several million dollars in grants for WIPB. Much of the credit for the station's success goes to Patti for her keen eyes, great sense of humor, due diligence, and excellent questions to which I found good answers. That success also belongs to an extraordinary team of Program Directors, Development Directors, and Engineers, all of whom generously shared their expertise and genius to make WIPB and me look really good. For each of them, I remain eternally grateful. We succeeded handsomely, and the new station built in the Ball Building in 1988, during my tenure and because of our programming, in large part with the help of the Speaker of the Indiana House, Bob Dailey, is testimony to that. I recognize that God has placed the right people on my teams, again and again. The evidence is unequivocal.

So for most of what you are reading, others must share much of the credit. For the difficulties and mistakes made along the way that allowed me to finally ask Jesus to take control of my life at the age of thirty-one, I bear full responsibility. I'm just glad I didn't muddle through more years trying to do what Frank Sinatra sang of in "My Way." At that point, I'd had enough of living my life "my way," and I was ready for something better. I found it, as you'll see in the parking lot of WISH-TV on October 15, 1975, two years to the day before I married Linda... Oops. It appears that I ran out of battery in my laptop. That's a not-so-subtle signal that it's time to let you check out the Beginning, and see how the "joust" that emerged as this book, commenced.

In various ways known only to me, each of you, as family or close friend, or curious reader has enriched my life and added to my "trust walk with God" and my willingness to grow and learn more about Him. However, you should recognize that my wife, Linda, is not responsible for what is in this book: I am, and I have continued to thank God for guiding me to remember the things that would add to this recitation and disregard the ones that would detract, throughout its creation.

Chapter 1

The Beginning

We sat at the breakfast bar. Here we were, having Thanksgiving 2017 in our son Steve's house. He and his wife, Staci, had fixed an incredible meal. Steve had baked a great turkey. Stevie had fixed his usual Vegan lunch salad, and we were all sitting around, talking after most of the meal had been finished. Maybe we were on dessert by then. Our daughter Kirsten's children, Addison and Aubrey, were there. Steve and Staci's boys, Steve and Ben, were there, and they were all asking, "What did you do before you met Grandma? Were you always a professor?" I had chosen to sit with our grandchildren instead of the full table of adults where I usually found my place.

This wasn't an ordinary Thanksgiving after all. They wanted to know... So I told them a story, and their eyes glistened with rapt attention. That was the beginning. I had never thought of writing an autobiography before. Then, there it was in front of me. Should I ask? And I did: "If I wrote about all the things that happened before Grandma and your parents entered my life, would you read it?"

"Yes," they chorused. "Oh yes! What were you doing when you met Grandma?"

So I resolved to write an autobiography. You're now in on where this book started. Did I want to do this? No, not until they asked me to. But now that I'm started, I simply must finish… (That's easier said than done.) If you've ever started on this journey, you know it's longer than it seemed that sunny afternoon there lingering over our pumpkin pie, too much to eat, and lots of love and laughter.

"Where do I start? I asked myself. "Where does it all begin?" I was clueless.

The Minnetrista Cultural Center is a community gathering place and museum celebrating the industry, arts, and heritage of East Central Indiana.

Weeks later, The Minnetrista Cultural Center (now "Minnetrista") called me to ask if I would be willing to do an interview about the painting show we had done at our PBS Station I had managed from 1976 until 1993. Along the way, we met and worked with Bob Ross, the soft-spoken, talented painter who painted his way into the hearts of tens of millions of Americans and ultimately, through his YouTube channel and other venues, into many tens of millions all over the world, with his "mighty brush," his wet-on-wet oil painting techniques, his wacky sense of humor, and irrepressible optimism.

We loved Bob at the station, and people in their homes and on their devices, made Bob Ross the most watched painter in all of history. He still is as I write this in 2023. Only now, living through the Covid-19 Pandemic, Bob has become the comforting presence to many more millions, looking for sanity in a world where hope is harder to come by than a pizza delivery-person without a mask. It is strange indeed and not something anyone would have wanted or anticipated when I first started writing this book.

I gave Minnetrista the interview with the condition that they would provide a transcript. They agreed, and as I revisited my life, the recorder capturing my thoughts and memories, the stories that are my life came spilling out. This was a beginning.

For the sake of my grandchildren who now number "nine," I am writing this book and limiting its length, so as not to bore them nor give them more detail than I should. We all have secrets, and some are better left where they now rest in peace, in the decades of my past.

There are others, however, the "meat and potatoes" of my life, that bear revisiting here. I hope they will intrigue you, cause you to laugh, cause you to be amazed and to cry, and to relish the idea that we are all human and depend more on the grace of God than our own intellect, God-given gifts, subterfuge, or unwillingness to go the extra mile. I wish I could say I have not been guilty of any of these at one time or another, but I don't want to play the spoiler. Initially, I was never very good at "coloring inside the lines." From very early, that was a problem and also in strange ways, frequently a blessing. My curiosity prompted my energy and also many of my dilemmas. You'll see...

Chapter 2

Beginnings

My life began in 1944, two years after my brother Fred, who was already a toddler at the time of my arrival. While he was born in a little Red Schoolhouse on the outskirts of New Albany, Indiana, I was born in town at Silvercrest Hospital, where my twenty-eight-year-old mother went into labor early on a Sunday morning in July.

My parents' first jobs had been as high school teachers in Clearspring, Indiana, a small town in Jackson County in southern Indiana, following their graduations from Indiana State Teachers College in Terre Haute, Indiana in 1938 and 1939. They lived in a small upstairs apartment in town. And my mother taught Home Economics and English; my father taught Science, Music, and Physical Education classes.

Two years later, they found themselves in New Albany where my father continued teaching, and my mother stayed home with my brother while expecting me. During the summer following my birth, we moved to Terre Haute to live near my dad's parents, with World War II still in full fury. My father had decided by then to return to school and get his Master's Degree from Indiana State, and got a job working in a smokeless powder plant in close-by Newport, Indiana, to help with the war effort and pay the bills.

After a year of working in the factory and taking night classes, my dad decided working full time and being up half the night with an infant in the house, wasn't working, so he enlisted in the Army in the summer of 1945. Before he was called up, the recruiter called my dad and told him not to report because the war had ended in Europe. And it was about to end in Japan; the recruiter said they probably wouldn't need him.

As it worked out, that is exactly what happened. The smokeless powder plant shut down, and my mom and dad moved on to Goshen for my dad's new job there, teaching chemistry at Goshen High School where the Principal, Tom Starr, was married to Grandma Linda's mother's sister, your Great Aunt Emma Starr. It was fall 1945, and though I was to reconnect with those very same families many years later, at that time in Goshen, the Starr's and Loat's and Needham's never met.

Grandma Linda Loats had been born in 1943 in Youngstown, Ohio, while her father was in the US Navy. When Henry Loats left the Navy in 1946, he moved to Ball State Teachers' College to begin teaching Industrial Education classes, and the rest is history. He and his wife, Ruth Ridenour Loats (born and raised in Modoc, Indiana about ten miles east of Muncie) moved to Muncie in 1946 for good, and Linda lived near the Ball State campus with her parents until she married Steve Slavin in the summer of 1964.

Grandma Linda was an exemplary student at Ball State Teachers College and graduated in three years after attending fall, spring and summer semesters and living just west of the Industrial Arts Building in Westwood with her parents. Linda was also very active in her Pi Phi Sorority and was an outstanding, serious student with a loaded schedule. She was a Home Economics and Science major and graduated in three years and a summer Magna Cum Laude with a 3.92 GPA. That's one of the reasons I always say when she questions me, "You're right, Linda." And she almost always is.

I have a special sign I found that fits her and is on her desk, since I bought it: "Mother/ Wife/ Boss!" Grandma likes that, and so do I, most of the time. Linda lived there with her parents near Ball State until she married Steve Slavin, following her July 1964 graduation, and moved to Indianapolis where Steve attended Indiana University Dental School.

While he finished his DDS, Linda taught at Ben Davis Junior High School on the west side of Indianapolis. They lived there until Steve graduated, and then, along with Linda's "tummy bump" (Kirsten), returned to Muncie in June 1967 to go into practice with his father, Chuck Slavin, and later, Steve's brother Chad, in the Slavin Dental Clinic.

A word about Linda's marriage to Steve, and Linda's three children: Kirsten, Steve and Brian. Shortly after their move to Muncie, Kirsten arrived in mid-July 1967. She attended Mitchell Elementary, Storer Middle School, and Northside High School. She was a popular cheerleader for six years, a beautiful dancer and excellent student and gymnast and lived with us in Muncie until she attended Indiana University in the fall of 1985.

There, Kirsten became a Kappa Alpha Theta, danced in the IU Modern Dance Company, majored in Telecommunications, and met her first husband, Tom Housand. They were married in 1990 in Muncie and lived in Cincinnati, Indianapolis, and then South Bend where Tom completed his MBA at Notre Dame. Shortly after that, they moved to Elkhart, Indiana where Addison, their first child, was born in April 1997, with Aubrey quickly following in late December 1998.

Addison and Aubrey both attended Indiana University, just as their parents had. Addison graduated in 2018 and went to work with Abercrombie and Fitch in Columbus. After one year with that company, she moved to a better position with Target Corporation in Minneapolis for a great new job working from home during Covid, and living closer to her boyfriend, Michael.

Aubrey (Aubs) graduated in 2021 after doing design work for the Indiana Student Union. She works for a wonderful start-up called The Farmer's Dog which is headquartered in New York City and is continuing her design work in their advertising program.

Unfortunately, after eighteen years of marriage, Kirsten and Tom divorced, and after seven years as a single mom and dating Eric Hammonds, Eric and Kirsten married in October 2019. Eric has his own business with his father, Tom, and Eric's daughter, Caroline, is majoring in Industrial Design at Purdue University. Meanwhile, Kirsten and Eric are proud of their girls' professions and collegiate choices, and Kirs and Eric continue their own successful careers in manufacturing and payroll services.

Kirsten's brother, Steve, was born during the time of the *Apollo 11* Mission that landed man on the moon. Steve has always been involved in numerous activities along with his work, and it truly seems his feet have yet to touch the ground. He is always busy at something and has the energy of a shooting star.

Steve also grew up in Muncie as a Northside High School Titan, and like his sister, began Indiana University in the fall of 1987. Steve had a great time at IU, majoring in Economics, Acoustic Guitar, and serving as Fiji social chairman before graduating in the spring of 1991. He immediately started coaching tennis at the Muncie YMCA and then became an Insurance Broker for Northwestern Mutual Life. Next, Brian and Steve created the rock band, Clifton Wells, honored Grandpa Loats with *The Loats Letters'* CD album and played dates in Muncie, Indianapolis, and surrounding venues part time for the next three years. While the band was a dream come true, it didn't make enough to survive, and other options had to be explored.

In the interim, Steve gave up insurance, continued as a YMCA Tennis Pro, and earned his Stock Brokerage credentials. Then in 1995, Steve fell in love and married Staci

Smiley of New Castle. Their first son, Stephen Douglas was born in 1998. Ben showed up in September 2000, and the rest is history... They celebrated twenty-five years of marriage in November 2020. See Steve or Staci or their boys for more details. They have had an exciting life and moved more than all the rest of us combined. Staci is a Decorator with Inland Interiors, and Steve is the Managing Broker for Coldwell Banker Real Estate in Muncie.

Their son Steve is now in the US Army stationed in Colorado Springs, and Steve and his younger brother, Ben, have both completed internships with Disney World in Orlando, while receiving high marks for their work ethic and follow-through and offers of jobs there, when they graduated. Steve interned in Hospitality. Ben interned in Business Management. Ben, who graduated from Ball State's Miller College of Business in 2023, is considering management jobs in Indiana and Florida and is planning on marriage to fiancée Kaylyn Hewitt by the year's end.

Grandson Steve has committed to his second stint in the Army and will be moving to his next assignment shortly, where he hopes to complete his ranger training and earn a promotion.

Linda's youngest, Brian, was born in May 1974, and for that summer and the next year, there were three small children, a happy wife, and a new Muncie School Board Member in their beautiful Queensbury home. Earlier that year, their father, Steve, had joined his father in the Slavin Dental Clinic in Muncie, and had been elected to the Muncie School Board with Linda going door to door to help him win the campaign. It was a happy time, and they looked forward to a bright future.

Then in early November 1975, Steve and his brother, Chad, cousin Sam Wearly, and Steve's friend Ron Wiehe flew down to Arkansas on a weekend fishing trip to Mountain Home, Arkansas. They had great fishing, but as they were taking off from the grass strip there into a crosswind,

Steve and his close friend, Ron—in the copilot's seat—were killed instantly during take-off. Steve was regarded by all who knew him as a careful pilot with an instrument rating, but shifting winds and gusts that day, caused unexpected turbulence, and the Piper Cherokee never cleared the trees.

Chad and cousin Sam Wearly, in the back seats, were gravely injured, and they both recovered eventually. Steve and Ron, in the front seats, died in the accident. Life had changed forever for Linda and their three children. Brian had been born in May 1974 and was 18 months old when his father died. It was a difficult time for Linda and the kids. Life would never be the same. Along with the community who had loved Steve and Linda, they all mourned his loss and the dramatic change that had come so quickly to their eleven short years together.

In 1974, I was still working at WISH-TV in Indianapolis, oblivious to what was happening in Muncie. That was destined to change.

Brian grew up in our Queensbury house, attended Michell School, the Halteman Village Pool (on his Big Wheel tricycle at four years old), Storer Middle School, Muncie Central for one year, and three years later, graduated from Delta High School where he was an outstanding swimmer. For a short time, Brian was a volunteer Young Life leader, and went to Young Life Camp in Colorado and Minnesota, and as a Freshman, Brian attended Taylor University.

Brian majored in Art his freshman year at Taylor but wanted the challenge of a more diverse Art Department and transferred to Ball State for his last four years. In 1997, Brian graduated with his BFA in Fine Arts from Ball State, having mastered pottery, drawing, painting, jewelry, and sculpture. He loved working with his hands and would have favorably impressed his Grandpa Henry Loats who died in 1985 and had taught Industrial arts and was an artist himself. Brian's favorite memories with me were attending the Clay Courts

Tennis tournaments in Indianapolis and the Reds Baseball games in Cincinnati.

After school, Brian sojourned in New York City for 7 months, but returned to Muncie to study Massage Therapy and Yoga, and for a time, played bass guitar in the band, Clifton Wells. In 1999, he fell in love and married Laura King, and they had two children: Arianna in 2001 in Muncie, and after their move to Middlebury, Vermont, Elliott was born in July 2005. Brian and Laura worked at the Middlebury Food Coop for ten years together. But after fifteen years of marriage, Brian and Laura divorced in 2016.

In 2017, Brian married Jennifer Stefani, and they live in Middlebury where Jennifer has a Counseling Practice, and Brian is a Massage Therapist. Jennifer has two children, Sofia, attending Williams College in Williamstown, Massachusetts, and Nathan, as I write this, a sophomore in high school. Brian and Laura's eldest, Arianna, finished high school in three years. After Circus Acrobatics Training at Loft Aloft in Chicago for two years, Arianna further perfected her juggling and acrobatic skills at the Quebec City Circus School for two more years and, just this year, auditioned and was hired for a four-month Mediterranean cruise. Brian's son, Elliott, has finished high school in three years and is planning on a Burlington school where he can complete his senior high school classes and get dual college credit as he searches for an engineering school where he can focus on a mechanical and engineering skill set. Elliot is now busy researching engineering options for college and his passion for jet airplane flight simulators and the baritone saxophone.

When I came on the scene, Linda was busy with Dental Wives' activities, Muncie Symphony League, and her children, and using Steve's life insurance policies to rebuild their lives and keep the home fires burning. She was working hard to keep the kids engaged with family, church, and friends and beginning to recognize she wanted and needed a husband to help with her children.

Linda was dating some and not necessarily looking for someone from "Showbiz" to light her fire, when I came along. Then, after a casual lunch and an afternoon of my shoveling crushed limestone in her backyard, her life changed forever. What a surprise!

In the interim, John Bowen, Ted Fullhart, and other men stepped in to work with the boys, and Linda and I will always be grateful for their generosity of spirit and for the time they dedicated to our boys as they continued to grow and develop friendships and family ties.

Chapter 3

Grandpa's Early Days

Now, let's skip back in time and go back and pick up the story of the Needham family once more. It is 1946. We had just moved from Terre Haute where my father did NOT report for the service and World War II on the advice of his recruiter. Instead, my dad got a teaching contract with Goshen High School to teach Science and Chemistry, the same school where Linda's Uncle Tom Starr was Principal.

At first in Goshen, my mother and father and my older brother Freddie and I lived in a pink stucco house with two bedrooms in the downtown area. My brother and I shared one of those rooms and lived there just over two years.

When I was four, my sister Nancy was born. Anticipating her birth, my parents built a new house on East Jackson Street, just outside the city limits East of town. We had a three-acre triangular pasture there where our Guernsey cow was free to roam, and a big lot for our house and the Truck Garden we planted each spring. The pasture was ample for our cow and a great place to play. It also had thistles everywhere, but they didn't bother Dolly Cow.

We loved the new house and the property where my father had built a huge swing and we had a long slide. We moved in just before my sister, Nancy was born in May 1948. With three bedrooms and a basement and a huge yard and pasture, we had lots of room to play. In the spring, we helped plant a substantial vegetable garden that we helped to weed and care for. My mother canned all kinds of vegetables: corn, beans, tomatoes, carrots, potatoes and fruit so we would have that to eat through the winter. We couldn't afford to buy canned vegetables and fruit all year round. On all sides, neighboring farmers planted fields full of corn, and we loved to play in them, especially in late summer when the corn grew tall, and we could play hide and seek among the stalks. We also built a large treehouse there in one of the trees in the nearest fencerow.

We had many wonderful days there at what my parents called, "Dolly Farm." It was like a continuous playground with our three-acre field and things to do, and the animals we had to play with and feed and clean up after...chickens, a pig, and our dairy cow. The pony came later and left the same day. What a disaster...well, I worked hard to provoke that—I wished I hadn't! But I was a rascal. I was always one-upping my older bother to get attention, and I made a costly mistake.

Four things I remember from living there: first, when I was four, my mother was washing diapers for my new baby sister (Nancy). Mom was in the basement where the washer was and also the clothes lines so we could dry our clothes indoors when the weather was bad, even though it was winter. We didn't have an electric or gas dryer. Although they were invented in 1937, home dryers did not become commonplace until the early 1960s, and because money was tight, we were not one of the early adopters.

To be safe, my mom always boiled the cotton diapers to make sure they were sterile and clean, since disposable diapers didn't come along until 1957 when Proctor and Gamble bought out Charmin Paper Company and experimented with paper diapers for the first time. Because of that, mom would boil them on the stove upstairs, bring them down to the basement, wring the hot water out, let them cool, and then hang them up to dry on clotheslines to take advantage of the furnace heat down there.

Second, my dad had taken my brother and me fishing a time or two and always warned me not to get into his fishing tackle box because of the sharp lures and fishhooks, and a knife or two. In spite of that, I was inordinately curious (I was always curious) and wanted to check it out. Telling me not to get into it just made me more curious. Years later, as I was living with my Grandmother Grace Boblitt Needham during my second year at Indiana State, she told me that I was very much like my father. I took that as a great compliment. It may have been more of an insightful observation that my dad had also had an insatiable curiosity, whether it was a good idea or not. I know I've occasionally been guilty of that failing myself.

Back to the basement in Goshen. In early December 1948, one morning, as my mother was washing my sister's diapers, I went down the basement stairs to see what she was doing. She was out of sight, around the corner of our large coal furnace, and when I went downstairs, there, in plain sight from where I stood on the stairs, wide-open on top of the work bench, sat my father's fishing tackle box. "Oh boy! Finally, a chance to check it out," I reasoned.

I quietly crept down the stairs, looked around for my mother who did not know I was there, and squeezed my legs in between what turned out to be "a pail of hot diapers" and the work bench. I was fiddling with the lures and knives and looking in the tackle box, when all of a sudden, I heard my mother coming around the furnace.

I turned to run. But as I twisted around to go, my legs abruptly caught between the bucket of boiling water and the workbench. I was busted! (We didn't know that word at the time, but you know what I mean.) I got caught! I faltered and lost my balance, sitting down in the boiling water!

"Yeowww!" The pain was unlike anything I had ever experienced, and it curdled my scream! "Yeowww!" I shouted again—and my terror filled the basement! Pain like nothing I'd ever even imagined wracked my small body, and I screamed again and again. My mother rushed to my side, lifted me under the arms and started to peel off my long underwear only to recognize my skin was stuck to it, and my boiled skin was starting to peel off. She was frantic!

I kept screaming, as she charged up the stairs, carrying me, her hands under my armpits, holding me away from her body, boiling water dripping everywhere.

I was screaming! I couldn't stop! She rushed to the phone—calling the ambulance; me SCREAMING IN THE BACKGROUND!

It is all a dream now, but then, it was a nightmare, punctuated by short breaths and screams. I was crying, and so was my mother. I'm sure she blamed herself, but neither of my parents ever spoke to me about it. No words were needed.

The pain was unbearable. I rode in the back of the ambulance on my belly, with my mother at my side. When I got to the hospital, they gave me pain medication, and then an ice bath to stop the burning. Then they put salve all over everything. The ice bath didn't totally stop the savage pain, but it helped.

After a while, I drifted off to sleep, and when I awoke, most of the pain was gone, and I was alone. I was on my stomach and was to remain there for the two weeks I lay in the hospital. I couldn't believe what I had done, and it was less than two weeks to Christmas. I wondered if Santa would find me in the hospital. What a terrible mistake I made, right before Christmas. I wished I hadn't disobeyed my father and played in his fishing tackle box. I never should have.

That was a tough lesson about learning to do what I was told. My parents never punished me or brought it up again. But I hurt for a long time and had to stay hospitalized until they could remove all the large blisters from my third-degree burns all over my behind. It was a tough and painful lesson.

The only positive memory was that Santa Claus came to see me in the hospital Christmas Eve, after all. He brought me two Hershey Bars and told me he was sorry I wouldn't be home for Christmas. He was right, but I enjoyed the chocolate bars he gave me and have always remembered that Christmas because it was the first one where I spent Christmas Eve alone—that year, in my hospital room. I remember, even now—I had been naughty and deserved to be punished. I guess in an indelible way, I was disciplined, far more than my parents would have if they had caught me and paddled me. What a mistake!

Fortunately, I survived without permanent damage, but for a long time, I had scars on my bottom as a reminder that rules matter and may be for my own good. My curiosity made me a slow learner.

Three other events at Dolly Farm stick in my mind: putting on shows for our gang of friends as a "Saturday Afternoon Hayride" (like the one we heard on WSM Nashville where we listened to the Grand Ole Opry Saturday nights on our radio). This was before we had television. My brother Fred and I would borrow my dad's tennis racquets for our shows and pretend they were guitars. Then we always invited all our friends from our neighborhood (maybe seven or eight of them would come) and we would stand up front on hay bales and pretend we were playing our mock guitars and sing Opry Songs like "The Tennessee Waltz." I dreamed then that one day, I would be standing on the stage of the Grand Ole Opry and singing to "my darlin…" just like I heard on the radio. Little did I know that years later, I would indeed stand on that very stage.

Second, my classmate, Judy Strang, was the first to have a small, round black and white TV in her house. Her father was a Contractor, and they had a big house. We heard about their TV and were really curious. We couldn't imagine it, but we wanted to see their TV.

Nonetheless, it was the early 1950s during the Polio scare and the Strang's weren't allowing anyone to go inside their house. It was too dangerous. We only got to see their TV a few times, and we watched it through Judy's glass storm door, sitting on the concrete steps where we could see and hear it.

Our favorite TV shows were *Howdy Doody and Buffalo Bob* and also *Super Circus* with Mary Hartline. It was the most magical thing I had ever seen. We didn't get a TV until a couple of years later. But watching it and seeing it for the first time really was a treat, and I hoped for the day when we might have a TV to look at that would make it so our family could more fully discover what was going on in the world.

Two years later, in 1952, we finally had a small round black and white TV, and we watched Britain's Queen Elizabeth II's Coronation from Westminster Abbey in London where Grandma Linda and I went to church on Sunday on our 1996 trip to England.

Watching that incredible coronation from halfway around the world was the most magical thing I had ever seen... images from across the world, happening right there in our living room. It was black and white, but it was beautiful, and we were excited to be participating in the Queen's Coronation, live from Great Britain. Wow! What a treat. I think I fell in love with television right then and there.

The last thing I remember from Goshen, clear as the daylights, was when my dad bought a pony for us when I was six. The good thing that turned out to be really bad was my brother was 8 and we had been going to the movies on Saturdays when we would walk downtown with a quarter each and would go see the cowboy movies starring Roy Rogers, Gene Autry, Pat Buttram, Hopalong Cassidy, or Tom Mix. We would see how they would get into trouble with putting burrs under someone's saddle, and everyone would laugh when the burr made the horse buck them off.

Chapter 4

Trying to Get Noticed

I was always trying to do something to win everyone's attention over my brother who would always obey all the rules. So when my dad brought a brown and white Pinto pony home as a surprise, he saddled it up for Freddie to take the first ride.

When my brother and dad went back to the shed for the bridle, I snuck a couple of burrs under the pony's saddle. Our pasture was full of Thistles, and I grabbed a couple of burrs. In the movies, cowboys got bucked off and never got hurt. I had seen Gene Autry's comic sidekick, Patrick Buttram do that, and I knew it wouldn't hurt my brother either, so I quickly went to work.

Freddie didn't see me do that, and neither did my dad. When he put Freddie on the pony, it began to buck and buck and buck! I was laughing, but my dad and Freddie were not laughing. My brother was screaming, and my dad grabbed the bridle, calmed the pony down, and helped Freddie out of the saddle.

Unfortunately, my dad decided then and there on the spot that the pony was too wild for two little boys to ever be able to ride it on their own. The next thing I knew, my dad was driving us to the farmer who had sold him the pony, returning the horse trailer he had borrowed, and giving our pony back to him, saying it was too wild for us to ever have any use for it. I was crushed. I was afraid.

I never told my brother or my dad what I had done with the pony when I was six until my father had had a stroke in 1995 at the age of seventy-nine. I was talking with my dad in the hospital one night, after he had his stroke, and when I told him, he said to me: "If you had told me the truth then, you would have gotten to keep the pony. I never knew you did that."

I know he forgave me for that and a lot of other stuff, but as it turned out, we never again had a pony of our own because of what I did. I still regret that, all these years later, but it was not meant to be, I guess. When I told my brother recently when he was eighty and still living in a long-term care facility, he said he never knew I had done that. He also wished I had told the truth at that time, but I wasn't secure enough to know what good would come from it. I just knew I would get paddled, and I just said nothing. I didn't want to take the punishment. That was a mistake. I was never meant to be a cowboy.

That fall, I went to school for the first time. There was no kindergarten, so I went to school with my brother on the yellow school bus, Freddie to Third Grade, and me to First Grade at Waterford School a couple of miles from town. When we got there, we were enrolled and were taught to read, write, and begin to do some simple math. As a part of my homework, we also were asked to memorize John 3:16 and recite it for the class. And in my class of about twenty-five, I was the first person to stand up in front of the class and recite it. "For God so loved the world that He gave His only begotten son, that whosoever would believe in Him would not perish but would have everlasting life." I wasn't really sure what all of that meant, but I learned the verse and got to stand up and recite it.

When I finished, my teacher, Mrs. Mast, thanked me for memorizing that verse and gave me a Red Paperback copy of the Gospel of John. I took it home, and my parents were really proud of me. I was proud that I had done that too. It was my first academic success and the first time I remember being rewarded for doing something good. I liked that feeling! As I look back on it, there was nothing wrong with that assignment.

Today, people feel differently since the activist judges started ruling against the inclusion of anything religious in schools in the early 1960s. Before that in America, it was fine to include assignments like that, and to talk about God in school and trust in God openly. I know it wasn't wrong. The Constitution doesn't forbid that, and neither did my school.

I've watched the changes, and even taught Media Law classes at Ball State University in the 1990s. Forbidding any religion in the schools is a recent judge-made ruling and trend that doesn't follow accurately what our founders had in mind for America. That's why In God We Trust was chiseled back into the wall above the Speaker's Chair of the US House of Representatives in the Capitol Building in Washington, DC, where it was originally engraved when it was rebuilt in 1815 after the War of 1812. Now, talking about God in school is no longer allowed in America except in religious schools that don't receive funding from the Federal Government. In my opinion, that is so wrong and so un-American.

I also remember clearly how we went to see our first color film ever in Goshen in 1952 of *Lassie Come Home* at the movie theater, although it was premiered across America near the end of World War II. The westerns were all sepia-tone or black and white, but the first color film we got to see was this one about the beautiful Collie named Lassie. We had a Collie/Shepherd mix named Tippy who was just like Lassie, and she was beautiful and smart and loved to play.

Shortly after I was six, we were in church one Sunday like we always were and mom and dad and my brother got up in the middle of the service to go and take communion. I said I wanted to go too, but my mom and dad told me I could not do that because I would not understand what communion was about until I was older. I remember sitting in the pew and crying because they all left me to sit there alone. I felt I was being punished and that because I was not always a good boy, they were making me sit this one out. I was devastated. They were right. I did not understand.

Back home again, I was inventive and often got us in trouble. For example, I taught my older brother how to pull out the drawers in the kitchen and use them as a step ladder to climb to the kitchen counter and reach above the cabinets to where my mother and father kept the cookie jar. That way, we could reach it and get cookies without them knowing it. At least that's what I thought. One day, my father came in and saw what I was doing, and he gave me a whipping. He told Freddie never to do that again, and he never did. Dad was right: I was the sparkplug.

In 1953, after a couple of years in our new house, my father came home from teaching and told us he had lost his job as a teacher in the high school when he failed the Superintendent's son in his chemistry class. The boy did failing work, and my dad gave him an F. When it came time to renew my father's contract, the Superintendent said dad was no longer welcome to teach at Goshen High School, and my father had to find another job. He decided to buy a Veedol Gas Station instead of teaching and go into business for himself. He did pretty well but worked very long hours.

My curiosity got the best of me another time when my father brought home a pistol from his Veedol gas station. I saw that he put it in his top dresser drawer and wondered what it would be like to look at it. Cowboys had pistols, and I had never seen one close up.

My dad had accepted the pistol in payment for repair services to someone's car, and he had agreed to hold it until the man paid his bill. I had other ideas, and the next day when my father was at work, I climbed up on a chair, opened the top drawer, and pulled the pistol out. I showed it to Fred who was serving as look-out, and I spun the cylinder in it. It had bullets in it, but I didn't pull the trigger or anything. I carefully put it back in the drawer, returned the chair to the dining room, and forgot all about it. When my dad opened his top dresser drawer again where he had hidden the gun under his clothes, he saw that it had been moved.

That night, when he came to dinner, he showed us the gun, told us he noticed it had been moved around, and that he was taking it that night to another person, and it would no longer be there in the house. He said he didn't know who had it out, but he looked straight at me, and I know he knew I had again broken the rules by getting into his drawer. I remember being surprised at how heavy it had been. I did try to put it back just the way it was, but he knew. We never saw it again.

Chapter 5

Cedar Lake, Indiana: Living on a "Real Farm"

Two years later, after moving to a different job in Chicago, my father moved us to Cedar Lake, Indiana, twenty-five miles from the Sherwin Williams Paint Plant where they made paints and inks. He was to work there the next twenty-seven years as the supervisor of a quality control laboratory where he tested incoming raw materials used to make the company products. He would take a sample of the liquid chemical in the railroad tank car, in a little cuplike cylinder on a stick, about half the size of my little finger and, on the basis of what my father's laboratory analysis of the contents showed, either accept or reject the delivery of that tank car with the thirty thousand gallons of chemicals it held.

That process amazed me: they could accurately determine the quality of the chemicals from that one small sample. His job was to use a Gas Chromatograph to analyze the chemical components in the shipment of those liquid chemical components that would ultimately make up the paints and inks that Sherwin Williams produced in his plant. He loved his work and supervised a laboratory crew of 4 chemists that were kept busy supplying high quality components for the broad offering of products Sherwin Williams made there.

Meanwhile, my brother and I had moved with our family to Cedar Lake, Indiana, and to Lincoln Elementary School. We had sold our new home in Goshen and were renting the Hired Hand's House— a large three-bedroom house where the owner of the Turnquist Farm had 280 acres, thirty-one head of dairy cows, several horses, a hundred chickens or more, a dozen hogs and several dogs and cats. This was like moving from the farm to the circus. There was lots more to do—many more things to play with—animals galore—and lots of chores we got to help with—UGH! The chores were fun at first—milking cows, helping with the haying (loading bales of hay on the wagons); shoveling manure—more UGH! And STINKO! Lots of it was fun. Some of it was real work. We learned a lot in a very short time.

We were again in seventh heaven with acres and acres to wander when we weren't doing chores at home or doing homework. With Freddie and me in fourth and second grades, we didn't have much homework and had plenty of time to survey our new digs.

We also had another empty bedroom upstairs near our room, with hardwood flooring, and in bad weather, we would draw a chalk circle on the floor and play marbles for hours at a time. I had a whole coffee can full of cat-eyes and steelies and a few shooters (larger marbles) and It was wonderful. I don't remember going to church there, but I'm sure we did. It is something we always did, every Sunday, and then we would come home to a big Sunday dinner that my mother had put on the stove in a pressure cooker before we left. It was always a great time together. Shortly after arriving there, my sister Mary Elizabeth was born in May 1952.

My memories of Cedar Lake come in two waves—the farm and the school. Turnquist Farm was like a step up toward heaven...so much acreage, woods and fields, a creek and a lake, and so many new animals to learn about and help feed, collect eggs from, milk the cows, and clean the barn by shoveling manure.

That sounded like fun, but in truth, it was a job that really stank bad. We would wear rubber boots, cover our noses with bandanas and use flat-blade shovels to put the cow manure we shoveled into a manure spreader wagon that the farmer would drive out to the fields and spread on the fields as fertilizer. It was a long time ago, but it is easy to remember that smelly job. I was only 8, but I remember it was not my favorite, and I did not like this part of farming nor, later, after I had done it a few times, getting up in the morning before dawn to help with the milking. I only did that a few times, but it made me appreciate farmers that did that every day of their lives. They milked early in the morning and again late in the afternoon.

The best part of farming was the rainy season when the fields would flood. It was kind of scary, but not when we decided to be like Huck Finn and Tom Sawyer. Larry Turnquist who was a couple years older than my brother decided we all needed a raft, and he and my brother built it out of two fifty-five-gallon drums and some wood planks wired onto the drums. Then we found a pole to maneuver ourselves around. I got to go too. It was reckless and dangerous, but it was an exciting adventure just like we had seen in the movie *The Adventures of Tom Sawyer*.

We were off on our adventure, got on the raft and away we went. The water was deep, over the top of the fenceposts, and we rafted from field to field. We were never told not to do this—we were just having a great time!

However, we ended up getting scolded big time when, afterward, we came into the house with the rich, sticky black mud caked all over our boots. Boy, did we get it. We had to clean up the house and also our boots. And we were never allowed to go rafting again! Darn! It was fun, if a little dangerous. As I look back, I couldn't even swim then, and the water was over my head every time we crossed the fenceposts.

So much for our "Adventures of Tom Sawyer foolery." We were grounded and forbidden to ever do that again. I didn't break this rule. My mom and dad were furious! We were definitely not going there again. But there were lots of other things to do. We played hide and seek, jumped off the bales of hay after climbing way up in the Hay-mow and leaping off, into the soft piles of hay, ten to fifteen feet below, only to climb up again and do it all over. It was dusty and hot and sticky, but we loved doing that, especially on rainy days. I also loved chasing my brother and his friend, Larry all over the farm.

Often, when we played hide and seek, Larry and my brother, Freddie would get tired of me tagging along, and suddenly, I was completely alone. So I had to find fun for myself. One day, after they disappeared, I discovered this beautiful kitty cat. It was different from the orange and white tabby-colored cats—the mousers we had in the barn, but it looked like a cat to me. However, I had never seen a cat like this before. It was black and white with a white stripe from its head to its tail. I chased it round and round and finally into Larry's grandmother's drive-in basement where she parked her car. The car was in it, and I chased that kitty around Grandma Turnquist's car a couple of times before I lost it. Then I headed home.

Woe was me! As I walked in the door, my mom started yelling at me. "Get out! Get out! Get back out on the back porch and take off your clothes. Why were you playing with a Skunk!"

"What's that," I asked, as she scrammed me out the door. I started stripping down to my underwear.

"No, NO!" she shouted. "Everything comes off. You're not putting any of this in our house. Get your clothes off and go upstairs and start a bath. I'll be up in a minute." She grimaced. It was a cruel lesson for me.

After two weeks of trying to air my clothes out on the back porch and a couple of Lye-soap baths, Mom burned the clothes. The smell would just not come out, and I was soon wearing my brother's old hand-me-down clothes from the year before that didn't fit right! Whatever, but they were the only clothes I had left. We got to buy one new set of clothes (jeans and a long sleeve shirt or two) for each school year from the Sears Mail Order Catalog, and we always outgrew them before we got new ones. But that year was different. I lost my jeans and shirt in this folly. After that, I always stayed far away from Skunks. That was a good idea, don't you think? El-Stinko! Ugh. AND I lost my good clothes.

I hadn't done anything bad on purpose. I had an allergy that caused me to have congested sinuses, and my nose would often need blowing. I didn't smell things very easily, so I never really knew what I had encountered, chasing the Skunk. I never even smelled the Skunk after it sprayed me. But Oh Boy! Everybody else did. Then my mom asked me a great question: "Why did you do that?" There went that year's set of new clothes. We were close to the wire on our finances, with my new baby sister. Now there were six of us to feed and clothe, and my dad was the only one working and commuting twenty-five miles each way each day to the South Side of Chicago for his work. We needed to move closer to his work.

Chapter 6

Time to Be a City Boy

When I turned eight, we moved to the south side of Chicago, to Dolton, Illinois—one of the many suburbs. We lived in a second-floor rental apartment with two bedrooms, an old-fashioned claw-footed tub, and a large living room, dining room, a kitchen, and a basement. We were only to live there for two years, but some pivotal things happened there to help me focus on what I wanted to be and who I was. I was not the angry, disobedient, self-centered person you have read about above, at least not totally self-centered. But I was confronted with things I did not understand and did not accept, at least at first.

Let me give you a few illustrations. First, we were able to see my father more than I remember ever seeing my father. He was not commuting one hour each way to work and was home when I got up in the mornings and when it was still light out and he drove into the driveway after work. All of that was new, and I was happy about that. My brother was in fifth grade, and I was now in third grade, and I was busy making friends and beginning to understand more about God. I was curious about who God was and we still went to church every week, as we always had.

My dad was good at surprising us too, beginning with Christmas the first year we were at 300 East 144th Street.

He came home one night and said he had rented a trailer for a friend of his so he could hide a train set in our basement and take it over to him Christmas Eve to surprise his son. When my dad arrived with the train set on two 4 x 8 foot pieces of plywood with train stations, snow, and houses and barns and railroad crossings all glued on—it was like, "Wow! This is SO AWESOME. What a lucky kid to get all this! It also had two transformers to run the trains. So dad asked us to help carry all that stuff in and stacked it near the wall so he and his friend could haul it out Christmas Eve after everyone went to bed so the man could surprise his lucky son.

We were really envious because it was a super-nice set, and we didn't even have a train, although we did have a real-life train, half a block away—the Chicago and Eastern Illinois Train tracks and switching yard was ever-present and noisy and just half a block East of us where they humped the box cars throughout the day, and sometimes into the night.

However, the train set wasn't for someone else. Christmas morning, my dad took us downstairs to the basement to stoke the coal furnace, and there it was—all set up for my brother and me to play with. It was one of the best Christmas presents ever. We loved the surprise and also learned not to believe everything my dad said around Christmas—you never knew if he was "blowing smoke" to surprise us as he did several more years in wonderful ways. We loved the surprises and didn't care when he told us white lies to snooker us with gifts we never imagined we would receive.

Like I said, the real trains were just about a half block east of us, and the Conductors sometimes threw us pieces of chalk if we saw them and called out "Chalk? Chalk?" Almost always, they would throw us smaller pieces of inch thick chalk that we would use to mark up the sidewalk for games like Hopscotch. It was also fun to run alongside the Caboose and call out to the Conductors for chalk, especially since they always smiled and laughed and threw some to us. We knew it wasn't the safest thing to do, but we didn't do that often, just when we were out of chalk.

We also harvested tadpoles from the ditches along the tracks each spring that often turned into frogs we had to release from the "live box" where we kept them when my dad wasn't taking us fishing. We also kept a Garter snake once, but it had an awful smell, and my mother quickly ordered it out of the house as "persona non grata!" I think we might have had it for a week, but it stunk. So it HAD to go. It belonged in the grass, not in our bedroom.

At this new place, my mother and father were very busy with my sisters, 2 and 6, and my brother was beginning to play a trombone and baritone in the band. I was intrigued since he practiced every day. Did I want to play a trombone? I looked it over and decided I would rather play a Cornet. So I started taking lessons and began to play in my school's band in fourth grade. I could sing too, and in fourth grade for the Christmas program, I sang a solo at the end of "Oh Holy Night."

Two things about that. I loved being the soloist. And my voice was changing. I missed the high note at the very end because my voice broke when I sang out "Oh Night Divine!" OUCH! Double OUCH! At that point, I decided I would never ever, EVER again sing a solo (at least until I could figure out where my voice was). It was no longer unwavering and soprano… it was bouncing irresponsibly between soprano and broken baritone. I wasn't singing ANY more solos. I was mortified. I could hit the notes, even the high ones, "most of the time," but sometimes, without warning, my voice broke. Jettison that! I'm done! I didn't sing again in public for about three years.

At the end of fourth grade, however, I did wear a tuxedo and a mustache and for the first time, I was in a play and was the villain in the role of "Mr. Memorize." As the villain, my job was to punish everyone who could not or would not "Memorize" the things they were supposed to do. My job was to discipline those who refused to comply by forcing them to eat Chalk-Dust (cut-up marshmallows). We had a lot of fun, and I loved acting on stage. It was easy, and I loved the costuming and play rehearsals. I also sneaked a few pieces of the prop "chalk-dust."

When the play ended, everyone in the audience cheered and cheered. I loved being the center of attention. It was the most fun I had had since beginning school. And I was encouraged because I had little trouble learning my lines, and I loved being deeply involved in the storyline of the play.

It was also at about that time that I was picked to be catcher for the Little League team "Pittsburgh Pirates." I loved being the catcher because I was in on every single pitch when we were on the field. I was catcher for four years, and I think I wrecked my knees because of that. My dad was the coach. I also joined a Cub Scout Pack and a Boy Scout Troup and went on camping trips with Cub Scouts, my Webelos Pack, and my Boy Scout Troop. I loved camping because our family had always camped on our vacations. We never stayed in a motel as a family growing up. We always either stayed in campgrounds or went to relatives houses for a visit.

When I graduated from Scouting, I joined our Explorer's Post. Each summer, my dad organized a trip to Ely, Minnesota where we canoed into the Quetico Provincial Park, an area of over 1 million acres of lakes and streams on the border with Canada and the Boundary Waters Canoe area in northeastern Minnesota. There, we portaged in all our equipment and everything except the fish we would eat for lunch and dinner, if the bears didn't break into camp.

One night, however, the bears did swim to the island we were camping on and scared the liver out of us! To keep the bears from eating all our food, we hung all our food in knapsacks on ropes, up in the trees, but the pots and pans still smelled like food, and the bears scattered them all over the camp. It was 2:00 AM but fortunately, though we had a close call and were scared, no one got hurt.

The closest I ever came to a bear was when we were portaging between two lakes, and my father, who was in the front of our canoe told me to turn around and see if we left anything behind at the last portage. We never heard it, but when I turned to look, there stood a black bear where we had been just seconds before. I looked quickly, kept paddling, and called back to my father: "No, nothing left, except that bear there, and he turned and laughed and kept paddling. It was closer than it sounds, but no one was hurt, and we were the last ones to push off our canoes. Thank God for that.

When I was ten, I remember beginning to get interested in reading the Bible. My parents had gotten me a New Testament and encouraged me to go to Methodist Youth Fellowship at our church, where my parents were sponsors. I began to be interested in what God wants us to be and to do with our lives. But I was still having problems with following the rules.

One day, for example, shortly after I had gotten a BB gun for my birthday, I was sighting in on a bird just above me and ready to shoot it and kill it when my dad pulled into the driveway. That would have been fine if I had been sighting in on a Sparrow. They were fair game, I had been told, but this was a Robin, something my dad had specifically warned me to leave alone and not shoot. I did not shoot, but he saw what I was doing. He got out of the car, and he was angry. My dad asked me, "What were you doing with that BB gun?"

I said "I was just sighting in on that Robin, but I wasn't going to kill it."

He asked me, "Do you remember what I told you when we got you the BB gun—how you had to leave Robins and Bluebirds alone, but you could shoot Sparrows since they were dirty birds?"

And I said, "Yes dad, but I wasn't going to kill it."

And then he said, "Give me your BB gun."

I handed it to him, and without another word, he broke the stock and the gun over his knee and handed it back to me.

"You're not old enough to realize when the rules cannot be broken," he said. "You might as well throw that in the trash. We're not getting you another one." And that was the end of that lesson. It really hurt, and I still remember how embarrassed I was to have been lying to my father about that. I know he knew what I was doing, and I did know what I was doing. I just didn't know he'd catch me. I still hadn't figured that out. But I knew I didn't want to repeat that lesson. It stung! I had wanted a BB gun for so long, and now, it was gone forever.

That's not all. As a part of being in a suburb, there were lots of other kids around, and sometimes we would walk into town. One day, my friend dared me to steal something from the Dime Store, and looking around, I decided I could do that. When I got home that night, I was playing with the new red ball, and bouncing it off the wall in my room. My father came in to see what was making the racket, and he asked me where I had gotten the ball. I said, "Oh Johnny gave it to me." Of course, that was a lie.

My dad came back a little while later and said he had just talked to Johnny's father, and he said his son did NOT give it to you, and that in fact, he had dared you to steal it, and you did. "Is that true?" he asked.

I looked down. I didn't know what to say. "You can't do that, Jimmy, not now, not ever. Get your coat. We're going down to the Dime Store." I was mortified. When we got to the Dime Store, it was still open. My dad gave me some money and said, "This is your allowance. You are to go in and tell the owner that you took this ball without paying for it. Tell him you are sorry and that you want to pay for it and return the ball and that you promise you'll never do that again! Do you understand?"

I said, "I do."

"Okay," he said. "I'm going with you."

I got out of the car and slowly walked to the Dime Store door. My dad was right behind me. As we walked into the store, the owner was behind the counter. He asked me what he could do to help me find something, and I said, "No, thank you. I came to tell you that today, I took this red ball earlier, and I didn't pay you for it. So here's the money for it, and the ball. I am really sorry. I will never do that again."

And I started crying and walking out of the store. My dad was with me, right behind me.

We got in the car, and he praised me and thanked me for doing the right thing, even when it hurt so bad to admit that I had taken this man's ball without paying. What a difficult thing that had been to do. My dad hugged me and told me he loved me and was proud of me, even though I felt awful, and continued to cry. I was really sorry I allowed myself to do something I knew was really wrong, just to win a dare. I really meant it. I would never do that again, and I never have. I don't steal anything from anyone. I don't take dares. It is just not in my nature. Only later did I learn that stealing Mark 10:19 is one of the Ten Things God Forbids in the Ten Commandments he gave Moses on the Stone Tablets on Mount Sinai during Israel's forty years in the wilderness.

Knowing how I felt that day, I can see why it's a very bad thing to steal. It separates you from all who are working to make a living and do the right things, and if you steal, you are not only breaking God's laws, but you are taking something that someone else owns and not allowing them to do what they wish with what they own—what they have a right to. You don't have a right to it. They do! It is truly wrong, and on that day, I realized it, and how wrong I was to take advantage of that store owner and think I was getting by with it.

Sometime later, I was reading the book of John all the way through and when I got to Chapter 15, where the top of the page caption read: "I chose you," I was stunned! I didn't know whether God would be knowing I would be reading it that day or not, but it really scared me. It was like really personal, like Jesus was right there talking to me. And in a very real sense, Jesus was! As I came to know Jesus, I learned that reading the Bible is one way God speaks to me.

Here is the passage from John 15:16, and this was what it says: "You did not choose Me, but I chose you, and appointed you that you would go and bear fruit, and that your fruit would remain, so that whatever you ask of the Father in My name He will give to you." And when I saw it, I slammed the Bible shut and shouted out loud: "I don't want to be chosen!" I didn't know what all that meant, but I felt like I had had a glimpse of my future, and I wasn't going to get to choose what it would be. That scared me. My perspective was a little small. "I wanted to be what I wanted to be!" But this was a beginning. I didn't throw the Bible away. I just quit reading it for a while.

I was thinking that if I were "chosen," I would have to be a minister, and I didn't want to be like our pastor, Reverend Howard. He was a stocky, stodgy man who was balding, wore glasses, and had a mustache and white hair. I definitely did not want to be like him. I wanted to be what I WANTED to be, not "chosen by God to be what God wanted me to be." Wow! What an awful thought!

I remember that like yesterday, and I think God heard me and gave me the space I needed to find Him on my own terms. I really did not want to be a bad boy. I just wanted to be what I wanted to be, and I sure didn't know what that was then. I was too young to know and too immature to decide for myself. Time and circumstances were needed to allow me to come to a recognition that doing it "my way" was not the way to happiness. Little did I know.

When I was eleven, we moved to a new house on Evers Street with three bedrooms, 1 ½ baths, and a full basement. For the first time since Goshen, we were buying the house and not renting it. I remember cutting the grass and weeds for the first time. By the end of the second summer, it had become a nice lawn. What a surprise. I also learned that if I would mow the grass, my mom and dad would pay us for that. That was also new, and I liked that. My brother and I also helped my father build a two-story garage where he parked the car inside for the first time ever. We helped him, including hoisting an eight-hundred-pound steel I-Beam that became the primary support for the second story. Together, we used a block-and-tackle to ratchet it up ten feet into the air and set it on the two center posts to support the second story. Then, we nailed it into position and cross-braced it with 2×4s. Finally, we built the framework and walls that became the second story. The garage had a steep roof and an attic where we stored all kinds of things. It was an adventure and satisfying task to take it from a plan with cinders on the ground to a concrete pad to a two-story garage we helped build. Then to see it rise as a two-story garage was really something, and we helped build it. I got a lot of satisfaction from helping do that.

Tippy was our dog from the time I was born. She was a Collie/German Shepherd mix and about fifty pounds with beautiful gold and white fur and a black forehead and black patch on her tail with a pointed white tip. We had Tippy, our first pet ever, from the time we were very small in Goshen to our house on Evers Street in Dolton, Illinois. We loved her until she developed Pneumonia the winter she was 13 years old. It had been a very cold, wet winter. She was having a lot of trouble breathing, and we all cried a lot. We were scared for her. When we called my dad and told him, he hurried home from work to take her to the Vet with my brother. Unfortunately, Tippy was too sick and died shortly thereafter.

We were devastated, and when they got home, we had a little funeral service in the basement, and we buried her in the back yard under our plum tree in a wooden box. It was the first funeral I had ever attended, and we cried and were empty. Nothing was the same. We never replaced her. When Judy and I were married, we had a Welsh Terrier named Tiffany. When Linda and I married, we had Holly, a mixed breed who loved to chase squirrels. She died chasing a squirrel one day. After that, we had our goldfish: Mitchell, Marti, and Gras; Thumper the Gerbil; Mindy, the live-in wild dog who had six puppies; Whit, the cat with the tuxedo markings who died and came back; and finally, Abby, our Bichon Friese who was the best pet of all and died at thirteen in our Riviera home. That will do for our pet summary. We loved them all and spoiled them too. We trained some to do tricks, and did everything we could to keep them healthy. We learned that pets don't live forever except in our hearts. But every one of them was special and helped us learn responsibility and what unmerited love is like.

Moving back in time to when I was twelve, in our new house on Evers in Dolton, Illinois, Fred and I had our own upstairs bedroom again, all to ourselves unlike Cedar Lake where we shared our bedroom with Nancy.

On Evers Street, Mary Elizabeth (now Candy), and Nancy had the other upstairs bedroom, and for the first time, we got to choose the paint for our bedrooms. We loved the house and loved being only 6 doors from Dolton Park. Our Park was about fifty acres and had basketball courts, tennis courts, and Franklin School, grades first through eighth. It was an awesome location.

Franklin School was a combination elementary and middle school in one building. And for us, it was in an awesome location, and we had our track meets and tennis matches there. Every winter, the Dolton Volunteer Fire Department would build a rectangular dirt retainer ridge and fill it with water. Winters seemed colder then, and their homemade ice rink always froze solid. It wasn't very deep, so it froze quickly every year. To get ready, each year as our feet grew larger, we shopped at the Goodwill Store and bought used skates for one dollar a pair, and for the first time ever, we ice skated and played hockey.

I remember many times playing until my feet were numb. Then, we'd have to go home and wash our frozen white pinkies under cold water in the tub until they turned pink and were thawed out. When you skate that long, your toes freeze. And when you thaw them out, they really hurt for a while. But it was worth it. I loved hockey.

Then, every summer, we had the Volunteer Firemen's Carnival too, and we loved that, especially picking up coins under that roller coaster the morning after the Carnival closed down. Sometimes, we would find several dollars apiece in change. Our location on Evers was even better than the huge farm we had lived on in Cedar Lake. We never thought we would have such ready access to so much fun and be so close to our school. It was unbelievable.

It also held some temptations.

Chapter 7

You Got Trouble, My Friend—Right Here

I had wonderful teachers for each of my first five years in Elementary School, and I had a capable, creative, dynamic and energetic band director from fourth through eighth grade. He was so high strung that one day, when people weren't paying attention and talking, and they were obviously not prepared, our Conductor threw his baton so hard, it pierced a Sousaphone bell.

Later we heard he got in trouble, and he apologized for losing his temper. He had let his perfectionism and need to keep control get the best of him. Our band director was a great teacher and conductor but had a temper. We all learned a lot from him, and in spite of that one explosion, we never saw him angry again. We did have a very good band because of him, and after that, we all paid attention when he was on the podium. And yes, I was one of those talking!

In fifth grade, after seeing my class picture and my mother's "bowl" haircut, I decided I would go to the barber to get my hair cut. My parents told me I would have to pay for that myself, so I began to get part-time jobs and save my allowance. Somewhere there is a fifth-grade picture of me, and if you ever see it, you'll know why I wanted a regular barber to cut my hair the next time.

I think I only got 50 cents/week for allowance, so I jumped at opportunities to shovel snow during the winter all over our housing development where there were several hundred houses. Sometimes, because I was used to pushing myself, I would come home with $10 or even $15 dollars in my pocket. When I mowed grass, I could make as much as $1.50 per yard, and I mowed several yards every week. My parents also paid me to do odd jobs too that were not part of our everyday chores. We didn't get paid for regular chores like cooking dinner, shoveling coal cinders, or taking out the trash, but there were other opportunities, and I took them.

When I started looking for opportunities, I discovered by working hard, I could buy some of my own clothes that were above and beyond what my parents could pay for. That motivated me more than ever, because in seventh grade, we started to have boy/girl parties and I experienced my first kiss playing spin the bottle. If you don't know what that is, you'll have to ask me. I don't remember the kiss, but I remember the party, and I liked it. We had sodas and cake and a lot of fun. I think there were six boys and six girls. I kissed every one of the girls at least once. I had a lot to learn.

I also began to go to movies with one girl I liked and later to dances at the school. I walked her home and we talked for hours. We went to the "Sweet Shop" and got Green Rivers or Cherry Cokes and French fries. I felt that she liked me, and she did. That was my first crush, but not my last.

Needless to say, I was motivated to look good and to dress well. While I only went to a couple of those parties (and the parents *were* there, really), it was fun—way more fun than I had had before. It's amazing what that did to motivate my profit-motive, imagination and discipline. I looked for every opportunity to earn extra cash and hoped for the day when I would have a girlfriend of my own. That came sooner than I expected, and the day came when, with the help of my parents, I took a girl with me to a movie, paid her way, and walked her home. That was the beginning of a number of girls that I would call my "girlfriend." I had a lot of "semidates" in those middle-school years, and real dates in high school where I picked up and drove girls home; and I even "went steady" a couple of times, but I never got into intimacy.

One of the girls in our seventh grade class got intimate and pregnant, and we all knew about it and decided that was not for us. She had to drop out of school, and we never saw her again. So I saved that for marriage. But I really enjoyed kissing girls, and I did that a lot. I also knew I didn't want to get in trouble. It wasn't worth the price you would pay.

I also had a very hard lesson when I was about eleven years old. The Carnival came to town every summer, and the second summer we lived on Evers Street, I went to the Carnival as I had before. My parents had warned me not to play the Wheel of Fortune where you would put your money down on a number and if the spin ended up pointing to your number, you won double or triple the amount of money you put down on it. I went to the Carnival with no plans to play Wheel of Fortune.

Then, I went by that tent and was watching them play, and saw some people win, and I thought: "I'll just play it once!" So I put down a dime. I won! So I put down two dimes, and I won again. I ran it up to three dollars—a fortune in my world, and then I bet it all, and lost it all. Not realizing what I was really doing, I ran home, emptied out my piggybank, and went back and lost all that I had.

What a lesson! I was angry with myself and angrier still that I had disobeyed my parents, and angry that I had lost all my money. But I also knew I was not going to tell them or my brother, and I was NOT going to gamble again, EVER!

Later in my life, that lesson kept me from gambling when I went to Las Vegas for the National Association of Broadcasters' Equipment shows for twenty-five years in a row from WISH-TV in Indianapolis, and then from WIPB-TV in Muncie. In all that time, I never put a quarter, or dollar and anything in a slot machine or played Kino or Blackjack or Roulette—anything. I never wanted to discover if I was a "problem gambler." So I just never played the games in Vegas. Though I did watch someone lose $16,000 in about five minutes, once over his shoulder at a Roulette Table—it was more than I could take! That was more money at that time than I was making in an entire year.

I knew I had made a good choice to bypass that temptation. I still don't gamble. I've never bought a Lottery Ticket to this day, and I never will. I believe the Lottery's just a tax on the poor. Besides, by that time I had read through the *Living Bible*, and in Proverbs 16:33, David writes: "The Coin is tossed into the air, but its every decision is from God." Another translation says: "The Lot is cast into the lap, but its every decision is from God." This was a serious decision by the Disciples. When Judas betrayed Jesus and hung himself, the Disciples tossed lots to choose who the twelfth Disciple would be. To me, that proved casting lots or flipping a coin and asking God for an answer was very serious business, not something you toy with.

The Jewish Priests tossed lots to determine who would minister in the Holy of Holies each year; there are eighty-eight examples of casting lots in the Old Testament alone. Trusting God to determine the outcome of a serious decision also used the Urim and Thummim that the Jewish High Priest carried in his Breastplate and was used to settle arguments that were brought to him to decide.

Even King Solomon knew that the casting of lots put an end to disputes. They still use it to determine who has the ball in football games. There, it resolves disputes without question. It worked in Biblical times, and it works today. Only

42

God-fearing Jews and Christians believe God can determine what should happen by casting lots. They really believe our Sovereign God will tell them what choice to make by His deciding how the lot will fall. I knew from my experience in the park that God didn't want me to think gambling was "easy money." And I have always passed on that. I figured that if God wants to bless me, He'll have to do it some other way. And honestly, over the years when I look at what we've been given, He has.

I re-read this and have to say, I still don't see myself as a rascal. Although, if my boys had been like me, they probably would have had a rougher time with us than they did. Compared to me, Steve and Brian were very well behaved, and I don't remember them doing some of the shenanigans I did, but then, I'm not dead yet. There may be some confessions ahead. I don't know. But I'd be surprised. Like my dad, I love them both—all three—and nothing they have ever done or said, would ever have changed that then or will change my love in the future. Kirsten was and is the daughter I always hoped I'd have. So I have been the big winner in all of this. More on that later.

Chapter 8

Turning a Corner

What I've written here in the first several chapters is all true. Honestly, I was involved in more mischief, but you get the idea. I did wear a dunce cap once in second grade because I was always pestering other students when I got done early. "Yes, my teacher, Mrs. Scritchfield, really had a pointed Dunce Cap that she made incorrigible students like me, wear. But I was having harmless fun, and I always got my work done first. She did write me up as "incorrigible."

I was breaking new ground in our household and diverging from the always obedient and straight-A student my brother was to what I needed to do to be noticed and to compete for attention. I got the attention, not always the way I wanted it or the way my parents wanted to give it to me, but they did "give it to me" when I needed it.

And to soften my "corners," I did get disciplined far more than my brother Fred did. I didn't envy him that. I just accepted that there were risks to not obeying, and I pushed the envelope a few times. Well, more than a few times. I wasn't always a perfect student, either and was expelled from school in sixth grade. Yes, that's true too. My mom talked them into allowing me to come back after my three day suspension. I learned I had to keep my mouth shut sometimes, when I was really angry at a teacher.

I was not a perfect child. My parents loved me anyway, and I loved them with an undying love that continues to this day. My dad was my hero, and as I watched my mother die at ninety-six years of age and the way she handled the last fourteen years of her life without my dad, she became my hero too. She was a loving, great lady, who stayed alert and alive and giving to the very end of her days and was always saying, "I choose life."

I spent the next to last week of Mom's life with her in Denver at the Cherry Creek Nursing Center, and it was a wonderful time. She was in Hospice Care by then and dying with Macular Degeneration, congestive heart failure, and Cancer. In spite of all that—the Oxygenator, the wheelchair, and the Cancer—she was alert and alive.

Her roommate Norma told me when I came to see her that my mother was fine, except she was having nightmares every night and keeping their whole wing of the nursing home awake with her screaming and scary dreams. When I asked my mother about it, she said she just couldn't sleep. Then we got to talking, and I asked her if she had any "hold-backs"—things she wished that God had forgiven her for, but that He had never really forgiven her for them. She said, "Like what?"

And I said, "You know, Mom, I DON'T know. But something that you wish you had never done and that you wish God would forgive you for. Something only you would remember. And then she rolled her eyes and looked at the ceiling for a moment and said quietly so her roommate wouldn't hear: "Well there is one thing."

And before she continued, I assured her, "Mom, I'll never tell anyone what you say, but I think it will help if you tell me and we pray about it. Okay?"

And she began: she told me about something that happened when she was sixteen. Here we were, eighty years later, and it was keeping her up at night. And I said to her, "Mom, you know what? I think the only person who hasn't forgiven you for this is you!" and I was looking straight into her eyes. And then I said, "I'm sure God has forgiven you for this, long ago. So why don't we pray together and ask God to help you forgive yourself and cast your sins, including this one, into the ocean. The Bible says, and Corrie TenBoom told me in person when I had her on my Channel 8 *Teleconference* TV show—Corrie told me that when God forgives sin, He takes all our sins—past, present, and future—ties them up in a bandana with a large stone in the middle and casts them into the depths of the sea, and He posts a sign that reads No Fishing Allowed! That's from Micah 7:18–20. Did you know that?"

And my mother laughed as I prayed, and we both laughed and I repeated it again: "That's what the Bible says, Mom. 'No fishing allowed.' You're free. God has forgiven you and He is helping you, even now, to forgive yourself." And you know what? She did forgive herself right then, never to have another nightmare.

That night was the beginning of the last week of her life. She died the next Friday, never having that nightmare again, and in fact, the night after we talked and prayed together, she had a wonderful conversation with her mother and father and brother that amazed her roommate and me. I wasn't there, but when I met her roommate, Norma, for breakfast, she told me: "Your mother had visitors last night, and it was wonderful!" And she laughed. "It was her mother and her father and her brother who all died years ago, but it was the sweetest conversation, and she kept saying 'Oh, Mother—this, and 'Oh, Father, that…and it went on and on, but it was never frightening or loud or screaming like before. She was obviously at peace, finally."

One week later, seven days after I left her on Friday, she breathed her last as she reached out her arms toward the Light at the end of her bed, fell back at peace, and stopped breathing. My sister, Candy, was there holding her hands and praying with her, and she said it was the most beautiful thing she had ever witnessed.

We know where my mother is. I asked her once how old she was when she first knew about Jesus. And she answered, "Oh, I've always known Jesus since I was a little girl, and He has always been with me over all these years."

Chapter 9

The Biggest Step So Far

What this autobiography now needs to shift to from here forward, is about what God has been doing with me from the beginning. I needed His help from the get-go, and I still need it today and on into our futures. As you have observed, He has stepped in again and again to rescue me in tight places, counsel me with good advice, and keep me from serious consequences for things I did that were ill-advised. We're not done yet.

When I turned twelve, I went through the Catechism of the Methodist Church shortly after my confrontation in the garden with the "I chose you" passage in the Bible, and I was told to "remember my baptism (as an infant) and be grateful. and I was "confirmed" as a full church member and capable of taking communion—something I was denied when I was 6 years old and didn't understand it. But I have to admit, I still did not understand what I had done and who God really was.

A few years later, I was sixteen and went to a Billy Graham Crusade at McCormick's Place with 30,000 others. When Reverend Graham asked those who wanted to recommit their lives to Christ to come forward and we all started singing "Just As I Am," I felt my heart "moved," and I went forward for the Crusade Altar Call. I felt like I needed to acknowledge God and Christ before the world and for myself—before all these strangers—to know that God was with me and in me. Afterward, a Christian counselor prayed with me and invited me to go to a Bible study for the next six weeks so that I could more fully understand what Christ was asking of me. I agreed to try and do that and went back to where my girlfriend was sitting and drove home wondering what would happen next.

When I told my parents what I had done and asked them if I could take their car to go 40 miles each way to Des Plaines on the far west side of Chicago each Wednesday for the next six weeks, they said they thought that would be a good idea. These were follow-up meetings with a Billy Graham Team home discussion group, and my parents agreed. I don't know if they truly trusted me with the car and driving that far, but they did trust God in this, and they urged me to go.

These meetings were the first time where I listened to the discussions about Jesus as an adult, was questioned as an adult—experienced other adults listening to me expressing my thoughts, doubts, and questions, and I began to grow as a very young and immature Christian. I was surprised that mom and dad trusted me to make that 80-mile journey each week to be "coached" by the Billy Graham team, and it changed my life in the direction that only God can change a life. I listened, really prayed, and trusted that God was listening for real, this time. There was much more to come.

This is where I truly began to learn who I am and Whose I am, and I wanted the Holy Spirit to be a part of my life. I didn't really know exactly what that meant then, but ultimately, I knew I needed to know more. I wasn't yet ready to give it all away and let something or Someone else guide my life.

Chapter 10

Trippin' in Israel: Unforgettable

What Jesus has been teaching me since then through His Holy Spirit, however, is really the most important part of my life. It was then. It is now!

Only at sixteen, I didn't know what I know now and say to you, from forty-seven years of allowing Him to guide me, and listening to His "still, small voice"—"doing life His way is way better."

Most of all, I am grateful He has never left me and has been leading me, step-by-step, through most of my life and continues to lead me, moment by moment, day by day... It is the greatest adventure ever for a naughty, show-off nick-named "Howard." That's another story from 2010. I'm not sure it will make this book except as a Random Thought and later conversation. In Israel in 2010, God had my attention, again and again. It is hard to be there and never take your eyes off of Jesus. But that's what happens. God got my attention, and I decided to be "all in." When we get to the trip to Israel Grandma and I took, I even got the only nickname I ever had: "Howard!"

Well, why not tell you now? We had always wanted to go to Jerusalem. When I retired in 2010, Linda and I signed up to go to the Holy Land, Israel, with a Catholic Church group organized by St. John the Twenty-Third Retreat Center and one of our favorite people: Father John Kiefert. He and I are the same age, and he was to be the Spiritual Guide for our trip and the thirty-five of us who signed up to go. We were going in November 2010, and all of us were really excited. It was to be a Pilgrimage to the Holy Land, not a mere vacation.

We flew to Israel and landed in Tel Aviv. When we arrived, we were met by our bus and a Palestinian Christian guide who was to be with us for the entire 10 days. We immediately boarded our bus and took off for Nazareth where we were spending our first three nights. It was to be an incredible eye-opening experience. We had several people on our bus who were walking slowly and a couple using a cane, so we ended up stringing out our group and worrying our Tour Guide. Finally, to manage his frustration, he looked for someone who would "bring up the rear" and make sure everyone was accounted for. I was tall and young, compared to many others on the trip, and our Guide pointed to me and said, "Jim [reading my name tag], you'll be the one bringing up the rear and making sure we don't lose anyone." I agreed, and we proceeded. At the end of the first day, before he had really learned any names, we all had gotten on the bus, and I was standing there, ready to sit down, and our Tour Guide shouted out, "Where is Howard?"

Nobody answered. He ducked down the front steps, looked both ways, and came back up. And shouted again, "Where is 'Howard!' We can't go without 'Howard.'"

And finally one of the people on the bus figured out what was going on and said, politely, "You mean JIM! He's standing right here!" pointing to me. And our guide did a double-take, and then laughed and said, "Yes, I guess he is. I thought his name was 'Howard' And everyone laughed. After that, they all called me "Howard" and would say as we climbed onto the bus at each stop. "We can go now! 'Howard' is here." And everyone would laugh, including our guide. So for the rest of the trip, people called me "Howard."

The name didn't stick, however, except with a former professor from Ball State that I have known since 1978. When he sees me, he still says "How are you doing, Howard?" So now you know. As a child, I had a Christmas stocking with my real name on it, and it said "Jimmy Bob" since I am James Robert. But that's it! Nobody ever called me Howard again except for Dr. Pete. So now you know.

Chapter 11

My Job Now, Going Forward

I recognize now that I can best show my gratitude to God by how I share my life with you and everyone I meet. It's not about boasting except in boasting what the Holy Spirit does and is doing and has done to love others through us and change my life and their lives by giving ourselves away. These things have happened to bring glory to God, not to elevate me. If we get to help someone or help you, it is not so you'll owe us anything, but so you'll understand what we really believe and that we really love you as Christ loves…"wanting you to be the most loved, best possible YOU that you can be." Maybe you'll see Christ in us and share His unlimited love with others…your family, your children, the people you work with and meet, the strangers you get to help along the way…anyone God puts in your path and nudges you to engage… You may know this or you may never have heard it, but "Love is the only thing that exists where, the more you give it away, the more you have!" I believe it. I practice it. I know it to be true. Now, you know it too.

We truly want you to know God so that not only here but in God's Eternity, we will know you there and be with you and your spirit forever as God's continuing gift to you and to us. I don't see that as selfish. I see that as the most loving thing I can do for you, and it's my job to share His love for you. He loves you just as you are—as the precious, unique person you are—numbering all of your days from before you were born (Psalm 139:16).

Our lives never were ours; the Holy Spirit and Jesus and God have been a part of our DNA from the moment before we were conceived in our mother's wombs. Our lives are meant to be awakened in our perceptions by sharing what God is doing and singing praises for His incredible plan which includes every breath, every hair on our heads, every glance and sneeze, and every tear we have shed as we have walked this path, sometimes feeling confident, sometimes grateful, sometimes drowning in emotion, and sometimes feeling very much alone. And in all these times, whether we acknowledge it or not, it was often in the spaces between the confidence and the loneliness that He has carried us in His Arms, never far from His heart.

But I'm getting ahead of myself.

Chapter 12

Music Is My Life

In middle school and high school, I was also spending lots of time practicing my trumpet and playing tennis. With the help of my parents who let me play Cornet on a rented horn in fourth grade, for Christmas that year, they agreed to help me buy a beautiful silver Conn Constellation trumpet and pay them back at the rate of five dollars every month for four years. I was eager to have my very own horn, so I agreed to work hard to find a way to pay for that instrument, and I have had it all of my life and shared it with my boys and now with my grandsons, Elliott and Nathan. I think it is now our son Brian's to keep or give away or use for his benefit. Elliott tried it for a time but is now playing the Baritone Saxophone in his high school Jazz Band. Nathan is now playing the trumpet in his high school band, and I'm proud of both of them. I love the fact they are interested in music which was always a large part of my own life.

First, I sang. Then I played the Cornet; then the Trumpet; and finally, I sang some more in three Musicals and later, in the High Street Church Choir for fifteen years. My mother and father were also very musical. My mom played the piano, and my father played the Baritone and Trombone and taught music in his first job out of college. At one point, he wanted us to all be part of a Needham Family band. That never happened, but often as we travelled, we sang songs in the car, mostly church hymns and songs from our Scouting adventures. It was fun and a great memory.

Back to high school… Honestly, like a lot of young guys, I really wanted to be on the football team when I got to high school and catch the passes and carry the ball down the field for touchdowns. I was only 120 pounds, and about 5 foot 9, but I wanted to be a half-back. When I went to practice, and put on my pads, I discovered I had to run the Gauntlet a few times to see how well I could hold onto the ball. The team of Guards and Tackles and Safety's and other running backs would line up on either side, punching at the ball with their fists. I was not strong enough to keep the ball from being punched out of my arms. I would never be a half-back! I discovered they were trying to punch the ball out of my arms with their fists but were all hitting my hands and arms and soon the ball would go flying. They were only hitting my hands and skinny arms and chest and back, and I couldn't hold onto it. After two weeks, I realized I wasn't a football player. I wasn't cut out to be a football star.

So after a few very long weeks of practice, I turned in my helmet and pads and reported for Freshman Tennis Practice where I could play with a ball that I didn't have to defend from 60 merciless teammates. I was relieved and ready to do something I was built to do rather than something I wanted to do. There were no bruises and smelly pads and helmets on the tennis team, and I didn't have to wear a mouth guard. I liked that part. It also was all up to me to win or lose. It was an individual sport. I could not be a hero on the football field after all, but I could win on the courts. I loved tennis. My father was a star tennis player at Indiana State when he was in college, and my brother and I had been playing tennis with my dad since we were in fifth grade and moved to Evers Street, right down the street from the courts. I had found my sport.

I did well at tennis and also on my Trumpet in the Marching Band and Orchestra. And when it came to the band trip to Colorado to play concerts in the mountain state (I had never seen mountains before), I sold chocolate turtles to all our neighbors so I could go on the band trip and sit next to a beautiful blonde French Horn player, that I thought was the prettiest girl I had ever seen. I really was smitten with her. So 136 boxes of Chocolate Turtles and lots of annoyed neighbors later, I qualified to go on the band trip and play three concerts in Colorado. It was a train trip on a Vista-Dome passenger car with seats on the second level and *huge bubble-top windows with 360-degree views so we could see out of both sides of* the train and also straight up to the moon and the stars. It was really romantic. I sat with my "girlfriend" all the way out. But by the time we were ready to come back, someone else had gotten her attention, and she sat with him all the way back to Thornton Township High School where we were in school. I was really bummed-out and disappointed with that trip after all that time and all that work selling turtles so I could go.

I moved on, refocused my energies, and did well in my classes and by January of my sophomore year, we moved to a new high school—Thornridge High School—only six blocks from our home. There were lots of new girls there, and I was number one on the tennis team and played second trumpet. My Junior year, I became Solo Trumpet and played *A Trumpeter's Lullaby* solo with our band. If you've never heard it, you should check it out on-line. Check out Wynton Marsalis' version on YouTube. It is as beautiful today as it was then, and I loved playing it, standing out in front of the band and soloing. I also played Solo trumpet in the Dance Band, which hampered my dating relationships but also paid me $10 a week. I just never got to dance. In all, I think I had four or five girlfriends through high school, and then we all graduated and left those friendships behind as we moved on to colleges across the country.

During my summers in between my sophomore year in high school and freshman year in college, I worked as a lifeguard at the local Dolton Pool. I thought I had it made. I wasn't even sure I would go to college. Then, I was offered a music scholarship playing my trumpet at the University of Dubuque in Dubuque, Iowa that paid my tuition, so I decided to check it out. When I got to Dubuque after driving seven hours clear across Illinois, I discovered the University was only one large building on one city block with four hundred students.

My first high school, Thornton Township High School had 4,600 students, and Thornridge, the school I moved to my sophomore year and graduated from, had 1,300. I just couldn't see myself going to such a small college, regardless of the financial incentive. The only other school I had applied to was Indiana State University where both of my parents had graduated, and I decided to go there. My dad was happy with my decision and told me it was college or moving out on my own and paying all my bills. That was an easy decision! Indiana State was looking really good!

Chapter 13

Flunking a Physical
and My Master's

Indiana State was my first choice! I went to college to study Physics but because I won the lead role of Daniel Boone in the first play of the season, I changed my major to Theater the first week. Only after my father's death in 1999, did I discover in his papers that my dad also had gone to college to study Physics. When I changed my major to Theater my first week in school and called him with the "good news," he was surprised and disappointed and reminded me I had four years of tuition that my parents would pay, and the rest was on me. He asked how I thought I could make a living working in the theater. I told him I would figure it out.

That was a tough conversation. I stayed with Theater for my first two and a half years, acting in eighteen plays and musicals. I sang the lead in "Finian's Rainbow," "Oklahoma," and "Sound of Music" and acted in fifteen other shows. My mom and dad were always there, driving two hundred miles each way from Dolton, Illinois, to see every show I was in. After finishing all the theater courses, my junior year, I added Psychology as a major. I thought it was more interesting than being in front of people and pretending to be someone else. I was pretty good at acting, but I had become more interested by then in what was going on in my mind than in doing plays. It was the right change for me.

All of a sudden, I was studying Personality Theories, Freudian Psychology, Abnormal Psych, and Behavioral Psychology (or Rat Lab, as it was called). That was the class where I learned that consistency in my behavior determined how fast and how well my pet rat "Petunia" would learn to take a ping pong ball and put it through a wire coat-hanger I had bent into a hoop on the side of my Skinner Box. By the end of the first month in class, Petunia would jump into motion as soon as I put her in her Skinner Box and turned the light on. She became a blur as she went to work, nudging the ball to the corner with her nose to where the hoop was, picking the ping pong ball up with her front legs and putting it through the hoop, six inches above her, and darting across the ribbed bottom of the box for the food shelf where the pellet had dropped in place as soon as she "made the dunk." It was fun and surprising. When I came to class each day, Petunia was on my shoulder for the duration.

During my senior year, I began dating a girl named Judy who played the piano and organ at our local church where my Uncle Al was the pastor. After a while, we fell in love and two years later were married. I had received my Bachelor's degree in Theater and Psychology, and with my draft number at no. 30, I volunteered for the US Air Force and Vietnam.

When I reported for intake, I passed the written tests, but failed my physical. My doctor from home reported that I had Bronchial Asthma and the Armed Forces declared I was 4-F. My flying days were scuttled! No room in the Service for me. Only later did we discover that while I did have what appeared to be Bronchial Asthma, as an adolescent, what I really had was a severe gluten intolerance that made my chest vibrate when I was eating a lot of bread. Throughout my life, I have lived on Antihistamines until at seventy, I discovered my gluten intolerance and that by avoiding gluten in my diet, the allergic reactions I fought for sixty years all but disappeared completely. My childhood doctor never knew, and neither did we.

With military service off the table, I applied for a Graduate Assistantship in Radio-TV and entered Graduate School at Indiana State University. I immediately began studying Psychology and Radio-TV as a double major. I finished all the coursework for both Masters' programs but never did defend my Psychology Thesis, so I only received a Master's Degree in Radio-TV. And I decided that with being married, holding a full-time job and paying off my student debt, one Master's would have to do. I wasn't going back for another eight months of research in order to finish the Psychology Masters. I was interested in randomized concept formation in fourth graders but not enough to go back for eight more months of research and thesis writing. I had been in college six years. That was enough. My supervising professor said I would never get to hang out my shingle and be a practicing Psychologist. I told him he was correct! One masters was enough!

After receiving my Master's in Radio-TV in May '68, I went to work at WTHI-TV in Terre Haute as a Production Engineer. All of a sudden, we were doing TV forty hours a week, and I loved it. I ran camera, did lighting, ran audio, ran film and video-tape, and had a blast. The salary wasn't great and the Director was awful and cussed out everyone who did not jump when he said "jump." Other than that, it was a great job. Judy and I moved into Married Student Housing while she continued to work to finish her degree in Music Education. It was a happy time.

Along the way, my Pastor, my Uncle Al Mitchell, convinced me that England's King James did not translate the Greek word *baptizo* because the King did not want to be immersed for his baptism. The word *baptism* is a transliteration of the Greek word *baptize*, which means to immerse or make fully wet. In Hebrew, it is referred to as a *mikveh—*

an immersion. So King James, the same King James who ordered the "King James Bible," ordered the printers to print the Greek word *baptizo* in his King James Bible but not translate it. Then he would designate what the King wanted it to mean, not what it really meant, and he would not have to be immersed.

That same king, King James, also met with my ancestor, Robert Cushman in 1623 to negotiate and authorize the agreement with the Pilgrims (for which Robert Cushman was the "Principal Agent" to the English Investors (a group referred to in British history as the London Merchant Adventurers). Cushman raised the money for the Mayflower and also the Speedwell, and was with the Pilgrims when they originally migrated to Leiden, southwest of Amsterdam, in Holland to escape the oversight and disapproval of King James in the early 1600s. In 1618, the Pilgrims moved back to England because their children were learning Dutch, not English. Cushman and the other Pilgrim parents then set about devising a plan to go to the New World and create a settlement there where they could practice their belief in God freely. They were willing to take the chance they could survive and flourish by trusting God and His Providence in the New World and not having King James breathing down their necks.

Thus, the word *baptizo* came to be understood in England as a "sprinkling baptism" and was never truly translated into English and what the Bible really meant! John the Baptist did not "sprinkle Jesus." He immersed Jesus in the water of the Jordan River. Now, you too know the back story of what that word *baptism* (*mikveh* in Hebrew) really means.

When I read this in the Greek/English dictionary at age twenty-one, my Uncle Al, who was married to my Aunt Ruth (my father's sister), asked me, "Do you now understand what the word *baptism* means?" And I said I did. And then he said, "Have you ever been baptized?" And I said, "I guess not."

So I arranged to be immersed at church the next week, and I was. In many ways, it was strange, but certainly different from being sprinkled as an infant. Nonetheless, I felt like I had made a new and full commitment to God in front of many witnesses as the Bible requires. I felt I was moving closer to God, and I was happy with that, in spite of the very wet clothes and the humble nature of the experience. The Bible says in 1 Pet., "This water symbolizes, not the removal of dirt from the body but the pledge of a clear conscience toward God. It saves you by the resurrection of Jesus Christ..." (1 Pet. 3:21). It is what Jesus did with John the Baptist in the River Jordan when the dove alighted on Jesus' shoulder and a voice from heaven said, "This is my Son, whom I love; with him I am well pleased" (Matthew 3:17). Only later, in Israel in 2010, Grandma and I were "baptized again" in the River Jordan by a Holy Man (a Catholic Priest) named John. We thought at the time that was a significant and memorable parallel to Jesus' baptism that we would always recall. The Jordan was muddy and cold and came up to our thighs. It was about fifty feet wide and moving fairly quickly and separated Israel from Jordan. Father John whipped some branches of Hyssop through the water and sprayed us with the river water three times while we were standing there, getting all of us wet. It was a symbolic baptism for everyone, regardless of his or her personal history. Father John then went for a swim in the Jordan, something we will never forget.

My Uncle Al married Judy and me in 1967, and we honeymooned in Chicago on the Chicago Lakefront. It was short and sweet, and we went back to Terre Haute where Judy returned to classes, and I went back to work at WTHI-TV, Channel 10, CBS for the Wabash Valley. I was committed to be faithful, work hard, try to excel in TV and learn all I could. I worked very hard on the four-to-twelve shift which included the Six O'clock and Eleven O'clock news blocks and tape-recording public affairs programs and commercials from eight to ten every night. I was learning a lot. TV was fun.

Nine months later, I had had enough of my Director's swearing at me and everyone else, and also of my $85/week salary, and I started looking around for a better job. In January, I applied for an Assistant Director of Audiovisual Services job at the University of Guelph in Ontario, Canada, and in late February 1969 landed in Guelph, Ontario, Canada. We were excited about the new job and the salary that had just doubled for me. Judy was to join me in August when she completed her degree. Late in March, she called to tell me the Registrar at Indiana State had contacted her to tell her he had "misadvised" her and that she could not graduate until August 1970. We were shocked and angry. This was not fair.

No one in her family had ever graduated from college, so I immediately started looking for another job, closer to home. We felt like we had been betrayed, but there was nothing more to do. She did not have enough "Upper-Division Credits" to graduate, so I had to stay in Canada for an additional year without her or get another job, or she had to quit school—the decision was made. We both wanted her to finish her degree. I started looking for another position.

About that time, my Director of Audiovisual Services at the University of Guelph in Ontario, Dick Ellis, came to me and said he had not had a vacation in nine years—that he was taking off for two weeks—oh, and I was in charge.

So Mr. Ellis packed up and took off, much to my surprise and to my staff's delight.

The twenty-four staff members who were left, immediately called a meeting with me as soon as Dick was out of town. It was an all-staff meeting. I felt VERY uncomfortable about this, but I agreed to meet with them.

We started our meeting at 11:00 AM and finished late in the afternoon. They had hidden their grievances well, but ultimately, listed 18 issues they felt had to be resolved if they were to continue to work for Mr. Ellis. And they wanted me to find a way to resolve their complaints. They ranged from Ellis' refusal to call them by name (some didn't even think he KNEW their names) to wanting a new building to house our hopelessly overcrowded facility. We had twenty-six people in an old two-story house with basement (about 3,000 square feet) and it was VERY, very crowded.

I listened and took notes. As they began, I said to them. "Okay, here are the ground rules! I will listen to everything you say. I will make notes on what your issues are, and I promise you, I will do everything I can to correct these problems. I know Mr. Ellis is unaware of these issues, and you must promise me never to reveal that we have had this meeting. In the meantime, you will begin to see the changes you want to have, and you will know very shortly that I am working under the radar to make those changes. Do not reveal that we have discussed these and trust me. That is what we must do if we are to succeed. Do you all agree and promise to keep your silence?"

We made it through the two weeks, and everyone seemed to be working better as a team. For me, married just seven months before, I went back to Terre Haute to see Judy every two weeks. I would pack up on Friday afternoons, get in my new Pontiac LeMans with the big HO engine and head for Terre Haute, Indiana, six hundred miles each way. When I was in Guelph, I worked twelve-hour days, and worked hard to deal with the staff complaints. Attitudes were beginning to change. I began to make decisions. Dick Ellis let me run the show. It was a management clinic for me, with Dick guiding my decisions, all the while, letting me guide the internal culture. Things were beginning to change.

One by one, we were able to resolve each of the eighteen complaints. That is, all except the issue about a new building. When I left seven months later and moved to my new job as Eastern Kentucky University's first TV Producer in Richmond, Kentucky, God had answered all of my prayers, and given me the wisdom to deal with their issues.

God had also enabled my staff to keep their mouths shut and trust me. God also helped me persuade, cajole, and very carefully nudge my boss in the direction of calling people by name, repainting the entire building to suit our team, and all of the other issues except the most difficult one: having a new building.

My staff all kept their promise to me. Our Director was happy, the staff was happy, I was happy, and we became more efficient and better at what we were doing month by month. When people are happy working, it is amazing what can be accomplished. I began to recognize two sayings that I created or borrowed that I was convinced characterized life: "Should-be's aren't ARES!" (Just because things should be one way, that won't make it so), and "None of us is as smart as all of us!" They were practical reminders that to make every step forward, we had to create a plan, embrace it together, and keep working it day by day. That is what we did. And it worked beautifully.

Chapter 14

I Made It Through the Rain

When I left the University of Guelph, my staff surprised me with a very special book that has each of their pictures in it—you may see it someday where they all signed it in the back and provided their pictures and mine, sharing their love for me and what we had accomplished together in my seven months there as a twenty-four-year-old neophyte manager. I started there when I was twenty-four and left shortly after turning twenty-five. I had learned an enormous amount from them.

Everyone was older than I was except our student secretary. I knew I didn't know very much and that they all collectively knew a lot more than I did. I also used all the Psychology I had studied to shape behaviors and worked hard at implementing all I had learned in those Psych classes to persuade my Director and staff to do the right things. The miracle was, as Dick came along, he discovered he liked the way it was all going much better, and he morphed into a better manager and boss than he had been when I arrived.

As a result, I learned a lot, and gained significant confidence in my ideas and ability to manage and persuade people, and to direct activity toward a very clear objective, even when others set the goals. In the midst of that, my office mate—our Chief Artist, Leslie—had asked to repaint our office bright orange, and my Director and I had agreed. Much to my surprise, when I did my first hire a couple of months later and interviewed almost two hundred persons for our Chief Photographer's position (not a very good idea), I discovered something about color: when we took our office walls from off-white to bright orange, it changed everyone who came into the room.

After the change, the remaining interviewees would stop, transfixed at the door, scan the walls quickly, and then laugh as if someone had made a joke. And then, and only then, they'd introduce themselves and walk in. They all had big smiles on their faces because the room was just "not to be ignored." What a surprise. Later, when I managed Channel 49 in Muncie, we did the same color scheme: burnt orange for our studio carpet and matching chairs with chrome arms on our one set for all of our interview programs. And the bright orange worked its magic there, as well. People loved it—and SURPRISE! It went well with everything.

One other thing happened in Guelph that was incredible as God prepared me for what was to come. I assisted our Chief Cinematographer, Ray Pollard, in voicing a film of *Apiculture at the University of Guelph*.

Our Sister University in Africa was struggling with a blight on their bee population in their country and, being an Agricultural Research University like Purdue in Indiana, we were asked if we could send them a film that would help them turn their bee-keeping problem around and save their hives. So I did the voice-over for their film, and we sent it out. Before I left in September, we received word that what we had helped them to learn was already making inroads in solving their problems, and they sent a letter to our President thanking him for helping turn the problem around. I realized, then, that video does more than entertain: it can literally change lives for the better. I have always remembered that lesson and used it as a context for everything I have done in video since.

Chapter 15

TV Producer at Last

When I completed my Master's Degree in Radio-TV and all my Psychology coursework, but no thesis defense, I was hoping to get a job as a Television Producer. I wasn't really sure what that was, but I wanted to be in charge of writing, producing, directing, and editing of programs. My next job was to take on exactly that role: I was Eastern Kentucky University's first TV Producer. When I asked what that job was to be, my Administrator of Audiovisual Services said, "You'll have to show us what we need to do and then create the programs we need and want and put them on the air. They'll be representing Eastern Kentucky University (EKU) and air on Tuesday evenings in Prime Time and be distributed by the thirteen-station Kentucky Educational Television Network." Jim Harris continued, "I'm not sure what that should be, so make us proud!" That was my assignment. He was giving me my head to be creative and as good as we could be. I couldn't wait to get started. But I did.

Initially, I was to produce several televised classes for internal use at the University. And beginning in January 1970, I would begin doing documentaries for EKU that would entertain, inform, and reflect well on the University. That sounded exciting.

Then late in my first week there, I was sitting in the office talking with my Production Manager, and Jim Harris, our Administrator, walked in and asked, "Who would like to do a job for the President?"

I asked what he meant.

Harris said, "It's a two-week assignment that will take you out of Kentucky and where you'll be paid the same that you now receive from the University who will be reimbursed, but the work is not for EKU."

I asked what we would be doing, and he said that he wasn't quite sure. The EKU President had been contacted to provide two producers who could travel for two weeks in November and that we would be trained, and all our expenses would be paid. I said, "Just what does the President want us to do?"

And he said, "Oh, it's not our University President! No, you'll be working for the President of the United States, President Nixon."

I exclaimed, "You've got to be kidding! I'm not doing anything in November that I can't put aside for two weeks. I could go!"

And Harris said, "Okay, Needham, you're in. Anyone else interested?"

And at that, Rudd Parsons, a graduate student sitting there, asked if he could do the work.

And Mr. Harris, said, "That would be fine. I'll forward your names to the FBI for background checks, and they'll get back with you. Thanks for volunteering."

All of a sudden, I was possibly going to work for the White House. Wow! What a surprise. I had much to learn. It was my first week on the job at EKU. And the next six weeks would be tumultuous and exciting. I was pumped. Within the next week, the FBI had checked us out and said we were approved to go. We were to go to training classes in Lexington on how to use the equipment, and also finish filling out our paperwork.

When the fifteenth of November came, I was on a plane to Washington, DC, to work for the President. Six years later, to the day, I would be interviewing Holocaust survivor Corrie TenBoom on my WISH-TV talk show in Indianapolis, because of an act of God and action of the United Nations. We really have no idea what is in our future, do we? You'll see.

So on Saturday, November 15, 1969, we left Lexington, Kentucky, around noon and arrived in Washington, DC, before dinner. Shortly after landing, we had a quick dinner together and stayed in the Airport Motel, a place near what was then Washington National Airport—now Reagan International. We were to meet again at 5:00 AM.

Sunday morning early, we were picked up with our gear from the hotel at 5:00 AM and taken to the White House where we were checked in and led to the third sub-basement and a room I cannot remember. When we entered the room, all of the producers who were to deploy to the rest of the country were there and were asked to sit around a large rectangular table seating about a dozen of us. None of us knew what was coming.

Once we were seated, our host began by pointing to the displays on the walls all around us that highlighted the participants and the historic meetings that had happened in this very room. We were thrust into history and noted the important persons who had participated in managing the affairs of the United States from this very place. The White House staff wanted us to have a sense of history and of the gravitas and importance of the project we were about to embark on.

Next, the White House staff showed us the National Film Board film, *Jim Decker Builds a Longliner.* What Canada learned is that by using the film as a catalyst for change, the people of Fogo Island, Newfoundland, were able to voice their concerns and dreams and share them with others on the island and in the government. Ultimately, the film shows how one of the islanders built a longliner—a fishing boat using long lines—with the help of his friends, overcoming the problems of financing and the lack of tools and government support. The islanders figured out a way to create a profitable business and because of that, were able to remain on the island and continue their lives there. The Canadian government had been planning to force the citizens of Fogo Island to move to the mainland so they would not starve to death. However, the islanders' entrepreneurial spirit, mettle, and courage helped them get back on their feet and survive in place on Fogo Island instead of having to leave the island and their way of life there, for good. The transformation recorded on that award-winning Canadian Film Board film, was incredibly powerful! Wow!

The film we saw was the White House's way of planting in our heads, an idea they hoped to take advantage of, as we went out to gather information on video to help the 1979 White House Conference on Food and Nutrition find a successful way to resolve what seemed to be "intractable problems of food and nutrition in America's poorest communities." The outcome from the first and only White House Conference on Food and Nutrition of December 1969 was over 1,400 recommendations that were to reinvent our government's programs to help the poor upgrade their diets and lives and how they could successfully and significantly improve the quality of their lives and their nutrition.

The beauty of seeing this example which still resonates in my mind, is that, as I mentioned above, because of my work on the film, *Apiculture at Guelph*, and that success, I was already convinced that "video can change lives for the better." That's exactly what the White House and their experts hoped would be the case, and as you will see below, it worked, better than anyone could have expected.

We had been called into the service of President Nixon to help him address the food and nutrition crisis in America. He had assembled a team of experts to gather information and video for the Food and Nutrition Conference that was to take place in December 1969. As it turned out, that conference was transformational for America's poor, and without a doubt, what transpired in that period transformed us as well.

Chapter 16

TV Changes Lives
for the Better

This conference is the one and only White House Conference on Food and Nutrition ever held, and it resulted in
hundreds of different programs and ideas for federal projects that pioneered better ways to feed the poor and hungry in America and improve their nutrition. It was headed
by Tufts University President Jean Mayer and made many
major changes in the way the federal government assisted
the poor such as free breakfast and lunch for malnourished
children. We were proud of what we had done.

When we were ready to depart for our working assignments all across America, we were each given a half-sheet
letter from the Special Assistant to the President, Michael
White, printed on White House stationery which said,

> To Whom It May Concern:
>
> This person is in the service of the
> President of the United States and the
> White House Conference on Food, Nutri-

tion, and Health. Please extend him every courtesy. Thank You!

Sincerely,
Michael White
Special Assistant to the President.

That was literally our "Get out of jail, free" card.

White told us at that briefing to always keep that paper with us and to bring it out only when we were experiencing a problem where we needed special assistance from law enforcement or other civil authorities. He said that if we encountered "trouble," they would bend over backwards to help us.

As it turned out, I never had to use it. But Rudd Parsons, the EKU Graduate Student who volunteered that day in the office, did get stopped by an Arizona State Trooper one day, who pulled him over when Rudd was going 100 mph to get to the Phoenix airport and deliver the tapes he had recorded that day. When the officer came to Rudd's car, Rudd rolled down the window and said he was working for the President on a special project. Would he please read the letter?

The trooper took the letter, went back to his car, radioed his office, and came back. He apologized and asked "Mr. Parsons" to please follow him, and they took off at 120 mph and got Rudd to the airport in time to deliver the tapes to the airplane waiting to take off for Washington. Mr. Parsons did not get a ticket. He received the help he needed and a thank you from the officer for allowing him to be of assistance.

That tells you something about why people working for the President feel somewhat insulated from the general public and how it would give one a sense of special privilege in whatever they had been asked to do by the White House.

Two things happened when I was working on the White House project that are notable: I got food poisoning, and I was asked to stay and help our Unit Producer edit the video we had taken.

First, our Unit Producer was not well known at the time, though she was a veteran filmmaker from Paramount Pictures. Verna Fields was a twenty-year veteran of the film industry and a notable feature film editor with significant location work. We had a great time working together and successfully completed our project. Five years later she was the principal editor for one of the greatest blockbusters of all time on film: the original *Jaws*. Some of you may have seen it. If you haven't, it's worth seeing again, just to see her name in the credits as Editor.

For our work, we were sent to the small town of 8,000, Ellsworth, Maine where we were housed in a little motel. Our focus was the tiny fishing community of Stonington, about forty miles south, on the ocean, and our schedule was grueling. We would wake up at 6:00 AM, breakfast at 7:00 and work through with a short lunch break until about 6:00 PM. We then jumped in the car, raced two hours to Portland and sent our footage on to Washington, DC, for previewing what we had filmed that day. Then we would leisurely head back to Ellsworth and stop along the way for dinner. We always feasted like royalty on our expense account. Verna never found a bad restaurant, or so we thought.

Ten days into the project, on the night before Thanksgiving, November 26, we stopped to have a Maine Lobster dinner. I had lobster and steamed clams. It was delicious. We pulled into a sea-side restaurant about 8:30 PM, not unusually late for our routine where we were working seven days a week. Dinner usually happened about that time, and we were hungry.

That night, we got back to our motel around 10:30 PM, and I immediately went to bed. But about 11:00 PM, I got up, slightly nauseated, and headed for the bathroom. I had to vomit and then use the toilet. About every twenty to thirty minutes, I repeated the cycle. I would vomit and visit the toilet. Then, I would almost get to sleep, but after feeling alright, in minutes, I would be throwing up again. Every fifteen to twenty minutes, I would begin to feel sick again and repeat the sequence. Finally, about 1:00 AM, I went to Verna's room, and rapped on the door. She was immediately awake.

I told her what was happening, and she said, "Get your clothes on. You have food poisoning, and we're going to the hospital. You can't keep doing this. You'll dehydrate, and then you'll be in trouble. Wait until the next wave happens and get right down here. Then we're heading for the hospital.

I did what she said, and we arrived at the hospital about thirty minutes later.

When we arrived, she pulled up to the door and got out. The Hospital was totally dark. She ran up to the door and used her college ring to click on the heavy glass. Not too loud at first, and then with increasing urgency. Finally, a nurse stuck her head around the corner of the dark hall where a single light bulb shown and called out softly. "I'm sorry. We're closed. We don't reopen until tomorrow morning at 8:00 AM. Come back then." And she disappeared. "Oh-h-h! Not good!

That set Verna Fields off! Verna began rapping again on the glass in the door, much louder this time. When the nurse reappeared, Verna shouted, "This man needs to see a doctor! He's got food poisoning and he's completely dehydrating! Let us in!"

The nurse replied, "We don't have any beds, and besides, no doctor is on call right now. We can't help you." And she walked away again, into the darkness. "Big mistake!" Uhh!

Verna exploded! "Like hell you can't. I've got someone here who has food poisoning, and he needs to see a doctor.

"Whoa, Nellie!" That was a mistake. Verna was at the glass door, and now she was really mad, pounding on it with a fury like she would break it down. And I think she might have, but the nurse wisely reappeared and opened the door slightly, and in protest again, said in a louder voice, "I'm sorry, we can't help you! I told…" but it was too late.

Verna was in the door, dragging me in behind her and telling the nurse who was backing away: "Get him a gurney then if you don't have any beds. He has to have a doctor and a shot, or he'll be vomiting and having diarrhea all night. You can't just send us back to the motel. We're not going!"

Not willing to engage in fisticuffs with this crazy woman dynamo, the nurse showed up almost immediately with a gurney and had me lie down on it. When I had to vomit, I did. When I had to go to the bathroom, I did that. A couple of hours later, a doctor showed up next to me, gave me a shot, and I woke up eight hours later around 11:00 AM.

Verna was beside me. "How are you doing?" she asked. I said, "I think I'm alright. I think I got rid of everything I had."

She said, "That's normal. I've been through this before. You'll want to drink a little water—not much—and let your stomach settle. We're due in Bar Harbor in an hour and are going for a boat ride on a friend's yacht. Do you think you can handle that? We'll have food and drinks, but I don't think you'll want any of that. We will also have some water for you. Are you up for it?"

I said "Yes," and about an hour later, was gingerly stepping down the gang plank to the boat and going out to sea. Fortunately, I am not easily seasick, and I had no problems with that.

What I can tell you about this episode is this: "It helps to know what is happening. And sometimes, you have to basically decide that you 'will not be denied!'" That was what I saw in Verna Fields at one thirty in the morning! She was fearless and so determined! She knew what had to happen, and she showed by her actions and voice that she was going to get done what needed to be done. Verna was not to be denied! I slept all night.

I loved that woman and her resolve that came from seeing food poisoning before and knowing she had to take control. She was a great producer and a wonderful, talented professional who took great care of me that night. She was the Television Producer I hoped to be who handled whatever greeted me and "all other duties as assigned or NOT assigned but needed." She was in charge! There was no doubt in my mind or anyone else's. I had been given an incredible gift: a practical clinic in crisis management that I would need again, later. But I had seen Verna in action and knew that in a crisis, I had to make decisions, and on the basis of my convictions, I must follow through.

I didn't eat Lobster or Steamed Clams again for over twenty years. Actually, I have never eaten Steamed Clams again. I was told later they were probably the culprit, and I never ever want to repeat that night. "Burned once, shame on you—burned twice, shame on me!"

Finally, when we were ready to leave for home and our project was complete, Verna asked if I wanted to go to Washington, DC, to help edit the videos we had created. I called my boss back at Eastern Kentucky University and his answer was curt and to the point: "If you're not back in the office tomorrow morning, Needham, you're fired!"

So I got on the plane in Maine and headed for Richmond, Kentucky, and home. I always wondered what my life would have been like if I had decided to go to Washington and edit video, but that was not to be. Looking back, I made the right call. I didn't go back with Verna Fields, but I went home with a "lifetime of lessons."

Back at Eastern Kentucky University and its station, WKLE-TV 46, I went to work on monthly documentaries and the EKU Instructional TV series including a series on Shorthand and one on Accounting. I also did thirty-minute documentaries for the Kentucky Educational Television Network of thirteen stations, of which WKLE was one. I really enjoyed that and, over the months, recognized in looking at the work some of my student helpers did that some of them were very talented. I began to observe that I was better at identifying talent and directing them than actually producing the programs. I loved researching and writing them, but others seemed to eclipse me in their editing skills. That was both a surprise and an acknowledgement that I was better at managing people than pushing buttons. Others had better timing than I did, but I loved writing and producing programs, and I didn't want to give it up.

Some of my best programs were entitled *The Census: Who Counts* for 1970, *Blackthink: My Life as a Black Man and White Man* by Jesse Owens, *The Carpenters: Karen & Richard, Her Name Was Liberty* about the original understandings of "liberty" in the words of the New England preachers and our founding fathers from the early 1700s through the US revolutionary war, *Berea Community Schools: Open Concept Construction for K-12* about the first ever open-concept elementary-high school building with no interior walls between the rooms, *Mark Twain Tonight, Earl Combs of Old Kentucky*, Kentucky's first Major League Baseball Hall of Fame award winner, and two dozen others. It was a blast. I was finally in my element.

In August 1970, as we had planned, I stopped commuting weekly to see Judy in Terre Haute, and she joined me in Faculty Housing near the campus. Judy got a job at Estill County High School teaching music, where she worked until we moved to Indianapolis in May 1972.

In early 1972, I was called on the carpet by the Eastern Kentucky University President, Robert Martin. Until that time, I had never received anything but commendations for the documentary work I had done for the first two years. The content of my documentaries was something my Supervisor bragged about, and the Network appreciated our creative approach and the excellent production values. Content issues never surfaced once in that time period.

That is, until the EKU President began planning his coordinated effort to generate funding for several buildings at EKU he felt were necessary for the University's progress. EKU had the largest ROTC program in the United States, and we were at the height of the Vietnam war. The President thought that the documentary I had been preparing since November 1971 focusing on our outstanding ROTC program would distract from his legislative agenda to secure state construction funds he felt were absolutely necessary, and Dr. Martin did not want my efforts to bring attention to our ROTC classes that were contributing to the US acrimony over the conduct of the war. In other words, he wanted the ROTC documentary I was working on to just "go away silently" and not cause a stir.

Up to that time, I had the freedom to pursue my creativity, and my supervisor was very happy with my work. EKU's President decided, without seeing my work, that it might distract legislators from his agenda of requesting millions of dollars in construction funds, so he cancelled the documentary I had been working on for three months and decided to censor everything I did in the future. For me, that was the last straw.

I was disgusted and realized President Martin's censorship was all about politics, not my judgment or the quality of my work. I went to work on my résumé and three months later, had a new job in Indianapolis at the CBS station, WISH-TV.

Chapter 17

Indianapolis, Here I Come

The most interesting thing that happened in Richmond was that I found I loved producing television programs and researching and writing them, more than I loved directing and editing them. Secondly, I loved shooting the film and video involved, and I had a great eye for pictures. I was really disappointed by President Martin's abrupt censorship move, but I understood. And I was thrilled to be able to leverage my producing experience in Richmond into a mid-management position at WISH-TV, as its first Community Affairs Director. Here I was: my third "first-time job" in a row. Was that just a coincidence? Imagine that.

It was a heady promotion with a huge jump in salary. I moved from $9,000 a year to $13,000 a year. I was in the big time. By September 1972, I was making four times what I was earning in September 1968, and I was working in the market where I had day-dreamed, years earlier, I would someday get a chance to work. In 2023 dollars, that would be about $93,000. I was 28 years old.

When I worked at WTHI-TV in Terre Haute, and our station did the origination for *THE INDIANAPOLIS 500* each year, I had daydreamed of this day.

I was excited and honored to be working for WISH-TV, the top-rated News Station in Indianapolis and a part of the Corinthian Broadcasting Group of which there were five stations. As part of my new job, I began my friendship and working relationship with the Attorneys at one of the top FCC Law Offices in Washington—Covington & Burling. When I had questions, I would call them for advice. They were on retainer for us—they got a monthly fee—and I could call them any time I had questions. Not only was I the WISH-TV Community Affairs Director—I was the station's Legal Eagle—the person in charge of collecting and assembling the information for WISH-TV's License Renewal for 1976, and all the detail work that required. I am certain God knew I would need this background for my next job, and I had this experience handed to me. There are lots of stories there, but let me focus on the most important one.

My job was to oversee all our Public Affairs programs— our talk shows, our community activities, and our nonbroadcast public relations. In addition, I regularly interviewed the major community leaders in all the County Seats in central Indiana for seventy-five miles, and in Indianapolis and I fed the information I gathered to our News and Public Affairs program Producers. In my interviews, I would typically ask these leaders to tell me about the most important Problems, Needs, and Interests they saw in their community and sphere of influence and to write reports, summarizing their views.

I also served on boards of directors for non-profits where our station wanted a presence or where we had been asked to play a role like the Chamber of Commerce, United Way, the Urban League, and other entities, important to the station. I was one of the key substitutes our GM sent out to make speeches and talk about what the station was doing in the community when we were invited, and to attend dinners and other community meetings to which we were invited when the General Manager asked me to represent the station.

Serving in the community that way, turned out to be a busy part of my after-hours schedule. I would be attending dinner meetings several times a week, and Judy quickly tired of that and would not go, though she was invited. That turned out to be detrimental to our marriage. She wanted no part of the "roast beef and gravy circuit." She didn't want to participate, and I could not refuse to represent the station. That was my job. Because I was gone a lot, I did not realize it as she developed an interest in a colleague at her work—one of my golf buddies. Ultimately, he divorced his wife; Judy divorced me, and they got married. It was a difficult time and something I never saw coming.

Judy continued to teach music in Indianapolis, and I kept working at the station. When I told my boss, Bob McConnell, what was happening, he listened to my situation and then said: "Whatever you need to do, you should do it. But first, I'm telling you what you will NOT do. You will not quit your job. We love your work. We want you to stay with us. We are with you 100 percent, and if you need extra time off or counseling or other help, we will provide it. We are sorry this is happening, but I expect you to come to work and keep doing what you're doing. We will get through this together."

And I never doubted Bob McConnell meant it. He was wonderful from the time I heard about the divorce in July 1973 until it was final in April 1974. I had an important job, a supportive boss and co-workers, and I loved what I was doing. It was a very hard time for me, but I gradually accepted that I could not change Judy's mind, and that I had to adjust. And over time, I did just that.

That August, 1974, a program slot opened up for someone to host a program produced every Saturday for broadcast at 7:15 AM Sundays, called *Religion in the News*, and I asked Bob to do it. Since none of the newscasters wanted to fill the slot, my boss said I could do it as long as I did it on my own time and would do it without pay. I was glad for the distraction and was interested in the material and being on air. I jumped into it with both feet, and over that year, doubled the audience to 15,000 households. I experienced some success, and I was proud that in spite of this difficult time, I was making a difference. I was also learning a lot about the world of religion and how to put that newscast together. It was fun for me to get back into production again. I had missed it.

I dug into my work, we sold our house on north Pennsylvania in November we had purchased the year before, and I found a place to rent. Judy moved out, and we were separated and alone again. She kept our dog and bought new furniture from Kittles Fine Furniture, leaving me with a load of debt. I cut off our credit and started paying off what would today, be $30,000 in bills she had made for us. It was hard. But I resolved to do what I had to in order to get out of debt and restore my credit.

My father had always said that it was important to always have some debt so I would always have a reason to go to work each day. We did have some debt that was minor, but after Judy went furniture shopping for her new apartment, we had a huge amount of debt, none of which I was aware of until the bills started showing up, and I had to cut up our credit cards. That was the hardest thing to do— I could not trust her anymore.

I kept working hard at Channel 8 and eventually began dating again. Our divorce was final in April 1974, and I began dating a woman who had three children. She was also divorced from an abusive husband, and while the kids were very small and adorable, she was not the one for me. I dated a couple of other women in Indy too, but never felt a strong attraction to either one.

Chapter 18

Young Life: Getting Ready for What Is Next

Not long after that, one of our Ad Salesmen, introduced me to his sister Bonnie, and we began dating. She taught PE and coached gymnastics and volleyball at Carmel High School and was also a Young Life volunteer leader. As a result, I developed an interest in Young Life, a nondenominational Christian group for high school youth; and in the fall of 1974, I began going to Young Life Junior Leader training every Saturday so I could be a Junior Leader. Bonnie was a strong Christian and was reading a book about Corrie Ten-Boom. The TenBoom's were from Holland and had helped Jews escape from the Nazi's during World War II. Corrie was a survivor of Auschwitz. I was fascinated. Bonnie kept sharing Corrie TenBoom's books with me. I was enthralled by the TenBoom family's journey. I also was drawn to what was going on in Young Life, and really worked to understand why it was so successful.

I especially enjoyed the camaraderie of working with other young male leaders who were committed to Young Life and young people and were part of a great team doing something that obviously really mattered to the kids.

I was busy at work, but I loved this too. I was surprised a bit, but found a way to work it all in, and I liked working with Bonnie. Bonnie and I continued to date and work in Young Life at Broad Ripple High School.

Well, the Broad Ripple Club was just the beginning. In early November, the Young Life office called me and asked if I would be available to go on their annual ski trip. I told them I didn't ski, I had already used all of my vacation, and I could not afford to go. I was paying off my bills, had moved in with a roommate to cut my expenses in half, and just didn't have the money to go. They told me that if I went as a Junior Leader, I wouldn't have to pay for anything except incidentals. All food, transportation, lodging and equipment were included. As for skiing, they said, "We'll teach you what you need to know—no problem!" They asked me to ask my boss to see if I could take some time off without pay. So I asked God to show me what to say, and I walked into Mr. McConnell's office.

I vividly remember being afraid to talk to Bob about the time off, but I had already prayed about it and I had to ask. When I walked in the door, I asked if we could talk about an unusual request I had. He had me sit down and explain.

When I reviewed for him what we had accomplished that fall, and that I was caught up on my work, I asked if I could have a big favor. I told him about my volunteer work with Young Life at Broad Ripple High School and then North Central High School and how I had been invited to go on the ski trip. I asked if he could grant me three days off without pay after Christmas so I could go and be a Junior Leader and help with the 230 boys and girls going on the trip. He asked me about my work and where I was on the projects I had. Was I all caught up? I said I was, and he said, "Merry Christmas, Jim. Have a good time."

I said, "Thank you. I don't have any vacation left. Should I just tell Mr. Banta our CPA that I'm taking off three days without pay?"

And Bob said, "No, this one's on me. Have a great time. Thanks for doing this. See you the end of next week." And off I went. Little did I know I would have to be able to ski later for the family I was destined to inherit in Muncie.

When we got to Whitecap Mountain in Northern Wisconsin, I learned to fall down and get up again without taking off my skis, something you have to know to be safe on the slopes. Many of the Young Life kids had never skied before. I had not skied either, but I quickly got the hang of falling down with my skis on, and my job for the first two days of the trip was to show at least half of them how to fall down and get up again without removing their skis. That was hard at first, but by doing that, I met fully half of the kids, and we all had a good time. I had gotten comfortable on my skis as well.

At Whitecap Mountain, I did learn the basics of Snowplow Skiing, and two years later, after moving to Muncie and marrying Linda, my new bride and I took "our" kids skiing, and I was able to improve my skills and have a great time. One year after that, I taught our four-year-old, Brian to ski by holding onto his hands and snowplowing down the mountain, and later taught grandson Stevie to snowplow down the mountain, the same way, at Boyne Highlands. Skiing with Young Life had been a great gift, one I needed!

That trip to Whitecap was destined to be an important introduction to my new family, even though it happened two years before I even knew I would have a new family that would ski. And I was off to learn to ski and to help half of our campers learn to fall down with their skis on and get back up without endangering all the other skiers on the mountain by taking their skis off. They had to learn to roll over their skis with their skis grounded behind them and roll into a standing position. After doing that several hundred times, I knew how to do it too! I also ended up with two days to ski at the end of the trip after my job was completed, and I began to get the hang of how to snowplow ski myself.

At least, I could get down the mountain without killing myself or someone else. What I didn't know was that Linda's family was already learning to ski also, and that would be an important part of bonding with them when the time came. I was on my way, and without my knowing, God was preparing me for what I would encounter three years later.

Chapter 19

The Climb of a Lifetime

Bonnie and I kept working on Young Life that spring and had moved on to North Central High School. When the summer of 1975 came, I was also invited to attend Young Life's Frontier Ranch in Colorado with a group of two hundred students from Indianapolis, Gary, and Chicago. I didn't know any of them, but I was eager to see the Colorado Young Life Ranch property, and it sounded like a great vacation, so I signed on.

I took a week off to be a Junior Counselor with this rambunctious group of kids who were ready to have a great time at Frontier Ranch. There would be horseback riding, rafting, and a mountain climb, among other activities, and we all had the time of our lives. Frontier, a former Dude Ranch at 7,000 feet in the foothills of the Rockies, was where I met Skylar.

Skylar was a large young woman from Gary who had little confidence, partly because she was not in very good shape and significantly overweight. She was tentative about everything, especially when, in the middle of the week, we were scheduled to climb Long's Peak, a Fourteener with its summit at 14,259 feet.

According to OutThere Colorado, Longs Peak is the most dangerous and deadly mountain in the state, thanks to both the difficult 14.5-mile climb and huge drops. The other

30% of deaths on Longs Peak are said to have come from exhaustion, hypothermia, and cardiac arrest. I just found this information as I was writing this today. I don't know if Young Life still climbs Long's Peak. I do know that none of us knew that this climb was so dangerous on that day. Nonetheless, we all filed out of the buses at about 9:00 AM and were intent on being back by nightfall. We began the climb, which is not steep, about 10:00 AM, but from the bottom, you cannot see the summit. It didn't seem so tough when we started out. We just knew it was a long trip to the top.

Skylar was assigned to me and two other seasoned leaders, two guys and a girl, and we started up together. From the beginning, we knew it was going to be a challenge for Skylar and for us. She kept saying things like, "I can't do this. Just leave me behind and pick me up on the way back." We checked that out with our Frontier Camp Leaders and found out that our bus was to pick us up on the other side of the mountain. "No can do!" Staying behind on this side of the mountain was not an option.

When we asked our Camp staff guides about what to do, they answered cheerfully, "No one can stay behind. Everyone climbs this one. Just keep encouraging her. She had a physical. She can make this. Just help her keep going. We don't come back this way!" So we settled in to encouraging, nudging, pushing her from behind and beside her and giving her our hands and our backs, one step at a time.

Skylar complained and yelled at us a number of times. When we fell behind, we talked with her, and went over why we were all climbing this mountain, and that we would make it. She was never sure if we were trying to kill her or just get her to keep climbing. She really didn't know. Honestly, I didn't know either, but I trusted our Frontier Camp Guides, and we trusted God, and we kept going. Frequently, her friends would come back down the mountain a bit to encourage her, and she would start moving again.

As we neared the peak, after three hours of constant climbing and a few rest and water breaks, we still couldn't see the top. Since Long's Peak is a flat boulder field at the top, we just couldn't see it until we were almost upon it. But when we finally could see it, the final one hundred yards or so, Skylar did the unthinkable. She pushed us away, and started to walk on her own, without anyone's help. In fact, she almost jogged to the topmost stone that just sat there in the middle of that huge boulder field about half the size of a football field, and when she got there under her own power, she slumped down on the rock and began to cry. At first, just a whimper, but later, she sobbed. I rushed up to her and looked her in the face, asking if she was all right. And I'll never forget her face. This was the same angry face I had prodded and cajoled and teased up the mountain, but it was angry no more. Instead, she looked back at me, smiling through the tears splashing down her cheeks: "I never thought I could do it," she sobbed. "I never dreamed I could do it. I just didn't think I could make it."

And I added, "But you did. You did it! You did it on your own." And I gave her a big hug. Others were congratulating her too and we took pictures and looked at the view. It was 1:00 PM, four hours after getting off the bus. Over sixty peaks were visible everywhere from this mountain top, one of the highest in Colorado. Skylar had made it to the top, and we had been there to witness her quest, to encourage her, to trust God through all of this, and to make it possible for her to conquer her fear, stay on her feet, and summit one of the tallest peaks in the Rockies.

That climb changed Skylar. I'm not sure how, but I can swear it seemed that on the climb down, Skylar's feet barely touched the ground. And for the rest of that week, perhaps for the rest of her life, Skylar would never be the same. She had faced her fears, kept putting one foot in front of the other, given in, albeit grudgingly, to our persistence and nudging, and helping and pushing, and made the climb to the top and that incredible view. But even more, she had seen what God could help her do when she allowed herself to overcome her fear of the unknown, trust Him, and keep going. It was one of my proudest moments as a Young Life leader. I will always remember Skylar and the climb up Long's Peak "the most dangerous peak in all of Colorado" I learned just today as I wrote this. At least that's what the survey of most dangerous Colorado Mountains reported in 2019. Maybe she had good reason to be scared. But we made it. SHE made it! GOD made it possible! The impossible IS possible with God at the center of our focus—just another example of God's faithfulness when we trust Him…unforgettable faithfulness!

Chapter 20

God's Surprise: Who Is Corrie TenBoom?

By fall 1975, I had read two of Corrie TenBoom's books, and had managed to take on another WISH-TV program as host—*Teleconference* at 6:00 PM on Saturday nights. It was a call-in program where we had a guest or two and took questions from the audience. Fortunately, they were screened off-camera and handed to me as notes, to ask the questions. I liked the format, and though I was not paid for this program either, I enjoyed the better time slot and the fact that our audience was around forty thousand households. It was much more popular than *Religion in the News*. But I kept doing them both.

Earlier that fall, a friend of mine from Youth for Christ called to ask if I would have Corrie TenBoom on my talk show. I told him I knew about her and would be thrilled to book her. My program manager wasn't so sure. He had never heard of her. The show was set for Saturday, November 15th. But I was told if I didn't have a "news hook" by then—something related to a news story that would grab the audience's attention, I would not be allowed to have her on. I started pondering that, but also set up a substitute program.

And I started praying. If God wanted her on the show, some-thing would make that possible.

The group ascertainment interviews I ended up being in charge of, were set for September and October, and in the midst of those interviews, I was invited to go to lunch with Tom Wallace, the General Manager of the Christian Radio Station in Indianapolis. The program at that Rotary Meeting at the Indianapolis Athletic Club was a charismatic former football player named Bob Davenport who founded Taylor University's Wandering Wheels...a group that had criss-crossed America on bicycles more than forty-two times, and gone to many countries across the world to share their testi-monies about their faith in Jesus. I was intrigued.

When we got there, Tom found us a table with a good view, and after a quick bite of lunch, we settled in to hear the coach's story. Davenport was energetic, loud and sounded like a football coach, and he told how he had learned about Jesus after starring as an All-American Fullback at USC. What he found out about himself was that he was a lot more excited about what Christ was doing in his life than he had ever been about plunging through the line with the ball, and that the Wandering Wheels was the outcome of his passion and his commitment to God. He was really excited—almost too excited. I was a little put off and ready to go.

Tom asked me what I thought, and I said, "Frankly, he seems like a phony to me. I work in Television, and he just seems too pumped up to be real." Tom asked me to go up and talk to him. I said I didn't have time, but Tom went to the restroom, so I wandered up to get in line. There were three people in front of me, and as I turned to go, that line disap-peared, so I stepped up and looked him in the eye. "What do you like about giving a talk to a bunch of businessmen about your Wandering Wheels?" I asked.

And without skipping a beat, Bob countered, "What's not to like? I love telling how Jesus took me and made my life relevant and changed me and is changing all the kids that have ridden and are riding with me all across America. It's a trip for me, and it's a trip for them to see how people embrace them and their testimonies. I wouldn't want to do anything else!" After 30 seconds, I could see that his passion was real…that he really was energized by what he was doing and the kids whose lives he was changing, and I was impressed. He was authentic, and very polite. I turned to catch up to Tom.

When we got in the car, Tom asked me again, "So what do you think now?"

"I'm surprised to be saying this," I said, "but Bob's for real. He just has a fire in his belly that is amazing! I thought he was a phony, but he's not! I can see that now. He's just got something I don't have."

Tom quizzed me: "What do you mean?"

I fumbled a bit and finally said, "You know, Tom, I'm on a dozen boards of directors for non-profits and spend twelve to fourteen hours a day working at the station and helping people and giving myself away, and yet at the end of the day, I come up empty. I just can't do enough, regardless of how much good I try to do."

And Tom said, "Jim, what you're experiencing is what Blaise Pascal termed a "God-shaped vacuum in your heart which God put there and cannot be filled by anything except by God."

I said, "I don't know. I've been baptized, gone to church all of my life, went through catechism, went forward at a Billy Graham Crusade, and even got baptized a second time at twenty-one by immersion. What more can I do? I know who God is. I'm doing everything I can."

Tom had stopped the car by then in the parking lot at Channel 8, and he turned to me. "I have one question for you that might help. Have you ever prayed that Jesus would take control of your life, put Himself in the driver's seat of your life, and let you ride along and go wherever He would take you? Have you ever given your life over to Jesus and asked Him to take control?"

I paused for a very long moment, and then looking straight ahead, I dropped my head and said, "I guess not. I've really made a mess of my life. I've done all the things I wanted to do, and I can see I really can't make my life what I want it to be. In the midst of trying so hard, I come up empty."

And Tom said, "Do you have a good reason why you can't put Jesus in charge of your life right now?"

Somewhat bewildered, I paused for the longest time, "No, I guess I don't"

And he said, "Then pray with me."

And as Tom prayed with me, and I repeated the words, we prayed the sinners' prayer. I said I was a sinner and could not be what God wanted me to be and that my sins separated me from God. I prayed that Jesus would come into my life as my Lord and take control of my life and make me what he wanted me to be—and at the end, I thanked Jesus for coming into my life and taking me where He wanted me to go.

When I did that and repeated the prayer that Tom prayed with me, word for word, I lifted up my eyes, and the tears were streaming down my cheeks. I felt the world slip off of my shoulders—the weight was gone—the emptiness had disappeared! I was free again. And I sat there and cried and told Tom what I was feeling.

Tom asked me if I would join a group of similar men who were learning how to share their faith, and who were also trusting God with all of their hearts, and that they would share with me what I would want to do to be able to share what God had just done for me. And I said, "Yes, I'd like that."

Remember too, I was running full out: Young Life Junior Leader training, and also preparing to have Corrie TenBoom on my program, and doing my Saturday talk show, and serving on a dozen boards, and overseeing this extravaganza of interviewing dozens of community leaders with six television stations and twenty-five radio stations, yet here I was, crying—my tears falling as I sat in the front seat of Tom's car, having just given my life away to Jesus for real! It was an unforgettable moment.

Something had just happened! I was sure of one thing: something in me had changed, and I would never be the same. Jesus was in charge of my life, moment by moment, and I was no longer going it alone.

I went back into the station, and I was resolved that things were getting better. I kept working, finished the community leader interviews in the next couple of weeks and began to worry how I would ever get Corrie TenBoom on *Teleconference*. What I learned later is it wasn't really up to me. I prayed and asked for God's help. I didn't know what else to do.

As a matter of preparation, I read several newspapers every day to keep up with world news and Indianapolis news and also what was going on in our community. That was my job as Community Affairs Director/Administrative Assistant to the General Manager.

I had almost given up hope. It was late Friday afternoon, the day before Corrie was tentatively going on *Teleconference*, and I was looking at the *Wall Street Journal*, and there was my answer, Front Page and Center: "United Nations Approves Resolution: 'Zionism Is Racism' "—I had my news hook.

I ran down to my program manager, showed him the paper, and he said, "You'd better have someone from the Jewish community here that can help interpret what all of this means."

In my assignment to pull together significant community leaders, I had become friends with the Chief Rabbi of the Indianapolis Hebrew Congregation, the largest synagogue in Indianapolis, who had participated in our interviews, and

I immediately put in a call to him. Rabbi Saltzman answered the phone.

"This is Jim Needham from Channel 8, calling for Murray Saltzman. Is he in?" I asked breathless.

And the voice replied, "This is Murray Saltzman, Jim. How are you?" And I told him my story, and what had just happened.

I asked if he knew about my show *Teleconference*, and he said he sometimes watched it. I asked if he knew anything about Corrie TenBoom. And he answered, "Indeed I do. I know what she and her family did during the war."

He asked when my program would be on. "At 6:00 PM, tomorrow," I said.

There was a short pause. Then Rabbi Saltzman remarked, "I just looked out the window and I'm thinking that by 6:00 PM tomorrow evening, it will surely be dark, and the Sabbath will be over. I'll be there."

That's how Rabbi Saltzman ended up on my show with Corrie TenBoom. I think you can see how God steered me to just the right information at just the right time to make everything work like clockwork for Corrie to appear on my show and led to a fascinating half hour of lively talk, incredible insights, an embrace by Rabbi Saltzman of the TenBoom family's sacrifices (the whole family died in Auschwitz except for Corrie), and a growing understanding and amazement of how God had intervened or preplanned or something so that Corrie would be sitting next to me on that Saturday evening, November 15. It was to be an evening I never forgot and exactly one month to the day from when I had committed my life to Christ and Jesus leading me. Wow! Explain that! It was definitely not a coincidence. I was beginning to believe it was more a "God-incident."

As preparation, I did go to see Corrie speak at the Indianapolis Convention Center that very night, before she was on my show the following day. Bonnie and I sidled in and sat in the bleachers in a crowd of eight thousand, as Corrie was being introduced. She ambled up to the podium, this eighty-three-year-old "Tramp for the Lord" as she labeled herself, cleared her throat and moved the microphone in front of her.

When she began to speak, she straightened up and had a smile on her lips. I couldn't wait to see what would happen. She started by thanking God for what He had done for her and what He was doing here, bringing her to speak at the Bill and Gloria Gaither Praise Gathering for the second year in a row.

I had called Jim Gerard, the Noon Talk show host on Channel 6, earlier, doing my due diligence. I wanted to know what to expect, so I checked out what Corrie had been like the year before when she was a guest on Jim's show. Gerard warned me I would have to be on my guard because "Corrie will take over the interview. You'll have to cut her off. She has so much enthusiasm once she gets going, it's hard to maintain control. Just be warned," he said with a laugh.

And that's exactly what she did with my show and also that Friday night at the Convention Center. Once she got rolling, she straightened up and was no longer 83. She looked more like sixty or so. But she was no longer the old woman who had ambled to the podium. She was on fire with stories and thanksgiving to God, and challenges. She was a formidable speaker, and she commanded our attention for a full seventy-five minutes, and when she ambled back to her chair to thundering applause, her words were never to be forgotten.

I knew I had my hands full.

I had recommitted my life to Christ on October 15, 1975. I knew that. I deliberately put God in charge. Now what? Well, why did I worry? With God in charge, *Teleconference* was extraordinary, and many people called and two hung on to talk with me about the show. One caller said she loved the show and Corrie TenBoom, and that I was the rudest interviewer she had ever seen. She complained, "You kept cutting her off again and again. At least you could have let her make her point."

"Oh, but you see," I opined. "I believe like she believes. I was just—"

And the caller cut me off with a scream: "DON'T lie to me. Don't try and DIGNIFY your rude behavior. You're LYING to me. Everyone saw you. At least you could have been CIVIL with her!" And she SLAMMED down the phone.

There was a second caller who also would not hang up until she talked with me. So I took the call. I couldn't talk long...I had a *Religion in the News* show to do with Corrie as my special guest. In the meantime, Bonnie was talking with Corrie.

As soon as I picked up the phone and said, "Hello," the caller erupted: "Where did you get that shill of a Jew. He wasn't Jewish. Whoever Rabbi what's his name was, he wasn't Jewish. Did you see his body language? He started out facing away from Ms. TenBoom, and by the end of the show, he was virtually embracing everything she was saying and leaning into her, and it was DISGUSTING! How could you PUT someone on like that?"

I started explaining who Rabbi Saltzman was and that he was not only the Chief Rabbi of the largest Hebrew Congregation in Indianapolis but also a member of the US Civil Rights Commission, and the caller erupted again, screaming like the woman before. "THAT was no Rabbi and certainly not a Jew. Your show is so dishonest!" And she also slammed the phone down.

So much for being honest!

The interview with Corrie TenBoom for *Religion in the News* also went very well. And as a special treat, Bonnie and Corrie and I had a short chat with her after the show. We thanked her for including us in her schedule. She took a minute to autograph the book Bonnie had brought with her, and then she left with Paul Palmeri. Our time with Corrie was at an end. The people from Youth For Christ that had sponsored her and had called me months earlier to say they had chosen my show as the only show she would be on, were very pleased with the two programs and the guest Rabbi who had participated.

In my mind, God's hand was all over what had just happened. And I thanked Him for graciously orchestrating an incredible weekend. What an adventure, beginning Friday at 4:30 PM.

I wondered then, what will be next? I didn't have long to wait.

Chapter 21

How Do I Grow My Faith?

Shortly thereafter, the Indianapolis film premiere of Corrie TenBoom's life story, *The Hiding Place* was set to launch in December. I was invited as an honored guest to dine with Jeanette Clift, the woman who played Corrie in the film. Jeanette sat next to me at the dinner, and we had a great discussion. Jeanette told me how she had begun the filming with Corrie TenBoom while she was an agnostic…not sure what she believed, but in spite of her lack of faith, Jeanette won the part. She told me that after working with Corrie for a year—filming her story—she had accepted Christ and that making the film with Corrie TenBoom had dramatically changed her life.

I asked her what the secret was. What would she advise someone who wanted to grow his faith? Jeanette was quick to reply: "Corrie told me, 'Read Romans 10:17 'Faith comes from hearing, and hearing from the Word of God.'"

"I did that," Jeanette said, "and as I did, reading the words of God changed me. I became a believer."

So I went home that night and I resolved to do something I had never done before: read the Bible through, and I began that very night with Romans 10:17.

It is ironic that Bonnie and I had also been attending a weekly Bible class every Friday night, where a local Carmel dentist was teaching from the book of Romans. How timely—how strange was that? Another coincidence? I think not.

God was always going before me. I was beginning to see that and experience that. I praise Him now, and He never ceases to amaze me. Just today, I came home early from working out, and there, sitting on the driveway, was Linda's car. I wondered what was wrong with it and why it wasn't garaged. When the door went up, there they were. We had been struggling with how to get two two-hundred-pound bookcase units down from the attic so we could donate them to the Rising Hope Church Auction.

The workers from Habitat's Restore Shop had been to our home earlier in the week and checked them out. They apologized and told us they were not allowed to bring down heavy furniture from an attic, and they rejected them, saying "It's against our rules. For our safety and the safety of what you're donating, we're not allowed to move heavy items down from attics that are that large. You'll have to find another way to get them down." We were disappointed as they drove away with our old living room couch but left the bookcases behind. What would we do? I couldn't manage or even help to manage bringing them down. I said we'd have to hire some movers. That's what we would do.

When I got home and saw the seventy-eight-inch-high bookcases sitting in the garage in Linda's parking place, I asked how that had happened. Her answer: "It was a God thing. We had a couple of guys come by to do some other work, and when I asked, they said, "We can do that, and in twenty minutes, it was all done. Linda gave them a few dollars, and thanked them. How would we have known to ask God to provide two 250-pound young men who could easily handle those two bookcases and put them on the floor where the volunteers from Rising Hope could load them into a pick-up and deliver them to the church auction? We wouldn't have known what to pray for. But Jesus told the disciples not to worry about what to say, but when confronted by an unknown situation, to ask God for His help, and the words would be provided. Like Linda said, "It was a God thing!"

"We Thank you, God. We praise You for making provision for us in so many ways, too many times to recount fully here. But WE know, and You know of our praise, and we thank You for always going before us. I'm sure what transpired did not surprise You, even though it surprised us! You are an awesome and loving God!"

Back in 1975 again, the adventure continued in Indianapolis. I moved from our idyllic home on North Pennsylvania with the leaded glass windows to Williamsburg on the Lake. It was November 1973 when we sold it. I moved again in October 1974 when my lease ran out and I decided I had to cut my expenses again. A year went by with that roommate and in December 1975, I decided I was going to trust God and give ten percent of my gross check to God each month as an act of faith, and I wrote in my checkbook: "Out of Debt in '76." I still owed thousands of dollars for the furniture and furnishings Judy had purchased with our credit cards when she moved out. I just knew I couldn't keep living like this, and that I had to find a better way to pay my bills so I could get my head above water again and eliminate my debt.

I remember one particular week in Indianapolis, just before Christmas, when the six men in my Bible study at Northwood Christian Church met for our Bible study at John Casteel's house. John was a brilliant man who had been Editor of *Christian Century Magazine* for thirty-five years. As he approached his 80th birthday, his granddaughter had asked him what he had learned in his eighty years. He told us confidentially, he didn't want to treat her question flippantly, or say "Nothing," so he pondered her question and finally, came up with this concise reminder which he had written on a card for each of us.

This is what John wrote: "In the greatest of matters, before you have half as much information as you need to have to know for sure what you should decide, you have to decide. Whether the question is about life or death, or where to live or with whom to spend your life, or a surgery, or pulling the plug for an aging parent, or putting a pet to sleep, or what career you should follow."

"In every case, you will never have half as much information as you need to have to know for sure what to decide, and you will have to decide. If you don't decide, time and events will decide for you. So here is what I say: 'I believe Jesus is the Son of God, that he lived and died in Jerusalem for my sins and was raised from the dead in three days. Jesus lives today and through His Holy Spirit, dwells in me. So I consider what I know, thank Him for the gift of faith He has given me in His word, and ask him to direct me by giving me His peace about the decision. Then, claiming His peace, I decide."

"Finally, I thank Him for His peace and move on to the next moment in my life when I must decide again a difficult question. I trust that by relying on this process, God is with me with every breath, so I am never alone. And regardless of the outcome, I will be with Him now and after the decision I reach."

Since I really do trust that God is in me and works through me, John Casteel's advice has been one of the most valuable pieces of perspective I have ever received. It reminds me of what I chose as my "life verse" when I was in the Timothy Project and learned to write out my testimony for the "elevator speech" (thirty seconds) and the longer testimony (two minutes).

And I chose this set of verses because it is laser-focused for me on what I think is the most important element of trusting God in the moment. Here it is, Philippians 4:4–9 "Rejoice in the Lord always. I will say it again: Rejoice! Let your gentleness be evident to all. The Lord is near. Do not be anxious about anything, but in every situation, by prayer and petition, with thanksgiving, present your requests to God. And the peace of God, which transcends all understanding, will guard your hearts and your minds in Christ Jesus. Finally, brothers and sisters, whatever is true, whatever is noble, whatever is right, whatever is pure, whatever is lovely, whatever is admirable—if anything is excellent or praiseworthy—think about such things. Whatever you have learned or received or heard from me or seen in me—put it into practice. And the God of peace will be with you."

How could it get any better than that? Having the "Peace of God" about what I decide? I think that's PRICELESS!

One of the things that I believe makes Bob Ross so successful and approachable and enjoyable to watch is that as he paints, he becomes the personification of this admonition from Paul. Think about it. Bob shows all who watch, how to focus on what is true, noble, right, pure, lovely, admirable, excellent or praiseworthy—what a recipe for thinking about all that is good in what you are doing, and jettisoning, at least for thirty minutes, the negative thoughts that arise when you do something and say, "darn," or even worse. Bob says, "No, it's not a mistake. It's a happy accident." And whatever you've done, you can transform it into something beautiful.

Bob wasn't God, but he was superb at focusing on what was good and what could be good, and never on what was bad, ugly, or disappointing. We should all choose to be that way as often as we can. It's a highway to happiness and peace with God. If God is sovereign and knows all things, is always present, is always pulling for the best for us in what life has to offer, why would we not approach our thinking in that way?

Back to Indianapolis: To cut my expenses further, I found a roommate at The Landings, and cut my expenses from $500 per month at Williamsburg on the Lake to $200 per month, and moved in with this person I found in the newspaper want ads. That seemed to be a good idea! It was a good deal financially, until the unthinkable happened. I was on-air, live, on the set of *Teleconference* and realized that I had something crawling on my neck. Since my back was often sore, I would lay down on the floor and stretch before heading into Channel 8 to do my six-o'clock show.

That night, during my TV show, Teleconference, as I was asking questions live on the air, a flea was crawling up my neck toward my hairline, and I didn't know what to do. Finally, I touched it, and it moved away. Later in the broadcast, it showed up again. That was all I could take! I had a confrontation with my roommate when I got home that night. When I joined him in November 1974, he was alone. By December 1975, he had moved in a large black dog and also his girlfriend to live with him. I was finished!

I didn't know what to do, but I had developed a dear friend who was a Young Life leader. I called him, and he said he had a spare bedroom and would rent it to me for $150 per month. I was convinced I had to cut my expenses even further, so I tried to sell my car which now had 100,000 miles on it, but I couldn't get anyone to even call me about my ad. So I fixed it up, and kept driving it.

I moved in that very night with Andy Mayo, my dear friend and fellow Young Life Leader who lived in Broad Ripple just off of Meridian Street. He had no dog, and his girlfriend did not live with him. I was safe again. It was a rough passage, but a necessary one. No more roommates with dogs or girlfriends.

I attended church each week, prayed a lot, kept volunteering with Young Life as a Volunteer Leader, and did talks every week for groups of kids from North Central High School. Those talks about Jesus helped me when I volunteered later in 1988, thirteen years later, to teach the adult seniors Sunday School Class at High Street—a journey that would end up lasting twenty-six years. It also prepared me to teach at Ball State where I moved from managing

WIPB-TV, Channel 49 to teaching in January 1993, some-thing I never envisioned. Who would have thought? Why does God always go before us like He promises? As I look back over my life, there is no question that is what was hap-pening! He was preparing me for what would come next. God never changes, does He?

My wife, Linda, has a favorite saying: "God never wastes anything." I know she's right, and she is prescient to bring that up at appropriate times. When we were at the Gaither Praise Gatherings in Indianapolis many of the first fifteen years they held them, there was a comic once who said he had the most important thing to tell all of us guys, and the gals didn't need to listen (but they did!). Here is what he said, "Guys, memorize this, and you will always be happy! 'Happy Wife, Happy Life.' Did you get that?" And at that, Linda nudged me in the ribs and asked, "Did you hear that? What did he say?"

And I repeated it: "Happy Wife, Happy Life." And she smiled.

I've quoted that many times to others, and also to our children. I believe it's true because it IS true!

Back to Indianapolis and late 1975. I had committed myself to getting out of debt in '76. I didn't know how that would happen, but I was working hard to be approved as doing what I was doing to glorify God. That was my daily goal. *Teleconference* and *Religion in the News* were going well. In February, Bonnie and I broke up, and I started dating someone else. But that person did not ring my chimes. So I kept at it, doing Young Life and my shows and preparing Channel 8 for its upcoming License Renewal. Then, in April, I asked to meet with Bob McConnell, my GM, to talk about my future with WISH-TV. He told me I was doing a great job, but he did not see a real future anywhere for me at WISH: not in sales, not in News, not in Traffic or Accounting, and not where I was then, Administrative Assistant to the GM.

For the first time ever in my career, I was telling my boss I was looking at another job opportunity. I described it for him: General Manager of the PBS station, WIPB-TV in Muncie. It was licensed to Ball State University.

Since I had never shared with any boss I had ever had that I was looking for another job, I was shaking in my boots and worried he might fire me on the spot, but instead, he encouraged me. The former Channel 8 Program Manager, Dave Smith, had retired from WISH-TV a couple of years earlier and was then teaching at Ball State University in the TCOM Department and would likely give me a good recommendation, so McConnell said I should apply. He thought it might prove to be a perfect "fit" for me.

With my application in, and a positive recommendation from Bob McConnell on the way, I waited to hear from WIPB-TV. After a week or so, they invited me to come for an interview. In the process, the persons I interviewed with, asked me if I could create a station that was very strong in community programming. I told them I had been in charge of community content for all of the public affairs programs at WISH-TV for four years, and I was sure I could do the job. Then they asked what an example of good community programming would look like. And in my confidence, I said: "Well, I'm hosting a program called *Teleconference* on Channel 8. It is on tomorrow night at 6:00 PM. If you'll tune in, you'll find out."

As I look back on that, it was a pretty overconfident challenge. But I was confident that God was going before me, and I thought that taking that risk was worth it. Besides, the program that was airing the next night focused on Him. It was for the "I Found It" campaign.

In 1976, bumper stickers and billboards appeared across America that said simply "I Found It! YOU can TOO" Organized by Campus Crusade—now known as CRU. Disseminated through local congregations, the idea was that strangers would ask what had been found and you'd answer

"Jesus" as an opportunity to share your personal testimony or the four spiritual laws. According to CRU's material, the campaign was extraordinarily successful and 85 percent of all Americans were exposed in the course of its run.

So I said, "Tune in. You'll see." And the rest is history. My interviewers must have liked the program because early Monday morning, I received a call telling me I had been selected to become the second General Manager of WIPB-TV beginning May 25, 1976. My salary jumped by 50 percent. And I thought, "I might make my goal of paying off my debt by December after all."

Later when I came to the station, people wondered what had happened for me to surge ahead of the top candidate, a Vice President for the Maryland Center for Public Broadcasting in Baltimore. But I knew. It was "a God thing," not anything I had done. I told them what I had done, but I did not tell them what I thought and to Whom I had given my thanks.

To me, it was like a miracle. I told my GM about the job opportunity. He didn't fire me. He encouraged me. I had an insider at Ball State who had given me a good recommendation and had steered me initially at Channel 8 to get the job of Community Affairs Director, and it had all happened incredibly fast and with little effort on my part. It was too easy, or so it seemed. More to follow.

When I came to Muncie for the interviews, one of those I met with was Edmund Ball, the Chairman of the Ball Corporation Board and immediate Past President of Ball Corporation who was on the PBS Board of Directors. He had lunch with me and asked me a very pointed question. This is what Ed said: "I'm on the PBS Board and also still active at Ball Corporation. We have a number of meetings each year, and I sometimes am unable to attend those meetings. Do you feel confident you could attend in my place and bring back what you learn and keep me abreast of what PBS is doing if I had to depend on you?"

And of course, with the confidence I had gained from being in charge of the Ascertainment Interviews and License Renewal Project and my work for the President, and my work as a TV Producer for three years, I said, "Yes, sir. Absolutely. I know I can handle that."

And when the times came, and they did, I attended for Ed Ball and never embarrassed him and always left him with good reports that demonstrated to him later that he had made a good choice in affirming me for the GM position at WIPB.

When I got back to the station on the day I got the call from Ball State about the WIPB General Managership, I took the materials back to the "I Found It" campaign office in Broad Ripple, and found the desk with the names starting with K-Z. They asked me my name and I told them, "I'm Jim Needham from Channel 8 with materials we used on WISH-TV Saturday night."

When I said that, a woman called out to me from across the room, and said, "Jim Needham? Could I talk with you before you go?"

I turned in the bumper stickers and other materials we had used to promote the "I Found It Campaign" on our *Teleconference* program and walked to the table where she was now standing. "I just wanted to meet you in person," she said, looking up at me, "and to thank you for putting our program on your station, and for doing such a good job with it. I know it did a lot of good."

She continued, "I just wanted you to know you are an answer to prayer, actually lots of prayers. Last August when we committed to doing this 'I Found It' campaign, we were facing a roadblock of sorts because none of the Indianapolis TV stations, or Radio stations were accepting product and service advertising from advocacy groups like ours."

"So we organized our volunteers and started to pray for each of the stations and for each of the executives and management people at all of the stations. I had your name, and I have been praying for you every day since then, and the success of this program is the result of God answering our prayers. We asked that He would somehow change the minds of all of the stations and allow them to accept our advertising when it came time for the campaign to begin. Last February, all of a sudden, the stations all decided to accept our advertising for the first time in history, and we were off and running. And then you put it on your program, and it had a wide airing and a good audience."

"I just wanted to thank you in person for your role in this," she continued. Then she added, "How has this year been for you?"

I stood there for a moment and my eyes welled with tears, and I told her. "This has been the most incredible year of my life. I learned about Corrie TenBoom, and actually met her and had her on my program. I was given my own early Saturday evening talk show, Jesus came into my life, and I recommitted my life to Him, and I have a brand-new job that begins in about 3 weeks."

"I am excited!" I continued—"No, I am overwhelmed with gratitude and praise for God who has done more than I could have hoped for over these months when you have been praying for me! What a journey it has been, and I know it is only beginning. Thank you for praying for me and for helping to make this all possible."

I turned and walked away, filled with gratitude for much that I had not known, but also for what I now knew were truly acts of God. There was no other explanation I would accept but that God truly was going before me, that God was continuing to lead me and grant me His favor, and that He had opened these doors for His purposes. I had been blessed by what I would begin to call "Divine Appointments," something only explainable by allowing myself to recognize that God continues to intercede in the affairs of our lives, and in my life in particular. Wow! What a thought!

Pastor Rick Warren calls these events "God-incidents," NOT coincidents. They are not accidents in the history book. They are God Himself, staging the greatest adventure ever, and often, they go unrecognized. I resolved to try to point to them as they happen, or when I discover His hand is the driving force.

My favorite prayer when I'm parking for any event or appointment is to thank God for my parking place. "I just need one," I pray out loud, so the kids will recognize God is in the details of our lives. And while it seems trivial and a bit audacious, if we are to be in prayer constantly, as the Bible reminds us, why not ask for God's favor when you need a place to park? So it's routine for me to sing out my prayer. And it is routine when that single spot opens up to thank God in the moment. And while they laugh at that, I suspect they all remember those parking places opening up time and again and hearing my hopeful prayer. They KNOW what I believe. And they have often seen this solid evidence before that God is listening.

I remember a specific instance as we attended a Home-coming Football game at IU in Bloomington, Indiana, where I dropped the family off at my daughter Kirsten's favorite steakhouse. The football game had just ended, and the downtown side streets were packed with cars. As the family got out, I asked them to order me something to drink as I stopped the car at the curb.

Then, before they could be seated, I walked in the door. "Where did you park, Dad?" Kirsten asked. And I answered, "In the spot God gave me, right outside the door." They all laughed. Some looked out the window to see our car, right out front.

As I dropped them off, the car in front of the restaurant started, blinked its lights, backed out of its spot, and pulled away, and I pulled in. Why that has happened dozens of times is a Holy mystery to me, but also a reason to be convinced that God wants our attention all of the time, even in the little things. If He cares about every hair on my head (many are now missing in action), then parking places and a recognition that He is truly sovereign, by the driver, must merit a breath of His attention.

I don't brag for me, but for God's Holy Spirit who wants God to be ever-present in our thoughts and prayers, even for parking places. Thanks be to God for His attention to detail. From God's record so far, I'll keep praying. I know He is faithful. I'm the one that sometimes drops the ball.

Chapter 22

A New General Manager
at WIPB-TV

On May 25, 1976, I began work at WIPB-TV. I was to be in charge of a very small station with a total of 10 employees. To put it in perspective, I had just left a station and deluxe facility of 40,000 square feet that employed two hundred persons to fill the same number of hours on air as WIPB had. Our little station on Minnetrista was located in a century-old house of 4,600 square feet. What a contrast.

The first General Manager, Bob Faull, greeted me and took me around to meet all the staff. He told me he would be there with me for the first week and then would be available to me by phone as needed over the next weeks and months as questions arose for issues that we did not discuss during my transition with him. Bob also urged me to go to the Development Conference in Phoenix, which was coming up in June, and that I cherry-pick as much information as possible from other managers who would be there. The conference also gave me my first opportunity to network with other small stations that were successfully dealing with the same kinds of challenges I would be facing.

So I set that plan in motion, and in Phoenix, I went around introducing myself to every small-station manager I could find, especially those in the Midwest. What surprised me most was how open to sharing these managers were from small and large stations. I was beginning to build a cadre of advisers who were friendly and only too willing to share the lessons and shortcuts, many had learned the hard way.

Next, when I returned home, I began meeting the Eastern Indiana Community Television (EICTV) Board of Directors and our Chairperson for the Joint Advisory Board, the President of the Ball State University Foundation and our Joint Advisory Board, Ralph Whitinger.

One of the greatest blessings for me is that what I found on my EICTV board was a group of top business leaders in Muncie and a number of exceptional entrepreneurs who were not only my board members but my mentors. Ralph and Ed Ball were two of them, and I will always be grateful for their friendship and guidance.

Rather than immediately relocating from Indianapolis to Muncie, I decided to commute from Broad Ripple for a few weeks until I got my feet on the ground. I was still working with Carmel Young Life, so I was regularly taking part in weekly Young Life meetings there and working with Bonnie on meetings and group events as they evolved.

Back at work, I was beginning to wonder if I was the right person for the WIPB-TV job. All of a sudden, one by one, the staff members were turning in their resignations. I was having to hire new people, and I didn't have much time. One of the staff members told me that they were working on building the new Independent TV station, WFFT-TV/55 in Fort Wayne, that was owned by a Muncie Businessman who was hiring them away as needed. Bob Faull, the former WIPB GM was managing the construction and hiring my former staffers to help put WFFT on the air. I could see the writing on the wall. One of them even confided in me that they "all knew the station was going dark," and they wanted another job for security. They thought WIPB-TV was on its way out of business. I just shook my head. Their morale was low, and they collectively were convinced WIPB would not survive.

At first, I was upset with the theft of my WIPB staffers who were being lured away for more money and greater security by this systematic loss of talent. Later, I realized that as they left, God was giving me the opportunity to hire my own people. As I hired new staff, I looked for people excited about doing local production and that had a variety of experiences at other stations. I knew I needed energetic young team members who had significant production experience elsewhere and the desire to make WIPB a successful small station and that could help me create the burst of local programming that would help us to thrive in the months and years ahead.

I remember night after night getting down on my knees by my bed in Broad Ripple in Andy's apartment, asking God to reassure me that He had not moved me to Muncie and Channel 49 to fail. "What is the answer?" I wondered aloud. And then, there it was, right in front of me—in the Bible.

Someone had suggested that I read Proverbs, one chapter a day, and as I was reading it one evening, there was my answer, straight from God. Proverbs 11:14 said it as plain as day, "In an abundance of counselors, there is wisdom." Wisdom was what I needed, so I started systematically meeting with my board members: with Ralph Whitinger, with Ed Ball, with my first President, Tom Sargent who was fighting cancer and going to Houston for treatments every two months. And I regularly met with Oliver Bumb, the Ball State Vice President who oversaw the operations and the station's personnel matters.

In July I took the plunge and moved to Muncie's southwest side to a two-bedroom trailer home in Freedom Acres. It proved to be the same amount I was paying Andy, and I didn't have to commute 90 minutes each way morning and evening. I had worn myself to a frazzle commuting and welcomed a place on the edge of town where I could save over two hours of driving back and forth, most days, and get more sleep. The twelve-hour days I began with were leaving me exhausted, and I needed to make the leap to living in Muncie. It was a great decision.

In some ways, the early days at Channel 49 were a "difficult slog through the mud." But in other ways, as we moved through this passage, we found better employees, great enthusiasm that mirrored my own, and the ability to take on challenges and succeed, often with incredible results. People were loving what was happening at WIPB-TV, Channel 49, PBS for East Central Indiana. God was not letting me fail, and I was using His counsel and counselors—all of them—and God's trustworthy counsel was working.

My Promotion contractor, Sunny Spurgeon was also a great help. She was very wise, had been part of the founding of the station in 1971 along with four other women, and was our Promotion and Program Guide Consultant. She met with me weekly at first, and later monthly, and gave me priceless insights into the community and to persons I was meeting with. She was also close friends with Linda Slavin, the widow of a dentist that had passed away after a plane crash in November 1975. Linda had three children and had helped put the station on the air in the 1970–71 rush to buy Muncie's former commercial TV station, WLBC-TV from Don Burton and convert it into a PBS facility.

In October 1976, we staged a huge celebration and party for WIPB's 5th Anniversary. It was a big deal, and lots of people were involved. Linda was there, and I met her briefly for the first time. She said I helped her with her coat, and I probably did, but in the commotion, I did not remember.

I was heavily involved in Carmel High School's Young Life club at that time and dating Bonnie and thoroughly caught up in replacing departing staff members and growing the station. I was also getting involved in the community, making new friends, and involving myself in other ways that would benefit the station as we continued to produce and air ongoing programming, and create new programs as opportunities arose.

By the end of December 1976, I had replaced all but one of the staff members, and I was confident the station was moving in the right direction. I was still dating Bonnie, but shortly after the beginning of the year, we decided that we were not meant for each other and ended our relationship. She had helped me through a difficult transition, introduced me to Corrie TenBoom and Young Life, and was there through God's transformation when He guided me to recommit myself to Jesus Christ and hand my "steering wheel" for my life over to Him. That was the biggest and best decision of my life.

I will always be grateful that Bonnie loved her horse more than she loved me. We were still friends, but our dating relationship ended early in February 1977.

Chapter 23

Who Is This Woman?

In March, Sunny and Bill Spurgeon staged a party during a pledge week at Channel 49 and invited me to come. It turned out later it was a set-up specifically for me to meet Linda Slavin while she was my partner in doing a W. C. Fields' skit there, where I was WC, and she was my girlfriend. It was fun, if a bit contrived. While the skit only lasted a few minutes, it was long enough for me to get a sense of what Linda was like.

Unfortunately, WIPB-TV was doing on-air pledging that night, and I had to duck in and duck out after about twenty minutes. I'm sure she must have thought I was a bore as I did not stay long after our skit ended. The good part of that party was that I did get to meet Linda face-to-face for the first time, and she was very attractive, polite, nice, and easy to talk to. I liked her and would have stayed longer, but I had to get back to the station where we were pledging.

As Linda remembers it, I was there one minute, and gone the next. I was on air that night. It was a very brief introduction in a social setting. But I have to tell you: I was intrigued by her. Maybe I would get to know her better, later? I wondered?

I dated a Muncie woman from Ball State several times after that, but nothing really clicked for me. So I stopped calling her. I had had enough of dating non-Christian women. I was tired of playing "the dating game."

Then, one day, I happened to see an ad in the paper for a speech by Linda Slavin honoring her husband, Steve, who had been one of the founders of the Icerman Dental Clinic at Muncie Central High School. For some reason, I decided to go. I left the office and wandered in, just as she was being introduced by Dick Marshall, a close friend and School Board President. Dick was also on my EICTV Board and later, President.

Linda did a great job and was stunning in her turquoise dress and pearls. She was poised, beautiful, and professional. Again, I was impressed and stood at the back smiling as she sailed through what had to be a very difficult memorial speech, thanking everyone for the honor of placing the plaque there near the Clinic, and honoring her late husband, Steve. Linda and Steve had worked really hard to see him elected, and many of their community friends and well-wishers were there to celebrate one of the gifts Linda and Steve had given to the community and wish her well.

I watched as she greeted people afterward, and shepherded her three kids who were spit-shined and well behaved. Even then, they attracted me, and I wondered how she was doing it all. Sunny Spurgeon had been encouraging me to consider dating Linda throughout the year, even though I had been dating someone else. However, until that day, I had never seriously considered Linda, and then it was just a passing thought. I asked myself, "I wonder what she's really like? I think I'll call her."

As the crowd thinned, I got in line and introduced myself to her again and explained how I happened to be there. Then I met the kids for the first time. They were pleasant, energetic, and adorable. I could see she was a very capable mother and fully in charge. I had briefly dated a woman in Indianapolis who had three kids, but the timing was not right and I knew the difference immediately. Years before in

Canada, I had met a stepfather in Guelph with three girls. Ray Pollard was my Cinematographer, and I had always remembered him and how he had risen to the occasion and become a husband to a woman who had been widowed. He obviously loved them all. What a challenge, I thought. What a huge commitment. What a gift!

The very next week, one of our local program hosts, Al Rent, was in the station and asked if I played tennis. He said he and his wife were putting together a mixed doubles group and wondered if I would be interested. I said I was, but I didn't know any women in Muncie who played tennis. He said he did, and that Linda Slavin was a good tennis player and would be a great partner, if I could talk her into it. I had played tennis in high school and college and was pretty good in my prime but wasn't sure this was for me. It sounded like fun though, so I told him I'd give her a call and let him know.

The next week, on a Tuesday, I decided to call her and ask her to lunch. I got Linda's number from Sunny and picked up the phone. She answered on the second ring. I introduced myself to her, and then asked: "What have you been doing today?"

And she quickly answered without thinking, "Oh, I've been at my women's Bible study and"—she stopped, pausing abruptly, and then continued—"and—and I just got home."

There was a pregnant pause. She didn't go on talking, and neither did I. I wondered if I should ask what popped into my head and decided to take the plunge. (It was time for another twenty seconds of insanity where you decide to do what you think God wants you to do, regardless of the outcome—you become wholly vulnerable.) Mine was a very personal question. But I had to ask it: "Linda, who's the most important person in your life?" I stopped talking.

She hesitated for the longest time, and then kind of quickly stammered: "Jesus is. Who's the most important person in your life?"

And of course, I said, "Jesus is. I just had to ask. When I stopped dating women in Indianapolis and dated a few here, I discovered I didn't want to just date beautiful women. I wanted to date someone who was committed to doing what I wanted to do: put Jesus in the center of my life and do that with someone who was already centered on Him. I am thrilled to know that about you."

"Can I ask you one more thing?" And she said I could.

"Al and Linda Rent are starting a mixed doubles tennis group, and I wondered if you would be interested in being my partner in that and playing mixed doubles beginning in a couple weeks?"

She said it sounded like fun, and then I asked, "I'd really like to get to know you better. Would it be possible for you to meet me for lunch next Tuesday at the Cork and Cleaver at noon?" Linda hesitated a moment, and then said that would be fine.

We hung up, and I wondered what I was getting into. Only time would tell.

The following Tuesday, we met at the Cork & Cleaver for lunch. Linda was delightful, and we had a great visit. I really liked her, and she was fun to be with. When we finished, I asked her what she was doing the rest of the day, and she said she was shoveling crushed limestone for a Dental Wives Garden Party she was hosting that coming Saturday. She said her back was sore, but she was getting it done.

I jumped in, "I haven't done that for a while. I could take off work this afternoon and help you finish if you like."

Linda was proud, stubborn, and very self-reliant. "That's okay. I can do it myself" she said abruptly. But I wasn't taking "No." I really liked her, and I wanted to get to know her better. What a great opportunity. So I said, "No, I'm taking the afternoon off and coming over to help you. I'll be back in thirty minutes, and I took off for home and called in saying I would be out for the afternoon.

Linda obviously could do it herself. But I insisted. It turned out my job was to move a large stone fountain, and shovel a few hundred pounds of limestone, but by the end of the afternoon, everything was in place, and we had cleaned up. She dropped out late in the day when we were almost finished and disappeared inside. At around five, she came out to thank me and asked if I would be willing to stay for dinner. She said it was the least she could do to thank me for my help. I had been eating my own cooking for too long! What a payback! "Yes, of course," I said. "I'd love to."

When I went into the house, I discovered that the kids were already at the table and ready to eat. We sat down to eat, prayed for our food, had a wonderful dinner, laughed a lot and really enjoyed each other. About that time, Stevie piped up with a question: "Are you coming for dinner tomorrow night too?"

I looked at Linda, surprised, and didn't know what to say. But I managed, "Well, I don't know what Linda has planned, but I suppose I could if you wanted me to."

And Steve chimed in: "Well, I sure hope so, 'cause when you're not here, we only get hot dogs and French fries." Linda says that's not what happened, but the rest of us think it did.

In any event, Linda asked if I would like to come back for dinner the next night, and as she told me later, she called the fellow she had been dating later that night and told him that she was no longer available. I think she knew, even then, that we had something special. And as usual, she was right.

I shelved any interest I had in other women that night too. My heart was on fire, and I was amazed at how much I was attracted to Linda and this wonderful family that had appeared in front of me, as if by a miracle. As I look back, I think it was definitely God's gift to all of us. I suspect that Sunny had been selling this opportunity for quite a while, behind my back. I had a lot to be grateful for. Little did I know.

We continued to date and visit almost every day. We were growing closer, and it all felt right. Then, one night, as we were sitting on the couch downstairs, Kirsten came down and told me she was not happy, that she was afraid, and she wanted me to go home. She did not want me to hurt her or her brothers or her mother. Linda abruptly got up and took Kirsten upstairs and told her that she and I really cared about each other, that we didn't want to hurt her, and that she already knew me well enough to trust me.

Linda came back down and sat on the couch. We talked about it for a while. We knew we needed to consider Kirsten's words and concerns, but that we didn't really know what to do. I thought we should pray. We didn't know what else to do. Kirsten was the oldest child and doing what oldest children do: protecting her widowed mother and her family when she felt threatened. We understood that. I even remembered studying about that in school.

So holding Linda's hands, we bowed our heads and began to pray, asking God to help Kirsten to know that we loved each other, and that we loved Kirsten and Stevie and Brian. We asked God to help us know how to share how we felt with Kirsten so that she would know that we would work hard to protect her and her brothers, that we would find a way to show that our love was real, and that somehow, God would show us how to reveal this to Kirsten in a way that she would have no doubt that what we were telling her was true. As we opened our eyes, we became aware that all along, Kirsten had been standing there, listening to our prayer. And she was beginning to cry. We stood up and hugged her and told her we loved her, and we were so glad she had heard our heartfelt prayers. "We love each other," we told her, and she smiled through the tears, and just nodded.

She went back to bed, and she became my biggest supporter. I will never forget that evening or how quickly and completely God answered this prayer from the depths of our souls. God is good, and in Him is no darkness at all.

We thanked God that we had decided to pray and ask Him to intervene in what seemed to be an impossible situation, for us. For Him, it was easy, and it was permanent. What a great blessing that we prayed that night and asked Him to help us, and in asking Him for help in Kirsten's hearing, He answered our prayer on the spot. Never would we have known to ask for that kind of small but significant miracle. It confirmed to us again that our God is in the miracle business and is always present.

As I was writing this book, I asked Kirsten today about that and what happened to change her mind. She quietly said that when she heard us praying, God changed her heart. There is nothing more to say but "thank you Lord."

Shortly after that, on Linda's birthday, I asked her to marry me. And she hugged me with bright eyes and kissed me and said, "Yes, I adore you! Of course, I will." And we began to plan. We decided to consciously set the wedding as close as reasonable. We knew in our hearts it was right, but for the kids' sake and families' sakes, we wanted to put it off a reasonable period of time, and Linda wanted me to meet some of her most precious friends.

Chapter 24

The Approval Tour

That is when she asked if I was up for a short trip to meet some of her out-of-town friends that she and Steve had developed over the years. Of course, I was eager to do that. First, we went to Fort Wayne to meet with friends who were in School with Steve at IU, and we stayed the night. Everywhere we went, they asked if we slept together or apart. We had decided that was an issue we didn't want to model for our kids, so we never slept together until we were married.

We had a great visit with Mandy and Bill LaSalle there, and then went on to Elkhart where the Turnock family lived. Jack and Ann and their girls had been great friends and Jack had been in Steve's Dental Class at IU. There, we had another wonderful visit. I really liked meeting these friends, and I liked them all. They were really great people.

The last stop was to visit with Mary Jo and Tom Garling. They were vacationing that week at Grand Haven, Michigan, about one hundred miles west of their Portage, Michigan, home, and we met them at Grand Haven to stay with them on the beach. Mary Jo was the person who stayed with Linda and the kids for several weeks right after the accident and Steve's death, helping Linda in all kinds of ways. She was terrific.

This is where our visit got a little tricky. As we sat down for lunch on a picnic table close to the water, Kirsten, who had just gotten her new retainer, asked me to hold it while we had lunch. "Of course," I said. "I'll be happy to." And I put it in a napkin in my shirt pocket to keep it safe for her. When Kirs and Steve finished eating, they got up and ran to Lake Michigan to jump up and down in the waves. Brian, at three, was too young to do that by himself, so I volunteered to go with him.

As we jumped up and down in the waves, Kirsten came running back through the waves to me to reclaim her retainer. I reached for my shirt pocket—there was nothing there. I said, "Oh my God. I think it must have fallen out in the sand beneath the picnic table." We all ran back to the picnic table and got down on our hands and knees and started sifting the sand between our fingers. It wasn't there.

Kirs was crying by then, and Linda said, "Uncle Chad can make you another one. Don't worry about it. We'll get it replaced." But Kirsten was heartbroken. She had trusted me with something valuable—really important—a status symbol to some extent in her fifth-grade class, and I had let her down. I was crushed at my foolishness. Why didn't I just hand the retainer back to her when she finished eating? But I didn't! It was on me! We had to do something.

Linda and I hugged Kirsten, and Kirs and Steve went back to playing in the lake. I was crestfallen. I was so disappointed in myself, and I felt like we just had to find the retainer. Linda repeated that Uncle Chad could make another retainer, and I said, "We need to find this one. We don't know where it is, but God knows where it is. Let's look for it."

"Where do you think it is?" she asked. "In the lake?" We were standing on the very edge of the largest of the five Great Lakes—Lake Michigan. The waves were about two feet high and seemed to be washing in a northerly direction, to our right, along the shore. Linda shook her head. "What do you want to do?"

I swallowed and looked at the lake again, and then down at my feet. "Well," I stammered! "The retainer is not in the sand under the picnic table. We looked there. Right after lunch, I took Brian out to jump in the waves, and the retainer was probably still in my pocket. When it popped out, it had to go into the water. I never felt it."

"This is crazy," she laughed. "You're crazy. We have a light pink, clear retainer with a small wire, and you think we can find it in Lake Michigan, just by looking for it. That's nuts!"

"I know it sounds ridiculous," I blushed, "but let's pray about it, and look for it. I know it sounds impossible, but God is the God of the impossible. Just pray with me."

So we prayed. "God, you know where Kirsten's retainer is. We don't. Please show us where to look so we can find it and bring it back to her. She trusted me, and this is so important to me. It's the first time she has trusted me with something so important. Please help us find it. In Jesus' name. Thank you. Amen."

That was it.

We looked down again and it was clear that the waves were washing to the right, north along the shoreline. And I said, "Let's walk that way. Why don't you take my hand, you walk in the water, and I'll walk along the shore. And let's keep praying that God will help us see it when we come to it. We know it's here. He knows where it is. Please, God. Help us find Kirsten's retainer."

And we slowly started walking up the beach, silently, praying. And we walked and we walked, and we walked, and we walked, watching the water intently with every step.

And then, just as suddenly as we had discovered it was missing—thirty-five minutes after we had begun praying and walking and trusting God, Linda cried out, "There it is!" Suddenly dropping my hand, she reached down into the surf and picked it up—the tiny, barely pink, translucent retainer with its silver wire. The napkin had long disappeared, but there in Linda's hand was Kirsten's retainer. We hugged and thanked God, almost not believing what had happened.

We turned to look back to the place where it had been lost, and it was around a bend in the shoreline, completely out of sight. We were a mile and a half up the beach.

We walked and skipped back toward the picnic table, and at the end, started running toward them with the retainer in my hand. "We found it. We found it," I shouted! "Thank God we found it. God answered our prayer."

It was a huge event! We couldn't stop talking about it. God had answered another prayer, this one—for everyone to see and experience His faithfulness. It was a small miracle. No one could believe it, that little retainer, almost invisible in the water, found in a lake 150 miles wide and 300 miles long where ships have wrecked over the centuries because of storms, and many have lost their lives in this largest of the Great Lakes, and yet, we had found something so small, so insignificant in the overall scheme of things, and yet, we had found it.

We praised God for His faithfulness. And the miracle, I became convinced, was not that we found the retainer, but that we kept looking after there was no reasonable hope that it would be found. By trusting in God, we did find it, and Kirsten and everyone else was amazed that we had walked the mile and a half up the beach and found it in the water. We were surprised too, and very thankful we had trusted our sovereign, loving Father, and kept walking.

The last miracle that happened as we were getting ready to be married is that we set our wedding date for October 29. Then, our church called back to tell us the church was already booked for that date. We checked with Linda's Maid of Honor, Rosi Fullhart and discovered she was already booked for October 22. She asked if we could move it up another week, and so we did. We moved the wedding date to Saturday, October 15, and started sending out invitations and making arrangements for the reception.

It was a large wedding with over four hundred guests at College Avenue Methodist Church where Linda and Steve had been married thirteen years earlier.

It was a wonderful wedding with all three kids participating. As the service began, Brian started the ceremony by spreading flower petals up the aisle. The church was full of friends and family, coming together to celebrate a wonderful union of two people who had come together in a very short time, but were obviously happy for this day, and wanting to share it all with their many friends and family members. Linda's parents—Henry and Ruth Loats—my dad and mom, Fred and Jeanette Needham, my brother Fred and his wife Barb, Linda's sister and her husband—Lois and Don Schuhrke, and Linda's Sister-in-law and brother-in-law, Chad and Cindy Slavin. It was a blessing for all and a big occasion. The church was full and flowers were everywhere.

Everyone was there—many of the new friends I had made while managing the station for the first 17 months, Linda's friends from all the years growing up in Muncie, attending Burris, and graduating from Ball State, and of course Steve's friends and clients who had become close friends. It was unforgettable. Ed and Virginia Ball were there too and were to be fast friends until both passed away some twenty years later.

Only later did I learn that Ed had lost his first wife in a boating accident in Florida and married Virginia, and that they had three children together along with Ed's first two and Virginia's two boys from a prior marriage. They were a blended family, like us, and they always treated us like family and continued to be very close to us as long as they lived.

The other surprise as we looked back on it was that when the minister asked, "Who gives this woman to this man to be married?" the answer came from three very loud and proud children who had come to love me and were there behind us, waiting for that question.

"WE do!" they almost shouted, and everyone laughed. After that, Brian went back to the second pew, crawled up on the bench next to Ted Fullhart and immediately dropped off to sleep. He had been sleeping on the floor of the Bride's room just prior to the service, and after doing his part, closed his eyes for the rest of the ceremony. Steve and Kirsten were excited and watched closely as we took our vows, and the ceremony was completed. Somewhere, there are pictures of us walking back down the aisle with hundreds of well-wishers there to greet us and witness our vows. It was truly a great day.

It had been exactly two years to the day from the day I bowed my head in the parking lot at Channel 8 and asked Jesus to take the driver's seat of my life and take me where he wanted me to go. We didn't plan it like that, but I cannot believe it was anything less than another miracle and vivid reminder that God was and is sovereign in the affairs of our lives. We were grateful for that then and continue to recognize and be grateful for that now.

Looking back a couple of years, Linda's first husband, Steve, died in a plane accident on a weekend fishing trip to Mountain Home, Arkansas in November 1975. What a terrible tragedy. Everyone was in shock. My first marriage had failed in Indianapolis in 1973, and I too had been in shock, but in a different way. I do not believe God planned either of those events, nor do I believe they surprised him.

However, as the fog and pain cleared for each of us, God's plan somehow allowed a way for Linda and me to meet, fall in love, and join each other for a second chapter of what would prove to be a wonderful life. It is not what we went into our adult lives expecting or wanting, but it is what we got, and we are grateful for where we have traveled together, what we have today, and for whatever future lies ahead for us and for you.

There was more to come.

Chapter 25

Vacations

In 1978, our new family went on our first big vacation. Our destination was Ed and Virginia Ball's Ranch at Ortiz Mountain, New Mexico. We stayed in the Ball Compound with the Ranch Manager, Mrs. Blackshear, and we had a great time. On the way there, we visited my parents at their resort in Baxter, Minnesota on White Sand Shores Lake northwest of Minneapolis, where we caught 40 pan fish the first evening and had the best and longest visit with my parents ever.

From there, we visited Wall Drug, in the "metropolis" of Wall, South Dakota, dipped our toes into the Badlands, had a flat tire in Wyoming, and briefly saw Red Rocks Amphitheater, southwest of Denver. Next, our itinerary took us to the cliff-dwellings at Mese Verde, and after a few hours there, our tired crew took a nap as we headed southeast to Golden, New Mexico and Ortiz Mountain Ranch, 40 miles south of Santa Fe. What a trip and what an adventure was in store for us as we all became "dude ranchers" for a few days.

We spent three days in Ed and Virginia Ball's palatial adobe hacienda with our host, Mrs. Blackshear and had the time of our lives. Though Ed and Virginia were travelling elsewhere, Mrs. Blackshear made us all feel at home. As our time slipped away, we were dinner guests at the home of the ranch Foreman, Horatio Pargus and, after some cajoling and stories about the thirty-thousand-acre Ortiz Mountain Ranch, its history and what it was like when the Balls were there, we agreed to accept the invitation Ed Ball had extended when he asked Horatio to stage a small round-up for us one morning, and let us help with the branding, castrating, and inoculations of thirty young steers. Thank you, Ed, I think.

Honestly, the cowboy life seemed glamorous to us before that morning, but what we did there was the hottest, dirtiest work I have ever done, and I had worked midnights for a summer in a Sherwin Williams factory during college where the nighttime temperatures hovered at 130 degrees, and we had to take salt pills to prevent dehydration. The Ortiz Ranch Roundup was fun, after all, but it was anything but glamorous. Just ask Kirs, Steve or Brian—it was a memory like none other.

We had a great time, however, as we always did, and visited an Indian Reservation, Santa Fe, and the Grand Canyon. What a whirlwind trip and a great vacation. Many more would follow.

In 1979, we went to Calloway Gardens near Atlanta for a week and met the Albees—Bob, Luc, Todd, and Ryan. Our kids all participated in the circus program there under coaching by the students from the Florida State University Flying Circus. All day long, they practiced juggling, tightrope walking, and acrobatics. While they were having a blast, living the Circus life, Linda and I and Bob and Luc played golf until we retrieved our kids each day in time to grab some snacks and Muscadine Ice Cream and watch the daily performances of the Winter Garden Ski team. It was a vacation like none other. Water Ski Shows, Muscadine Ice Cream, and night-time movies in the woods. It was a great park-like vacation destination, and we returned for three summers to this incredible place.

Years later, we actually arrived for a brief visit in time for the incredible Azalea Festival in early April and saw the most awesome collection of Azaleas in America, all in full bloom. Amazing! It would be worth going back for one more time. Maybe YOU will get to see this amazing blaze of gorgeous flowers Calloway Gardens has collected in this incredible touch of heaven. God sure makes it unforgettable.

Beginning in 1983 as Steve's tennis improved, we migrated to Hilton Head, South Carolina where we eventually bought Marriott Grande Ocean Time Shares in 1994, and where we still vacation today. Over the years, we have used our Marriott ownership points to travel the world by trading in Marriott weeks for foreign travel. We still love Hilton Head and go there, at least one week a year to pamper ourselves and visit with Linda's sister Lois and brother-in-law, Don Schuhrke. It's a wonderful vacation destination that always feels like home.

We love the beach there at Grande Ocean and have travelled to many places around the world because of that Marriott ownership which we trade for air miles, guided tours, and weeks of vacations in other countries. We are so blessed that we are able to do that and are healthy enough to travel at our ages—now in our late seventies. Only God knows how long that window will be open. Thus far, we've been to all fifty states, almost every country in the Caribbean, all of the Central American countries, the Panama Canal and Columbia in South America. We also have been to many of the countries in Europe, and a number of times to Germany where Jockel and Anne live, and several times to Great Britain and Ireland.

While we are well traveled, we still have a few destinations we would like to go to, but the COVID-19 virus put a damper on our plans, and we are not sure we will ever be able to visit Africa or Greece or New Zealand, three places we would really like to have checked off on our Bucket List. But we may only see them on the Travel Channel.

We have also been to China, Hong Kong, Macau, Australia, Korea, Mexico, and various places in Canada. Time will tell when and if we will leave the US again. Meanwhile, we are grateful for all we have been able to do, and for the eight mission trips I took to Honduras during my parents' tenure building the Utila Methodist Community College there. We are grateful for the Ball State University, College of Architecture cadre of students and professors who designed and helped us build the Teacher's Residence there to help defray the required housing allowance for the mission school Principal.

Chapter 26

Missionaries to Utila

Three years after our visit with my parents in Brainard, Minnesota, they had sold their resort and begun their ten-year adventure as Educational Missionaries to Utila, the smallest and westernmost of the 5 Bay Islands off the north coast of Honduras. They went in response to God's call for teachers that they heard while attending their church meeting in Spring Hill, Florida, in July 1982, where they had retired.

That night, at that meeting, my mother turned to my dad and whispered, "Fred, when we were young, we said we wanted to be missionaries. Well, we could do this." And they went forward as the meeting ended, asked a lot of questions, and volunteered that night to go to Utila in December and begin working in the school there. My mother was sixty-six, and my dad, sixty-seven. They were always adventuresome, but we never saw that coming.

When I heard the news, I chided my father about retiring to a Paradise Island in the Caribbean. "What is that all about?" I asked. "First, you travel around the world for three months to celebrate your twenty-fifth anniversary, and then you head out to a beautiful island in the Caribbean where they don't even have phones or television. Some retirement," I teased.

My dad quickly responded by airmail post—no phones or TV on the island at that time—just short-wave phone patches. "Come on down and see it for yourself," he wrote. "Let us know when you're coming. We'll show you the island and the Quays" (the Keys). So I saddled up and visited in early 1985. Was I in for a surprise! No running water. No electricity after dark. No-see-ums—(biting gnats), every-where, and no regular sanitation. This was NOT my idea of paradise.

We did visit a small round island about two hundred yards in diameter named Paradise Island. Like the idyllic symbol of the Caribbean, it was all Coconut Palms and white sand and beautiful, and the water was very warm—around eighty-five degrees, but that was the extent of the dreamy island life. No one lived on that island. It was purely for show.

Actually, Utila was a very poor, undeveloped island that had been part of British Honduras until 1859, and then was ceded to the Republic of Honduras on June 1, 1861, and joined mainland Honduras on that date. The 750 people on the island when my parents arrived, were getting along as best they could. Most things, including paving streets, were done by hand. It was a big help to my parents that many of the islanders spoke both English and Spanish. And as a result, it was easy for my parents to teach in the school which was located in the church Annex, about four feet above sea level, twenty feet from the church and less than twenty feet from the bay next to the church.

However, it was not easy for my parents to receive permission to teach in the school. That came later. When they first landed on the short, 2,200-foot crushed tabby and sand landing strip with ocean on either end, in December 1982, they were met by the local pastor in charge of the school who told them they were not needed, and they should go back home. My Uncle Jim Cushman (for whom I was named) and his wife, Bea who had come along to help, were disappointed and discouraged by this confrontation,

139

and they decided there on the landing strip that if they were not wanted, they were not willing to fight the rejection they encountered. They discussed it briefly with my parents, said their goodbyes, and got back on the plane to return to their home in Oregon. A very long trip turned into a huge disappointment, and my parents were left alone on the island to figure it out.

My father and mother did not sleep that night but lay awake and prayed, silently and together. At about 5:15 AM when the roosters all over the island started crowing as they did every day as I discovered on my first trip to Utila, my parents were still wide awake. By then, my dad felt God telling him to go see the Pastor at the Methodist Mission House.

My father got up, dressed quickly, and went to the Methodist Mission House, and when he saw a light inside, went to the door and knocked. When the pastor came to the door, my father told him that God had brought them to Utila and they had promised a Utila Resident undergoing Cancer treatments in Tampa, that they would be there to greet her when she returned home, and they had decided they would stay to see her come home.

Furthermore, my father told the pastor that he and my mother would be staying on the island until God sent them home. That morning, my dad also asked for a meeting where my Mom and Dad could formally meet with the Utila Methodist Community College (Honduran High School) Board of the school. The pastor agreed to arrange for that.

Indeed, the pastor did arrange the meeting as he promised, but the nine-member board did not agree to meet right away. Even though the request for their meeting was made in early December, the Board's meeting with my parents was delayed until they had lived there on Utila for eleven weeks. It was late February when my folks were finally invited to talk with the school board, and nothing came of it. The board listened, and my parents told the board what they felt God had called them to do. The board seemed emotionless. They told my parents they had their two High School graduates from Great Britain, teaching the students what they needed to learn and needed nothing more.

The Board thanked my parents for their interest and dismissed them into the night. My parents walked home silently. The woman they promised to meet in Tampa had not arrived, so they decided to stay and see what they could learn about the island and its people. They would go to church, participate in community life, get to know people, use the short-wave radio to call my two sisters, my brother, and me and wait for their friend to come home to Utila from her Cancer treatments, and when their pre-purchased airline tickets were able to be used in late May, they would go home. That was the plan.

My father and mother were very social people, so it was not hard for them to strike up conversations. Most of the people on the island which had been British until 1861, spoke English, so my parents were able to do business, have conversations, and learn a lot in a very short time. They enjoyed the new friends they were meeting and the adventure.

Because of my father's heart attack when he was sixty-two and his heart surgery, my mother and father got up early daily and walked the two miles to the East end of the island where the Tabby and sand airport runway was and back every day. In the meantime, they helped fix up the place they were renting and got to know a lot of people on the island through church and through their use of the Short-Wave radios that my parents' new Utila friends and fellow church members regularly used. As a result, word spread that my parents were former teachers and had come to the island to teach, if needed. Conversations blossomed, but no one suggested that my parents should plan to stay and teach in the UMCC School. They packed to go home.

However, by the time my mom and dad went to board the plane back to the U.S., in May 1983, a group of interested parents whose children were in the school, came to see them off, and before my parents climbed the ladder into the plane to return to the United States for good, the children's parents stepped forward and asked if there was any way my parents would consider returning in the fall and becoming teachers in their (UMCC) United Methodist Community College school.

That was the beginning of a ten-year odyssey and mission trip when my parents sold their savings bonds, bought a piece of land, spent their resources, and cajoled and begged, and asked for financial help and work teams from churches all across America. Anywhere they had lived or had relatives or dear friends, they asked for opportunities to pitch the mission of that little island school, and God touched people as they talked, and opened their hearts and their checkbooks and supported the school with gifts and with numerous mission teams from across America over the years.

Each summer for ten years, when my parents returned to the United States, my mother and father would go to churches where they had belonged or where their kids and their families like ours, belonged, present their slide show, share an exciting update on what God was doing, and ask for financial support. There were always "love offerings" taken, and my parents used that money to fund the school over all those years. My father and mother had lived in numerous places, and their four children welcomed them to their home churches and helped them raise the dollars needed, to pay for American Volunteers who worked for very meager salaries. The rest of the funds raised paid for the expenses of operating the school. My mom and dad never took a salary nor asked that their travel expenses or housing be paid, but always took care of those expenses from their own savings and retirement income.

As a result, the school thrived and grew. There were many challenges along the way, and I visited in person 8 times to see what they were doing, and to bring three work teams to Utila from High Street Methodist in Muncie, where we helped finish the second story of the school and built the Teacher's Residence for the UMCC School Principal.

Work teams regularly came from Baton Rouge, Louisiana; New Orleans; Muncie, Indiana; Dolton, Illinois; Beaumont, Texas; Tampa and Spring Hill, Florida, and Clemson, South Carolina. Wherever my parents had lived or had children live over the years, my parents did presentations and asked for help in building and operating the school. And when they spoke in churches, the people were generous.

In talking with Kim Funez (one of the students in my parents' first UMCC class in 1983 who still lives on the island of Utila, in the UMCC in October 2022), the UMCC School had one hundred and fifty-five enrolled students. The school is now self-supporting and has realized what my parents only dreamed of: a Honduran Principal, five Honduran teachers, and the ability to pay their own bills without annual gifts from a dozen churches throughout the U.S.

Chapter 27

My Parents and Their Last Days

My parents retired from the Mission field in 1992 at the age of seventy-seven and seventy-six and returned to live near my sister, Nancy, in Bourbonnais, Illinois. My father had a stroke in 1994 in Colorado while visiting my youngest sister, Candy Kingsbury and died in Illinois in 1999. The last four years of his life were spent in convalescing in a nursing home and in living with my mother in Bourbonnais where they continued to be active in their church. I was very fortunate to have had many long talks with him during the three years he spent in Bourbonnais and was able to visit him the very day he died on February 26, 1999. He died 1 hour after I left for home that Friday afternoon.

I will always believe until my dying day that he knew he was dying and waited for me to leave. When I got ready to take off, he said he wanted to pray with me, and I helped him to stand up because he wanted to hug me and mom and the live-in nurse that was present all the time, the last several years, to help out with him. My mother wasn't strong enough to do that, but we stood together, as he requested, and prayed together, and then he shooed me out the door, saying, "I love you, and I want you to get home before it gets dark."

I left at about 5:00 PM. My mom called my wife Linda an hour and half later and said that he had died shortly after six. So Linda met me at home and told me of the phone call. What a blessing to get to see him one last time. I was so grateful. I was supposed to see them right after New Year's, but the weather was so bad that year, that I waited until February 26 to drive the two hundred miles to see them. Fortunately, he waited to see me, and I will always be grateful to him and to God for enabling me to see him and tell him I loved him, one last time.

When I asked my parents' minister what his recollections were of my mom and dad, at my mother's funeral in 2013, he said, "They were regular participants when they could be, in the choir and on the Missions committee where they always brought their love for others into the room and their love of Jesus which took them to Utila in the first place.

He told how they were a great example for all of the members of their church who marveled at what they had done beginning at age sixty-seven. My mother lived to be ninety-six and died in Centennial, Colorado, where my sister, Candy Kingsbury, lives. My mother lived in Westminster Village in Muncie for two years, followed by four years with my sister, Candy, and three years in Cherry Creek Nursing Center near Candy, where mom died in March 2013. My mom and Dad both loved Jesus and young people and their children and grandchildren and kept up with them to the end of their lives as best they could.

The last year of my mother's life in Denver, I visited her eight times because it was clear that she was losing ground. She was in Hospice the last time I was with her in February 2013. My mother and I did a lot of talking that last week as I visited with her, and she asked me to share our family history with you.

So at least in part, this book is my effort to keep my promise to you and to keep the promise I made to my mother the last time I saw her. To her, family history was always really important because from the time she was a little girl, she knew about how our ancestors came over on the Mayflower. "Really?" I said, "Tell me more." And she did. She gave me the little black book we have, published in 1940, that has the history of the Cushman family (her maiden name was Cushman).

That little black book, *A Few Cushmans of the Elkanah Branch, Descendents of Robert Cushman The Puritan*, chronicles the Cushman family from Robert Cushman who was born in 1577 to 1940 where it records Jeanette Elizabeth Cushman marrying my father, Frederick Homer Needham, on the side lawn of her mother's house in Bloomfield, Indiana on July 30, 1939.

My family history is important, so I need to briefly touch on that. My wife, Linda, has been doing Ancestry.com research on her own family background for the Loats clan which dates back several generations to the Auf Friesland Islands off the northwest coast of Germany and northeastern Netherlands.

In the process, Grandma checked on me and discovered that my ancestry goes back and includes Myles Standish who was in charge of the Mayflower Company's Security detail and was on its maiden voyage in 1620. It also includes Robert Cushman.

Our direct ancestor, Robert Cushman, the Principal Agent for the Mayflower Company, is also one of my forebears, and one of two persons who negotiated and signed the "The Charter from King James for the Plymouth Colony" in London in 1623. Cushman and Edward Winslow signed the Charter in London for themselves and their associates and planters in Plymouth in New England in January 1623.

This Charter enabled the Mayflower Company to be able to live in the New World with the King's blessing. While in London, Cushman also negotiated the support of The Merchant Adventurers (a group of supportive British Entrepreneurs) who provided funding for the Mayflower, the

Speedwell and the Fortune and other subsequent journeys to Plymouth for the growth of the New England Colony for the first seven years of the Puritans.

Cushman came over to Plymouth in November 1621 with his son, Thomas. When Robert Cushman returned to England in 1622, to negotiate the Charter with King James, Cushman left his son Thomas in the care of Governor William Bradford of the Plymouth Colony, and Thomas never saw his father again.

In 1625, Robert Cushman died in London of the Plague, never having returned to Plymouth. Robert's son, Thomas Cushman, later married Mary Allerton who came over on the Mayflower and was the longest surviving member of the original Mayflower trip in 1620 and died in 1699 at the age of 83. Thomas, known as "Thomas the Elder," was later an ordained minister and supervised the assignment of ministers to the pulpits in the New England Colony from 1649 until his death in 1691.

Thomas Cushman's father, Robert Cushman, was born in England in 1577. Robert's father was Thomas Couchman. Although spelled differently, the Couchmans of England had their deepest ancestry in Kent with Cranbrook at the center. Predominantly they were cloth makers, Flemish in origin, who with other countrymen came to several regions of England at the invitation of King Edward II around the year 1336. The Flemish Couchmans were likely from what would have been today's Belgium or Holland.

My parents' families were all believers. Our families have a long history of trusting Jesus in the midst of crises, like the Depression and the 1918 Flu pandemic, and theirs is a practice of depending upon God and trusting Him, throughout their lives, in good times and bad. Robert Cushman was part of the group of English Separatists who took their families and children to Holland in the early 1600s to avoid the persecution in England of Christians who did not want to be part of what became the Episcopal Church under King James. When they found their children were all learning Dutch instead of English, they concluded they needed to be back in England but quickly looked for another land where they could be free to practice the religion they believed the Bible teaches. Finally, in 1620, they embarked on the Mayflower and Speedwell, only to have both ships turn back when the Speedwell began shipping water. Cushman stayed in England and continued to raise money from the London Merchant Adventurers and sailed for Plymouth on the Fortune in 1621 with more recruits, supplies and resources. After arriving in Plymouth, Deacon Robert Cushman, preached the first sermon ever recorded in America. It is still available online.

Robert's son, Thomas Cushman, familiarly known as Elder Thomas Cushman, arrived at Plymouth, Massachusetts in November 1621 at fourteen years of age with his father, Robert. When Robert returned to England, Thomas continued living with Governor William Bradford until he married Mary Allerton in 1635 or 1636. They were married for fifty-five years, and he and Mary had seven children. Thomas was ordained Ruling Elder in 1649 and served in that position until his death. He held a highly important office in the Plymouth Colony and was a participator in the First Indian treaty with Massasoit and Samoset, which continued unviolated by both parties for over fifty years.

Because of this history, it is significant to know that my mother's family is descended from Elder Cushman's fifth child, Elkanah, who was born in 1651 and lived until 1727 in his seventy-seventh year. Many in my family have lived long and healthy lives, and my mother, Jeanette Elizabeth Cushman Needham was blessed in just that way. She died on March 3, 2013, having lived 96 years and five months.

As I visited with her in the week before she died, we did two things that really mattered to her: first, we called many of her friends and relatives that she kept in touch with over the years from all over the United States, and also in Honduras where my mother and father were missionaries to the Island of Utila, the westernmost of the five Bay Islands from 1982 to 1992.

We had a great time, and apparently, according to my sister, I "wore her out." I left on a Friday, and a week later, my mother passed away with my sister, Candy and her husband John Kingsbury, at her bedside. She was at peace with God and with her family and friends. Like my father before her, I am convinced she had waited to say "goodbye" to many persons that week, and I helped make that possible.

I am also at peace. After I left her, she never got out of bed again. She only sat up once and that was to greet a former church choir member who brought her a favorite dessert: bread pudding. She sat up in bed, when she was offered some, and while she had not eaten much or had much to drink, she had a couple of bites of that bread pudding and remarked: "That is really good!" And then she lay back down, never to sit up or eat again.

Secondly, in the week before that, she asked me to promise that I would share her Cushman heritage with you, so here it is. This is what she believed, and it is what I believe.

"God is sovereign"—my mother knew that and depended on that promise about His character. God knows the End from the Beginning. We are not puppets, but we are His children, and in spite of the free will He gives us, He knows what we will do in every situation. And regardless of our imperfections and inability to always do what is "right in God's sight," He loves us and through His son, Jesus, has provided us with a means to be with Him forever. All each of us has to do is choose to trust God and believe that Jesus is His only Son.

This book has recounted some of those adventures where God has rescued me and helped me to believe and know that He is God and is always with me. I am writing this to make sure you know what I am convinced is true and that this connection with God can be true for you too. All you have to do is confess to God that you have sinned, like we all have, and accept His gift of death on the cross in our place. It truly is that simple—that easy. A simple prayer like "God, forgive me, for I have sinned against You. Thank you for saving me, I want You to save me in Jesus' name" will open the door for you to eternity. Yes, it truly is that simple. God's got this. You just have to accept His incredible gift to have His peace. As you can tell from my stories, it is the better way to live your life. I am not perfect—just forgiven. And because of that, I have God's peace—it's a gift He's ready to give you too when you ask for it. All you have to do is trust Him.

All of us are sinners, not the least of us, me. You have seen my disobedience and foolish decisions. I was never perfect, though I sometimes was able to avoid the penalties acting out brings, and, Yes, sometimes I have wished I could have gone back and made different decisions. Regardless of what we do, God loves us—you and me—and He wants us to be with Him when we leave this world. We do not know how long we will live, but David, who as a very young shepherd boy, killed the giant Goliath, also was inspired to write Psalm 139:16 where God gave David these words: "You saw me before I was born. Every day of my life was recorded in your book. Every moment was laid out before a single day had passed."

When I was there in Colorado with my mother for my last time with her, we confronted the reality of her congestive heart failure that was taking her life and we reaffirmed our faith in God and in each other by praying together the Lord's Prayer and the 23rd Psalm, two of her favorites.

The last week I was with her, February 16–22, 2013, we read a lot of scriptures, sang songs from lyrics available on the Internet (which amused her), re-told family stories, and prayed and cried.

My mother was a Needham, married to my father Fred in 1939, but before that, she was a "Cushman," mindful—

kept in her mind—that her ancestors were from the Elkanah branch of the Cushman family—some of the pilgrims who helped settle this land and came over on the Mayflower. She was not proud—she was mindful of that (that's different) and she wanted me to share this with my children and grandchildren, and all those who are a part of our family...children, grandchildren, and those who call Linda and me, "Mom and Dad." I am convinced that those whom you love are your family. That's why you received a free signed copy of this book. Your promise is to "read it" and someday, write one of your own for your "family," whatever that turns out to be. Meanwhile, YOU are children of "the promise." That was my mother's way of saying, "You're in this family too."

Here's what she meant by that: My mom was very aware that her ancestors were from the Elkanah branch of the Cushman family—so who was the Biblical namesake, Elkanah? 3,300 years ago, in 1300 BC, before Israel's first king, Elkanah was the husband of two wives: Hannah who was barren, and Peninnah who had several children, and who mocked Hannah for being childless (see 1 Samuel). So Hanna prayed and prayed for a son; and finally, Elkanah became the father of Samuel, the Prophet, when God answered their prayers through Hannah.

All of his life, Elkanah followed and honored God, and Elkanah trusted his wife, Hannah, when she said she was praying for a son. When she (Hannah) finally got pregnant and had this son (she waited until this only son, Samuel, was no longer nursing, and then, as she had promised God, Hannah and Elkanah took Samuel to the Temple and consecrated Samuel to the Lord to become a priest.

And though Samuel was her only son, in fact, their only son, Hannah's husband, Elkanah, said, "Hannah, do what YOU think is best. And may the Lord make His promise to you come true." And God blessed them for their obedience, and Elkanah and Hannah had three more boys and two

151

daughters after that, to take the place of her first son whom she had consecrated to God, and God kept His promise.

As you may know, Samuel was not only a Priest before God but was indeed the 12th and last Judge of Israel. He was not just a Priest. Samuel was a Judge of Israel before God and also a Prophet of significance in the Bible. (I urge you to read 1 Samuel and 2 Samuel and see how important Samuel was in the history of Israel. Samuel was also the Judge who anointed Israel's first King, King Saul and also King David. Samuel's life is also a great story of faith, obedience, and ups and downs, just like our lives. And God is with you too, just as He was with Samuel.

As my mother and I visited there in the Cherry Creek Nursing Center the week before her death, my mother and I were reading about Elkanah and Hannah in 1 Samuel Chapters 1 and 2—and my mother told me, "As descendants of the Elkanah branch of the Cushman's, we are a people who "trust God completely, know that He holds our futures in His hands, and that we trust the judgments of our wives. We are grafted into that model, into that example of faithfulness, and trust, and love, and respect for our wives, and we are called to be God's people, not people of our own way.

And while she was telling me that, she was not boasting—no; she was reciting our four hundred years of family history in this country and hoping, she said, that I would share this history with our children and grandchildren so it would be remembered. And today, I have done exactly what she asked of me, through this book. By virtue of your being here and reading this, you are each "grafted in" to the Elkanah branch of the Cushman family. Elkanah and Hannah's faith journey took place over three thousand years ago; we are still called to be faithful, trust God, honor our wives, and know that it is God who holds our futures.

We are truly from a long line of Americans who came to this country seeking the freedom to worship God and to trust Him more than we trust ourselves. In my father—Fred—my mother found someone she could relate to, trust, respect and follow anywhere, even to that tiny island off the coast of Honduras—Utila—where the school they founded at God's direction with His blessings, continues to teach classrooms full of students—their reading, writing, arithmetic, and also computer skills and life lessons, and lessons about God.

When the minister met them at the airplane in December 1982 and said, "Go home! We have two English High School graduates teaching in our school. We don't need you here! Go home!" My parents said, "We'll stay for six months since our return tickets aren't good until May, and then we'll go home if you want us to."

As you know, sometimes things change and, in this case, they changed dramatically. When my parents approached the plane to leave the end of May 1983, a contingent of parents who had gotten to know my Mom and Dad came to them as they prepared to board the plane on the tabby landing strip, and said, "Oh Mr. Fred and Miss Jeanette, please come back and teach our students. They need you, and so do we!"

And my mom and dad did come back, and God blessed the work God had called them to. The UMCC, Utila Methodist Community College is thriving to this day. And they would say as I say here: "God did it!"

Chapter 28

Bob Ross and the
Joy of Painting

Along the way, we had an opportunity to help someone become famous: Bob Ross.

In 1982, Bob Ross and his business associate, Annette Kowalski, stopped in at WIPB-TV, the station where I was the General Manager, to see if we would be interested in doing a painting show for PBS. They had tried to do a painting series with a station just outside of Washington, DC, only to have that station, WNVC-TV fail to follow through. Bob and Annette were crisscrossing the country in a Dotson pick-up camper, giving painting classes, and happened to advertise in Muncie for students.

When they showed up on our doorstep, they had received over seventy applications for what was to be a one-day workshop. The great interest in their classes made it necessary for them to revise their calendar and come in and ask to speak with the Manager. My receptionist called me to come down and meet them, and we decided to take them to lunch. We talked about the possibilities, drew up a preliminary contract, and the rest is history. We agreed to finish the first series and put "Opens and Closes and credits" on each program from the WNVC series, and return those completed programs to the Joy of Painting Company. We also contracted to produce a thirteen-program WIPB-produced series to offer via satellite for other PBS stations to bid on and carry for the 1983 programming year. The *Joy of Painting*, as we know it today, was birthed at that luncheon.

The agreement with WIPB was that if we could get twenty-five stations to pick up the series, *The Joy of Painting* Company, as it was then called, would produce thirteen more programs with us. The first series was picked up by thirty stations, the second series was picked up by sixty, the third series was picked up by one hundred, and we were on our way. Ultimately, we did thirty-one series, each with thirteen individual programs—a total of 403 programs—before Bob died in 1995 at the age of fifty-two.

Now, because of Bob's popularity and his mantra of "no mistakes—just happy accidents," people viewing YouTube all over the world love Bob, his soothing voice, and optimistic presentation and teaching. Now there are over twenty-seven countries that regularly play Bob Ross programs on the Bob Ross Channel over YouTube. And there are other streaming services that make his programs available to hundreds of millions of other viewers around the world.

What Bob did, perhaps without knowing it, was to model the values the Apostle Paul talks about in Philippians 4:4–7 that I cited earlier—which I carefully chose as my *life verse* when I was in the Timothy Program. Deliberately deciding to routinely choose this attitude about what I encounter, helps me focus on what is good about everything in life instead of what is bad, disappointing, or frightening. And without knowing it, Bob Ross conscientiously chooses to focus on all the good we do when we paint instead of what we would commonly call mistakes—instead, naming them "happy accidents." Doing what Bob does changes the way we look at life and also helps us choose an attitude of gratitude over an attitude of failure. I think that is part of the magnetism of Bob and the "Joy of Painting" that Bob carries with him wherever he appears.

People love watching and listening to Bob because he focuses on what is right and beautiful, and not on what is wrong and ugly. In a way, it's the old adage that you can draw a lot more attention with honey than with vinegar. Honey is sweet; vinegar is bitter. What would you want to bathe your brain in? And Bob's encouraging words and affirmations, and observations of the beauty of this world, make him and his program an attractive place to hang out or paint along with him.

For many who watch and do not paint, they report that they finish the program and are literally at peace because they took the time to watch. In that comment, for me, I see the hand of God in all of this. After all, what Bob is doing is what the Apostle Paul recommended to "gain God's peace."

I'm not sure what Bob believed about God, but I do know that he always asked me to pray before every meal we ate together, and when I prayed, I asked God to bless Bob and the work we did together. And there's no question that God has done that—big-time. Bob's program is more popular today than ever, reaching maybe even one hundred or more countries (if the YouTube map in *Wikipedia* is to be believed). We don't know for sure where all his programs are available to those who can access YouTube. There are also thirty-five hundred CRI's—Certified Ross Instructors from America and many other countries that have been trained in New Smyrna Beach, Florida, where the Bob Ross ArtWorks Center trains Certified Ross Instructors to carry on the spirit and legacy of *The Joy of Painting.*

Secondly, when I was running the station, we created a televised auction—Telesale— in 1978. It was patterned after what we had seen as we attended the 1977 WCET-TV Cincinnati PBS on-air auction. WIPB's first auction, Telesale, raised $50,000. The second nearly $100,000 and we were well on our way to having the additional funds for equipment and staff to do all the local programming we could out of our 4,600 square foot Lucius L. Ball home, a Ball Brothers Foundation property on the banks of the White River. We were located just a few blocks north of downtown Muncie where WIPB-TV operated from 1972 until our move to a permanent home in the new Edmund F. Ball Communications Building on Ball State's campus in September 1988.

Edmund Ball was on our board and also on the PBS Board and was Chairman of the Ball Brothers Foundation and made the Lucious Ball house on Minnetrista available to house the fledgling WIPB station in 1972. That building, initially built in the 1870s and refurbished in the early 1900s, initially served as the station for six years—on loan from the Ball Brothers Foundation—but it ended up being the home of Channel 49 from 1972 through 1988, when the station moved to its permanent location on Ball State's campus, where it stands today. Ed Ball was also on our Eastern Indiana Community Television Board which oversaw the station's operations and funding, throughout my seventeen-year tenure at the station.

Third, we were the smallest station in the 1981 Advertising Test. In this Congressional test, only nine stations participated in the US to see if PBS stations could substitute regular Product and Service Advertising for our on-air fundraising. Congress wanted to see if we could substitute regular commercial product and service advertising for the then current Underwriting Announcements and on-air Pledging. We all worked hard at this test, but subsequently proved that regular Product and Service Advertising was not a sufficient substitute and did not raise enough new money to be able to replace our underwriting, auctions, and on-air pledging. Congress was disappointed, and so was I.

In the midst of that test, Bob Ross and Annette Kowalski showed up on our doorstep and gave us a new way to make money. For each "how-to" book that was requested showing how to do a Bob Ross painting in a series, we received one dollar. On some days, we received over four hundred letters with checks which were counted and sent on to the company's Herndon, Virginia headquarters. We were having a great time. Bob was fun to work with, and it was fun to have a real celebrity in our quiver to share with East Central Indiana, and with the world. Little did we know that Bob's program and popularity would grow to reach audiences and students in North America, Central America, Europe, Asia, Africa, and Australia.

Chapter 29

Other Notable Prayer Life Events and Our Accident

There are many events that were possible only because God answered our prayers. Here are a few of them, told in a shorthand fashion so you'll get the idea. They are part of the reason that I know God exists, that I know He answers prayers, and that I pray without ceasing as the Bible urges us to do, because I know God hears what we ask for, and Jesus tells the Disciples very clearly in John 14:12–14—two times, "I tell you the truth, anyone who believes in me will do the same works I have done, and even greater works, because I am going to be with the Father. You can ask for anything in my name, and I will do it, so that the Son can bring glory to the Father. Yes, ask me for anything in my name, and I will do it."

Now you see me writing this and questioning if I pray for anything for you. So I'll tell you plainly: Grandma and I pray for every one of you and ask God to give you the desires of your heart and to mold your desires so that what you hope and wish for are what He wants you to have that is better than anything you can imagine or ask. You are each in our prayers every night as we go to bed and thank God for giving you what you need to be happy and prosper. We ask for

God's favor to rest upon you and bring just the right people into your lives. Let me give you a few examples:

You've already heard about Kirsten's retainer, lost in Lake Michigan in August of 1977. We prayed and found it, remember? You heard about our praying for Kirsten to accept our love for each other when she ordered me out of the house—before we were engaged. And, in God's wisdom, God's answer was to allow Kirsten to sneak back down the stairs, stand in front of us, listen to our prayer as we prayed—eyes closed—and hear our hearts crying out to God, and seeing that—hearing that—Kirsten's heart was changed in a moment. When I asked her what happened that night, recently, those are the words she used to explain it. God changed her heart! When our friends, the Sparenbergs who lived down the street, were planning a wedding in their outdoor garden beside their house and morning storm clouds were gathering, I went to their house and told them to go ahead with their plans. God had told me to go back to their front door and knock and tell them that the storm clouds would go away, and the day would be perfect by 4:00 PM when the wedding was to begin, and it was!

And this was long before there were phone Apps telling us many hours in advance what to expect. It was cloudy, windy, and blowing, and I had just finished running for an hour and it looked like rain. As I approached our front door, a voice said to me: "Go back to the Sparenbergs and tell them the day will be sunny and bright by 4:00. Go ahead with your plans for the wedding. Everything will be fine!" And when the father, Jerry came to the door, he said they had just been discussing it and weren't sure if they should proceed.

But on the basis of what I told them, they went ahead with their plans and were at peace, and of course the day was absolutely perfect! How did I know? I actually was told to go back and tell them this, and they trusted that I was telling the truth. I was, and God proved it. Even to this day, any of the Sparenbergs who were there will attest that this is what happened. Remember, it wasn't the first time God had spoken to me or the first time He had fulfilled a promise. Ask them! Then you'll know this is a true report of God in action. I believe God answers our prayers for His glory, not ours. And he has done it again and again. Ask Kim or Kelly or Tricia or Jerry or Ann. They all remember this day—for good reason.

Here are some other brief reminders of how gracious and generous our God is when we ask: Brian going to Taylor University. He was worried he would find Taylor really challenging, and that he might not be admitted. Not only was he admitted to Taylor but he became the standout in all his art classes and had the courage and insight to transfer to Ball State for his BFA after the first year at Taylor where he averaged over a 3.0 or B. Well done, Brian. Thank you, God. Our prayer was that he would be admitted and that he would do well. Both prayers were answered.

Or take the time when we prayed that somehow Addison would get a good job after she graduated from Indiana University. She did not pledge to a sorority, so her contacts might be limited, we foolishly thought. Not only did she do very well in school but she ended up as President of the IU Student Foundation in charge of the Little Five Hundred. Last year, she returned for the celebration and the race and is finishing her third year in Supply Chain support services for Target Corporate offices after spending her first year working for Abercrombie & Fitch in Columbus. She got a signing bonus, travel expenses, and a great starting salary. She left Abercrombie after one year to take a better job at Target and continues there today, happy, challenged and well-rewarded for all of the things she did as an IU student. Again, our prayers were answered far beyond our greatest expectations. We just asked that she would find a good job after graduation. And she got a great job instead, and after her first move an incredibly great job. Thank you, God. That's way more than we were asking for.

Finally, one more illustration of how God answers prayer, in 2022, Grandma and I went to Florida for a vacation to work on my book, and relax in the sun. It seemed to be a good idea, but *it* ended up being an incredibly tumultuous winter with lots of surprises.

As we traveled south, I began having pains in my back that seemed to come from my left kidney. As the winter wore on and we struggled through the first couple of weeks, the pain grew sharper. We were praying that God would help us get well. Little did we know what we were asking. I went to our Chiropractor, and she treated me twice. Not having any success, she said she thought I had a UTI (a urinary tract infection) and should see my doctor.

Our doctor which we met with for the first time in March 2021 was on maternity leave, so we met with her substitute, an APRN Nurse Practitioner who checked me out and told me I had no infection. There was an office just below us on the first floor of our building where there were five Urologists, and she urged me to see one immediately. She said I had something that had to be addressed soon. Something was terribly wrong, and the pain in my kidney was getting worse.

All the while we're praying this will be something simple to resolve. That's not what God heard. On the twentieth of January, I met with the Urologist, and she checked me out. She said I had a very large prostate and that was blocking the flow from my kidney and sent me to have a CT scan the next day, January 21. On the way there, we pulled into a parking lot. I stopped the car to find the referral slip which was in my back pocket and was fishing for it with my foot on the brake when out of nowhere, a 2011 Lexus plowed into my side of our Odyssey minivan and hit the upright post right behind the driver's door, propelling us into a tree that was protected by a concrete curbing. We bounced over the curb, into the tree, and bounced back into the parking lot. The other car stopped, and so did we. I could not get out.

My door was jammed shut. The airbags had deployed, and Linda was shouting: "Jim, what have you done?"

Well, of course, I didn't know what I had done. I was sitting in the parking lot one minute looking six hundred feet down an empty lot and then looking forward across my left hand on top of the steering wheel and fishing with my right hand in my back pocket for my doctor's script for my MRI with the lab's address on it, "WHAM—without warning—the airbag in front of me explodes and the two bags to my left deploy and smash into my head, and Linda is screaming, "What have you done!" I had no idea. I had seen no one coming, and the parking lot was empty. And when the Lexus impacted us, my brakes were released so when we kept rolling toward the tree and Linda cried out: "Hit the brakes, Jim!" Nothing happened—the pedal went to the floor—because the brakes were released as soon as we were impacted, so we would roll forward instead of likely flipping over if the brakes were locked.

Almost immediately, we heard the automatic callback from Honda Link that is a built-in safety mechanism saying: "Mr. Needham, are you alright? This is Honda Link."

I was shocked to hear her voice, and so happy to hear from someone who was asking the right question. "Yes, we're fine," I said. "We're not injured. The airbags went off. Someone hit us, and we're fine, but I can't get out of my door."

The Honda Link operator urged us to calm down and take it easy. The Police, EMT's and Fire Department had all been called and would be there in five minutes. And indeed, very shortly, we heard the sirens and the deputy sheriff, fire truck, and EMT van arrived a couple minutes later. We were okay, and the driver of the other vehicle was also uninjured. It was only a few minutes, but it seemed like it was all happening in slow motion. I climbed over the console and got out of the car, and the other driver was there, alone, and had not been injured. He was happy that emergency personnel had been called and waited along with us for them to arrive.

The saga had begun. We didn't know what would happen next. The sheriff took down our information for the Police Report and called the towing company that would remove our vehicles from this huge parking lot that must have measured one hundred feet by six hundred feet long. As I sat there in the driver's seat right before impact, I was looking at a totally empty parking lot and had no idea we were about to be in an accident that would total our vehicle. This was the beginning of a very strange day.

As it turned out, the tow driver arrived shortly, and we called some friends to drive us home. Instead, they took us to my CT-scan appointment where they allowed us to be late and did the scan anyhow. That helped because the kidney problem continued.

That night, we prayed for the other driver, for our cars, for the insurance companies, and gave thanks that none of us had been injured. The other driver was also on his way to visit a doctor, and he also did not know at that time where he was going. I was hunting for my address, and he was taking what he thought was a shortcut to get to his doctor for some kind of test. It was a difficult day for both of us.

The next week, I went to my doctor, and she said my kidney was swollen, and that I would need to wear a foley catheter until we figured out what was causing the problem. My prostate was greatly enlarged, and I could not void my bladder. That was apparently the problem, so different tests were ordered, and I submitted to being poked and prodded until we got through those tests. When we were done, my doctor recommended that we do a TURP surgery that would create a pathway through my enlarged prostate and make a way for my urethra to pass the urine out so that the kidney which was swollen would be able to heal. Until I could do that, she left the catheter in and recommended that I go ahead with the surgery.

I had been reading online, and was convinced that being a Vegan, if I had the TURP surgery, I would bleed a lot, and that was not an option. I told her that, and that I would be asking someone else for a second opinion. I had already contacted a doctor in North Miami that did a bloodless surgery—an AquaAblation—which provided a three-day recovery. That was sounding real good. When I told my Urologist I was seeking a second opinion, she asked if I had any further questions. When I said I did, she said I should consult with the person that would do the surgery and that while she could recommend another Urologist in her practice, she would not answer the questions.

As we left the exam room, our nurse asked if we had any further questions, and we asked if the doctor had recommended anyone in particular. As a matter of fact, she had, and Grandma seized on that and said, "We'd like to have an appointment with that doctor then." I was not sure, but Grandma was sure, so I consented and went to the scheduling nurse. Shortly, we were leaving with an appointment for the next day.

We had been able to retrieve a rental car the day of the accident, so going back and forth to Naples—about an hour's drive—was not difficult. Linda went back with me the next day to hear what this other doctor would say. His name was Paulos Yohannes, MD. I looked up his name and history, and I discovered his name was Greek for Paul John. When we met with him the next day, we discovered he was from Louisville and had studied in New York and Kansas and was a pioneer in Robotic Prostate surgery. When we met with Dr. Yohannes, I told him I had looked up his name. "Why were you given that name which is Greek for Paul John?"

He laughed easily and answered that his parents were missionaries in Ethiopia and that he was named for the Apostle Paul and the Apostle that Jesus loved most, John. I blurted out that my estimation of him had just jumped from here (ground level) to above my head. "If someone has to do my surgery, I want it to be a doctor who can pray with me. Are you willing to do that?" And he said, "Absolutely!" And then we chatted about our personal commitment to Jesus, our churches, and that I most definitely wanted someone who believed in Jesus, to do the surgery. I was finally at peace about what to do next.

When we arrived for our appointment, we were on time, and Dr. Yohannes was five minutes late. Well, that was remarkably better than my former Urologist who had been one hour late for our first appointment, ninety minutes late for the second appointment, and an hour late for the third appointment. I was tired of sitting in the waiting room.

When I came back for Dr. Yohannes's second appointment, we came a half hour early, and I went to the bathroom. Yohannes' nurse came out three times in the first twenty minutes before I was due to have my appointment, and finally we got in to see him ten minutes early. We discussed what he would recommend, and he said it would be a Simple Prostatectomy which would take out the inner core of the Prostate and leave the mechanical elements that control the urine flow so that I would regain control of my "plumbing" within a week or two. I was happy about that prospect, and Dr. Yohannes prayed for me and our upcoming surgery as he had promised before we left to go back to our condo. I was still wearing my Foley catheter; it was painful, and I wanted to get rid of that as soon as possible.

As things worked out, I was to wear that catheter for forty-nine days overall. The only thing that comforted me was very early on, I realized that the Foley Catheter never leaked on me or the bed. It did wake me up every two hours during the night, so my sleep was somewhat fitful, but it never did leak. That was indeed a comforting discovery!

The date for my surgery was set for March 1. I contacted the doctor in North Miami and cancelled my appointment. Little did I know that was a brilliant decision. You'll understand shortly. The AquaBlation procedure uses high-speed room temperature water jets with a tiny footprint to destroy the tissue that is blocking the ureter and then wash it out with a saline solution so that the tissue that is destroyed is removed. Only after I had the surgery did I recognize that if I had the tissue that was destroyed removed, I might not have been able to discover that 10 percent of the tissue removed from my Prostate during my Simple Prostatectomy, had Adenocarcinoma cells in it and should be watched and re-tested.

That discovery was a gift from God who is always looking out for me. I was all set to take the 3-day recovery plan with AquaBlation until Grandma stepped in and said, "Let's take a look at what we can do here. Otherwise, I have to travel back and forth to North Miami." And when we found a truly Christian surgeon in Dr. Yohannes in Naples, I was eager to have him do the surgery and also to please Grandma who would have had to commute from Fort Myers Beach to North Miami if I had elected to do the AquaBlation, and never have known the underlying Adenocarcinoma diagnosis.

I consider the underlying Adenocarcinoma diagnosis a major add-on blessing from choosing Dr. Yohannes. I am back in Yorktown now, healthy again, and thanking God for the quick recovery and a happy wife. All of that is more than I deserve and more than many who have had my procedure receive when they have my diagnosis. I am so grateful to God for helping me listen to Grandma whose wise advice is almost always on target. There is no doubt that she has my best interest in mind, even when I disagree with her.

In this case, like Elkanah who respected the wishes of his wife, Hanna when she had her first child, Samuel, I listened to my wife and respected her heart and intention before God and was truly blessed.

Because of Hannah's faithfulness, after Samuel's birth, weaning, and dedication to the Priesthood by Hannah as she promised, God chose to bless these two faithful Israelites with three more sons and two daughters—all this to a woman who had been barren all of her life until her first-born, Samuel was born.

This episode in my life and in my memory of the story of Samuel and Hannah in 1 Samuel, reminds me that it is fair and right to respect your wife always and honor God with your promises to Him. My experience tells me that God always has something better in store for you when you do that. I hope I remember that and honor Grandma in that way, always. I hope you will also choose to show that respect for each other in your families and trust that God will bless you for doing what is right in His sight.

Chapter 30

God Prepares a Place
for Me in Korea

Earlier in my life, just after I retired from Ball State's TCOM Department (now the MEDIA Department), I was fortunate to be able to teach a summer session at the University of Incheon in Korea in the summer of 2010. At that time, I discovered I was only able to teach in Korea because I had been the General Manager of the station that had produced *The Joy of Painting*. When I was asked for my full résumé because I did not have a PhD, which they said was required to teach at their university, I mentioned the *Joy of Painting*. And instead of emailing me about it, the Chairman of the Media Department at the University of Incheon, telephoned me and asked about the *Joy of Painting* references on my résumé. When he realized I was the person responsible for producing the show with Bob Ross and Annette Kowalski, his tone softened and he remarked enthusiastically, "Oh, Mr. Needham, I grew up watching *The Joy of Painting* here in Korea. Of course, you can teach our students." For Korea, creating this incredible series was my PhD, and that was that. It was a wonderful 6 weeks in Korea where I was treated like royalty. I loved teaching the variety of students that I had—all fifteen of them—and they loved what they learned. What an amazing discovery and an amazing connection. Thank you, God! He had opened my doors, years before in the mind and heart of the Department Chairman.

When I arrived in Incheon, South Korea, I was taken to a hotel at the airport and given a room where I could catch up on my sleep and also begin to adjust to the fact that Korea operates thirteen hours ahead of Muncie time. After a good night's sleep, I was taken to the campus hotel where I was given a very nice one-bedroom apartment, and then asked to meet with the six faculty members who taught Media Studies to their engineering students who had an interest.

The campus was beautiful and brand new. I arrived at the end of their first year of onsite operations, and President Ahn, who had helped design the campus, was an ever-present addition, periodically adding finishing touches to his beautiful campus with his construction team. I saw him numerous times, checking out his buildings and grounds, and checking his punch-list of change orders with his team of engineers and contractors in tow. He also had an interest in me and had dinner with me on five occasions in the six weeks I was there. It was very special treatment for a small-town boy like me, born in the little town of New Albany, Indiana, sixty-six years before. Wow! That's all I can say. Being privileged like that was so far beyond my expectations, I just could not adequately express my gratitude to God and to President Ahn.

After my first good night's sleep in Korea at the hotel, the Media Faculty met with me and asked how I planned to teach their Korean students. The students all understood English, I was told, but they were reticent about speaking English. In fact, the professors said that as a matter of teaching technique, the students do not speak in Korean classrooms. The professors lecture, collect papers, and give tests, but there is no professor/student dialogue in the classroom. I said that would change with me and my approach to teaching Media Criticism. My students would have to talk.

The faculty expressed concern and disapproval. They didn't believe it could happen.

The reason this concerned them was my usual way of teaching Media Criticism was to present a basic outline for how to analyze media and then ask the students to discuss what their perceptions were of the media we were looking at. The professors told me that would never work with Korean students. I told them, "It will work in *my* classroom!" As I look back on it now, I was somewhat arrogant. I had worked with foreign students before at Ball State, and I was certain they would somehow begin to talk with me when I asked them to do so, clearly expecting them to respond.

I wasn't sure how that would come about, but I had never had a problem engaging students, and I was sure I could do that. I just didn't know how.

As the first week zoomed by, I could see what they meant. The students did not interact verbally with me much during that first week. We slowly and very systematically went over the details of what we were doing and what I intended to cover, and then I told them, we would be discussing our first media event the next week. My schedule was to teach Tuesday through Friday from 10:00 AM—1:00 PM, and then have Saturday through Monday off to organize the next week, grade papers, rest, and conduct personal business.

Teaching three hours a day was an unusual and difficult strain in a situation where I had to go over what I was saying slowly and repeatedly and systematically ask if anyone had any questions. That first week, I never got my first question. I began to wonder what I was going to do. I hoped I was communicating. I saw interest on their faces, and they were alert to what I was doing. I was going slowly and checking with them every minute or so. It was tedious for me, but important they get the idea and see the way I intended to teach them.

I had studied the strategies for successful teaching in a mixed language program and knew my students' writing in English would be better than their speaking. But I truly

believed they would be willing to talk if the issue was of sufficient interest, and I very persuasively "opened the door and
invited them in to 'our' conversation."

Since I like to work out daily, and know that working
out sharpens a person's abilities, lowers their stress, and
improves their ability to retain information, I went to the
brand-new Incheon University Gym on campus every morning at 6:00 AM. Remember, I was still on Indiana time to a
great degree, although Incheon is thirteen hours ahead of
Muncie time. Since I woke up early anyhow, and went to bed
early, it was easy to be at the gym by 6:00 AM.

The University of Incheon had spared no expense in
building a great gymnasium complex one block from my
hotel. It had all the bells and whistles, TV monitors on every
treadmill, and several large monitors around the workout
gym. I had been going to the gym every day at about 6:00
AM, to help myself adjust to the time difference, and I was
awake early each morning anyhow, so I figured, "Why not?"

The second Tuesday of my five-week semester, I
repeated my routine. I went to work out as I usually did, and I
had a great workout. I was beginning to adjust to the strange
hours and getting more and better sleep. That Tuesday was
the last day of going over the "basics" of media criticism.
Wednesday, June 30, was the day my class and I would
begin to "dive in and talk to each other" about what we were
seeing in the media.

When Wednesday came, I went to the gym, dressed
quickly in my running shorts and shirt, and came out of the
locker room only to be confronted with a young, good-look-
ing thirtysomething Korean male on every monitor. What
was I looking at? When I got on a treadmill to get my miles
in, I was facing a picture of the same young man on every
video screen. Something had happened. As I looked around,
there were obviously news stories on every channel featur-
ing his handsome face. He looked to be in his early thirties
and was obviously a well-known figure.

Confused and curious, I turned to the Korean man working out next to me and asked if he spoke English. He smiled and in perfect English, said he was the Asian Affairs Coordinator for the University of Missouri and was there to teach at their university for the summer and visit family. I asked him why this young man's picture was all over the media. And his reply stunned me.

His name was Park Yong-ha. He was a superstar, the top TV Star, singer and songwriter in Southeast Asia, and a very popular draw in his home country of South Korea and in Japan.

It's a terrible story, he told me. Park had just returned from a very successful Japanese tour where he had released eight new CDs and finished a sold-out concert tour in Tokyo the weekend before. When Park returned home, apparently, he found that his father, who was dying of stomach cancer, had taken a turn for the worse. In Park's anguish, he impulsively took a camcorder cable and hung himself, and was found dead on Wednesday morning, June 30. The country and his fans were devastated.

Park Yong-ha, superstar, extraordinaire, dead at thirty-two on June 30, 2010. What a tragedy!

I am a former Television Producer. I have produced documentaries and news stories. I knew what I had to do. This had happened overnight. The media was just delivering the story. It was the top and only news one could get that morning, and some of my students had been up since dawn, at least one travelling two hours by train each way to get to my 10:00 AM class on time. They would all know what had happened. We needed to look at it and discuss it. Where to begin?

As they had on Tuesday, they filed in quietly. No one was talking. I took roll. Everyone was present, and then I stood up and walked around the room. I showed them a picture of Park Yong-ha. "Do you know who this is?" I asked. They all nodded. One of them was crying. I told them how I had discovered the news, and then I asked, "Do you all know what happened last night?" And they all nodded.

173

Then I asked them the most important question that set the stage for the rest of the semester. "What do you think? When you do media criticism, you look at what the media is doing and ask yourself, 'What do I think of that? Is it true? Is it false? Is it fair? Is it exaggerated? Can I trust what I am hearing and seeing?"

I explained that in my classes, everyone is expected to talk. Each of them was expected to have an opinion. And I was the professor. I would ask the questions, and I would expect them to answer them, telling us all what they thought about what I was asking.

So I said, I will ask the question, and then I will listen to what each of you think. Park Yong-ha is dead. The media is talking about him—what he has done with his life and how he took his own life this morning. Are they being fair about what they are saying about him?"

"That's my question," I said. "Now it's your turn to talk." And I continued to emphasize that it was their turn to talk. I wanted to know what they each thought about what was happening in the media. I explained that I understood that Korean professors do not require their students to talk in class.

"I am an American, and that is how we teach in American Universities." I reiterated; "I want to know what YOU think now."

I stopped talking. After about three or four minutes, the smallest girl in my class, Adala Kim, maybe four feet, eight or so, sort of waved her hand a little, and I called her by name. "Adala, what do you think? Is the media being fair with what they are saying about Park Yong-ha?"

She sat there for the longest time, looked at her other classmates, and finally turned to me and asked in a very timid, soft voice: "Do you really want us to talk?"

And I immediately moved toward her where she was seated in a circle in our classroom and said. "Yes, Adala, that's exactly what I want to hear. What do YOU think about the media and how they are treating this terrible tragedy? How do you feel about it?"

And she began—quiet at first—she began to talk. And soon other hands went up, and soon they were all talking. Some were better at English than others, but they all had their opinions. We talked for the next three hours. It was thrilling and exhausting, but it was what I had come for. They were all participating: every single one of them. It was a new and energizing and innovating experience for them all, and for me.

I then gave them an assignment to summarize what was said in the class and post it on their podcast for me to read. I would read it that night and give them my ideas on what they had heard and seen. It was the beginning of a wonderful five weeks of international learning, and a treat for me and for them. How would I have known to ask for this to stimulate discussion? Things happen! And God had prepared me through all of my experiences to seize this moment and use it for His glory…to make this class a success for every one of us. I was stunned!

When we finished the five-week long class, they had all done well. As the second week of classes wound down, one of my students volunteered to guide me into Seoul, and helped me learn how to navigate the trains into this city of 25 million. They took the day off to accompany me to one of the Korean Palaces and showed me around. I tried to get others to do that, but only one volunteered.

Later, when I went to get a haircut, I thought my Korean was good enough for me to get the barber to do what I wanted. But when I showed her one inch with my fingers that I wanted her to cut off and shorten my hair, the barber thought I meant to leave only one inch, and I went to class the next day with a very close Kim Jong-un "skin the sides and leave a little on top" haircut that made me resemble Kim Jong-un. When I got to class, that day, they all laughed and pointed at me and teased me, saying, "Oh, Mr. Needham.

You got haircut!" And we all laughed as I explained what had happened. They all said they would have helped me if I had asked. I wish I had asked, but my hair all grew out, and I lived through it.

My six week experience at the University of Incheon was a delightful intermezzo between what I had been doing at Ball State for seventeen years as a TCOM professor and my escape to the world of retirement where my notion was I would get to do what I wanted instead of what I was being paid to do. What a big change in such a short time. But my time in Incheon had been miraculous in many ways.

There are many other stories I could tell you about my visit there, and I would love to go back. One comes to mind when I met Maria Valegas, the Special Assistant to the Mayor of Manilla in the Philippines. She was sitting in the lobby of our hotel, waiting to take her cab to the airport, when I sauntered in after class.

Maria stopped me by looking up and catching my eye, raising her hand as if to stop a car, and saying directly: "You're an American, aren't you?"

I said I was, and how did she know. She didn't answer, she just launched into her introduction about who she was and what she was doing in Incheon. She had been meeting with the Mayor of Incheon and said I should call his Assistant and get a tour of Incheon. She said I would never forget it, and since I had been busy teaching at the University of Incheon for the past six weeks, I should carve out one day to meet with the Assistant Mayor and tour the city.

That's exactly what I did! The Assistant Mayor was delighted to show me the city and drove me around in an official Limousine, showing me things I would never have seen without his help. Three things I saw will always remain with me: The General Douglas MacArthur Memorial and museum during the 60th Anniversary Celebration of the Allies' landing in Korea, the Incheon Maritime Museum, and the Yum Kwang Church.

MacArthur landed on Incheon beaches because the prevailing wisdom was that with the massive 35-foot tidal range and mud flats there, no one could ever land on the west side of the Korean peninsula, so it was left unprotected by the enemy.

Knowing that, MacArthur landed our troops during the three hours of high tide and split the country in two along the 18th parallel, and it continues to be split along that Parallel to this day with its DMZ Zone—The Demilitarized Zone where no Koreans from either side are allowed to live or be. If they are discovered there, they will be seen as spies and imprisoned or shot on sight. That is the reason none of my students could volunteer to take me there, even though I had been near the DMZ for dinner one night with President Ahn and his staff.

At the MacArthur Memorial, as tens of thousands celebrated the 60th Anniversary of MacArthur's landing, there were thousands of Post-it notes on the walls next to long sloping walkways with messages from Koreans. I still remember one in particular, that said, in English: "Thank you Dad for loving me and for sacrificing so that I could live free here in Korea. Wherever you are, I love you." And she wrote her name.

I saw several of these in English, obviously written by children of American GI's who went back home and didn't take their children with them or never knew they had fathered a child. None-the-less, everyone was wonderful to me. All of the Koreans I met, treated me as a special guest and made my stay very special indeed.

Second, we went to the Incheon Maritime Museum. That doesn't sound exciting until you know that it has a Diorama of the MacArthur Landing along with wing-footage film from the actual landing, and also a film that shows what happened on that fateful day as the battle began.

There was also a Diorama of the first time the Koreans built a Dry-Dock in 1910 and an explanation in Korean and

English about how there was a need for a Dry-Dock, and they built it out in the ocean because there was no way to excavate the ground along the shoreline. Much of Korea is rock. So the citizens just hauled stone and dirt to the ocean and dumped it in again and again, and finally had a rectangular Dry-Dock with Locks at the north end that they could open and let a ship sail in. Then they would close the locks, pump the water out, and work on the ship in Dry-Dock. Once repairs were completed, they would flood the Dry-Dock again, and sail the ship out.

One hundred years later, I was standing in Incheon on land that had been reclaimed from the ocean. Actually, the tallest building in South Korea, the Lotte World Tower, and fifth tallest building in the world is located on former sea beds that have been covered over with rock and dirt from the mountainous South Korean interior—hauled there by many horse-drawn wagons and dump trucks over many decades and dumped into the sea.

Because of that effort, the original shoreline on the west side of South Korea is now 6 miles inland from where the University of Incheon and Lotte World Tower, South Korea's tallest skyscraper are located. The campus, about a mile closer to the coast, is now just one hundred yards from the ocean. All of the land on which the University sits is re-claimed ocean. When you know there is a continuing complaint from China about Korea encroaching on China's rights to the Ocean, you now know how the Koreans learned they could create more flat land by the sea. They did it one hundred years ago, and they are still re-claiming land from the sea, much to China's dismay. It was fascinating to see that and realize how history has such a significant impact on our future.

Third, while I was there, I planned to go to the sister church of First Presbyterian Church here in Muncie. Yum Kwang Korean Presbyterian Church is on the north side of Seoul, so as my confidence grew, I wanted to discover if I could get there using the Seoul Metropolitan Subway system and attend church on the Sunday when our Mission Team from Muncie's First Presbyterian Church was to be in the city. I did go on my own the Saturday just before they were planning to be in church the next day, and I got lost downtown at Seoul Station. It was a huge subway station, and I looked for a map I could read.

I was standing there on the platform at Seoul Station, looking at a large wall map and wondering how to get to Yumkwang Church when a man approached me. He was Korean, wore a western style suit and tie, and in perfect English, asked if I was lost. I said I was, and that I hoped to go to Yumkwang Church which was north of the city, and I pointed to it on the map.

In perfect English, pointing to the stairs behind me, he said, "You need to go back to the stairs, go down those steps, go under the tracks, and go to the other side of the platform. Then he pointed the opposite direction and said, "Go north and get off at the third stop." I kept looking at the map for a long moment, memorizing what he had indicated, and then turned to thank him. My gracious tour guide was gone! He had already disappeared from the platform.

I looked around quickly, but he was gone. And I wondered if this was one of God's angels that have helped me other places. I'll never know, but I know he was there one moment and gone the next.

So I followed his instructions and caught the right train and ended up at the Yumkwang Presbyterian Church of Korea (a church of 17,000 members) after only four and a half hours on the trains, traveling by myself through a city of 25 million people. That was a little nerve-wracking, but I knew then, and I know now that God was with me and going before me.

When I was preparing to pack up and head to the airport and home, the University of Incheon Media Department Chair called and asked me to join her for a final debriefing over lunch. As we finished, she casually concluded with this:

"You know, Mr. Needham, we were skeptical that you would ever get our students to talk in your class, and that they might not benefit in the ways we had hoped for. Because of that, we carefully interviewed every one of them after classes ended, and we have concluded that our concerns about what would happen were without merit. They loved your class, and we would love for you to come back if that is something that can be worked out with Ball State University.

We had a delicious lunch, and I went back to my hotel to get my bags. I was smiling, and I was thanking God for allowing me to find a way to engage my Korean students in a tragic event they could not help but experience, and get a close-up glimpse of how we teach, how American students learn, and that their ideas were of great value to themselves and to each other.

When I went to the airport to go home, I discovered that my reservation had been changed. The airfare for my flight home had been upgraded from Tourist Class to Business Class. That was remarkable. When I got on the plane, the stewardess stopped me at the door, and ushered me to the stairway of the Boeing 747. "Your seat is up there," she said.

I was flabbergasted. "Are you sure?" I asked. She looked at my ticket, smiled, and pointed up the stairs.

Instead of sitting upright for the fifteen-hour trip, I slept most of the way, lying down, in Business Class. I had been "upgraded" as a bonus for what had transpired with my students.

When Linda asked how I had done in Korea, I smiled and said, "I slept all the way home. And I think I got an A+ for my teaching. What a wonderful experience in every way. I wish we could go there together someday." That may never happen, but for me, it was an adventure of a lifetime and another confirmation that God is still leading me, no matter where I go.

Chapter 31

Nazareth to Jerusalem: God Is My Witness

The next great adventure in 2010 turned out to be Israel. We had always wanted to go on a pilgrimage. We knew that good friends of ours in Muncie, Bibi and Saber Bahrami, faithful Muslims, routinely returned to Mecca each year for their pilgrimage, and we wanted to go to Jerusalem for ours. But we had never had the right opportunity. Then, we were invited to join the John XXIII Catholic Retreat Center in Hartford City, Indiana, and 35 others, and some of our best friends, and travel to Israel in November 2010. We immediately said "Yes" and soon were on our way.

A former Rotary member and close Catholic friend, Father John Kiefer was to be our Spiritual Director. We were eager and ready to go when November came, but a little reticent. We said we didn't want to make anyone uncomfortable when they had communion, but he formally covered that issue with all of us in our pre-trip session: "On this trip," he said, "regardless of where you worship, you will all take communion! Any questions?" Not one fellow traveler said a word to our Priest, and we were included in everything and had communion with everyone everywhere we went. It was unforgettable, amazing: even life changing.

We arrived in Tel Aviv early in the morning and boarded our bus to Nazareth, the city where Jesus spent much of his childhood and where we would stay for three days. We stayed at the Incarnate Word Convent attached to the Basilica of the Annunciation, visited the Basilica of the Annunciation and other sites, and had communion there.

One of the first places we went was the Basilica of the Annunciation where it is storied that the archangel Gabriel first appeared to Mary in her cliff-side dwelling. There in the lower level of the basilica, dimly lit and off to our left, was a rough-hewn stone altar in a small cave-like alcove, carved out of the cliff. Father John paused as we were preparing for communion and pointed. "Let's pause and consider," he said quietly, "what has been written on that altar over there. It is reported that this is the place where Gabriel spoke to Mary. And knowing that, you will see over there across the top of the altar, written in Latin, the words that make this place, very special indeed.

He read the words to us in Latin, and then in English. "This is what is written," he quietly said: 'In This Place, the Word Became Flesh'." Consider," he continued. "There is no other place on earth where this could be written, and it would be so!" My eyes welled up with tears as the meaning of his words overwhelmed me with my sense of wonder and worship! I was not alone. Who would not shudder in awe at this revelation... I was not alone.

Father John continued. "As we take communion here, look to your left—think for just a moment that two thousand years ago, in this place, Mary spoke to Gabriel and said these words of ultimate sacrifice: "Be it done unto me according to your word."

And then there was silence. Finally, after a few minutes, as we clumsily brushed away the tears, even as I write this here—recognition in our hearts, blazing through our minds, we finished communion with a deep sense that we had just experienced in the most holy place where we had ever taken communion... something way beyond communion...where Jesus began His journey on earth... It was something that is still with me as I write this—I will never forget!

We experienced lots of things in Nazareth and in the little town of Sepphoris, about three miles distant where Jesus probably went with his mother or father when he was a young boy. Sepphoris was a wealthy town in Jesus' day because those living there had devised a way to store water in cisterns and knew how to take best advantage of this knowledge to grow food and prosper, and their buildings were ornately decorated and sometimes included discarded Sarcophaguses, when available, in their construction.

When we were there, the remnants of a Roman Arena were also obvious, and Jesus might have come to that place as he and his family went to market. We will never know, but the mosaic tile floors and art and pictures we saw on their floor tiles, will always cause me to wonder where their wealth came from. It was such a contrast to the cave dwellings in the limestone cliffs of Nazareth, not more than three miles away, where Jesus had lived and where He "grew in favor with God and man" as a carpenter.

When our third day came in Nazareth, we were encouraged to visit a display of the Inn keeper's wife's paintings. She had spread them out for sale in the room where we gathered each morning for our day's briefings before we set out. Sophie Jabali had put out her oil paintings all around the room—some framed, many just unframed canvases, leaning against the backs of chairs. So at four forty-five, with fifteen minutes left in her exhibition, I went to see them.

Grandma Linda asked where I was going, and I told her. She told me not to buy any paintings—that we already had enough art all over our house, and she was right! So I promised. Then, when I got down there, I found I was really attracted to one painting as I entered, in the far corner. I immediately went to look at it.

Of all the paintings of desert-scapes, camels, donkeys, and some tents, as I glanced around the room, this was a painting of an old man with a red turban and a huge, bulky, cream-colored sack over his shoulder. He was walking, leaning over because of his burden. I told the painter, Sophie that this was her best painting, and I loved it.

The innkeeper's wife gushed—ready to make the sale: "Then, you should have it!"

I quickly held up my hand to stop her, and I explained that I could not buy it because I had promised my wife not to buy another painting. I explained that I was involved with a painter in America and had visited many museums and that this painting of hers was very good! I handed her a fifty-dollar bill I kept in my wallet for emergencies like these and said, "I can't buy your painting, but I'd like to give you this gift to encourage you to keep painting and buy some painting supplies. I can't buy your painting. I'm sorry."

And I turned to go. But Sophie would have none of it. She rushed to the painting, rolled it up in her hands, quickly returned to me and said, "If you love it, you should have it!"

I told her again, I could not buy it. It was priced at Two-hundred and fifty dollars, and while I had that in my room, I had also promised my wife not to buy a painting. Sophie said she had never displayed it before and had painted it in 1994 and wanted someone who loved it to have it. "You love it?" she groped for words—half questioning...

"I do," I said. "It's the best painting you have here. But I can't buy it!"

Sophie wasn't listening as she hurriedly thrust the rolled painting into my chest, and let it slip from her grasp. "Then you should have it!" But she had turned around as she thrust this unframed painting into my chest, repeating "If you love it, you should have it!"

I pushed back again, quickly reiterating my stand: "No! I can't buy it."

And she replied, "I know that! I'm giving it to you. I want someone who loves it to have it." And again she turned away, done with the conversation. I could almost hear her tears, as she began packing up her paintings.

I stood there helpless, clutching the painting she had left in my hands as I was trying to resist what she was doing. I said again: "I can't TAKE this."

Sophie said nothing; she made no eye contact; she continued to pack up her paintings; she never looked up. She never acknowledged what I was saying.

After a few moments, shaking my head, I turned to go. She was not listening to me...

When I walked into our room, I had the painting rolled up and under my arm. Linda asked: "What is that under your arm? I thought you were not going to buy a painting."

"I didn't buy a painting," I said.

Linda wasn't buying that! "Right!" she stammered and looked away. I knew this wasn't going anywhere good, so I said nothing.

Later, when we were at dinner, I called Father John aside and told him my dilemma. He said, "What's the problem then?"

I said, "I have the other two-hundred dollars, and I could give it to the Sisters of the Incarnate Word Convent where we are staying to give to her."

But Father John looked me in the eye, measuring my frustration, and said, "No, you can't do that! You can't spoil her gift. She gave it to you because the Holy Spirit prompted her to do that. You can't pay for it. Let it go."

And Father John walked away to get some dessert. I was frustrated. Later that night, I went to him again and said, "I don't feel comfortable about all of this. Why don't I just donate the money to the Sisters of the Convent and let them find a way to share it with Sophie."

And then, Father John confronted me once more, this time harshly—sternly thumping my chest with his index finger: "Jim!" he loudly bolted! "You have to learn one thing from THIS! This is NOT ALL ABOUT YOU! Sophie Jabali was prompted by the Holy Spirit to give the painting to you, and you can't give it back, and you can't pay for it." And thumping his big index finger in my chest once again, he said loudly once more: "This is NOT ABOUT YOU!" And he turned and walked away. I finally got the message.

I silently packed the painting in my bags when we prepared to leave. Later, after we returned home, I was leading a workshop where I was challenging volunteers to help raise money for the Cornerstone Center for the Arts. While I was also a volunteer, over the years, as a part of my community commitment, I had raised money for lots of organizations beginning with the Chamber of Commerce, United Way, Junior Achievement, the Cancer Society, and many others.

This was my third time at Chairing the fundraising for Cornerstone, and I had attracted a new group of people to help. They included Bibi Bahrami and her husband, Dr. Saber Bahrami and a number of their friends, many of them doctors and most of them Muslims who had never worked on a community fund-raising committee like I was chairing.

I had asked each of them to help us raise money for Cornerstone so they could learn how to raise money for AWAKEN, a program providing a school for children and a clinic in Afghanistan where Saber and Bibi were from, and where their school and clinic were serving thousands of people a year. And they were enthusiastic and excited to learn how community fundraising was done.

I told everyone who had signed up to be on our fund-raising team that we were all really blessed to live in America and be able to take time off from our jobs to help with this volunteer effort that provided opportunities for disadvantaged members of our community to receive scholarships to participate in the Arts here at a discounted price.

I also told them the story of the painting which had been a part of my PowerPoint and cited Abram as the Patriarch, the Father of each of our nations...of Israel, of

Christians, and of Islam.

Afterward, Bibi Bahrami came up and asked if I had the original painting that I had shown them on my PowerPoint, and I did. I pulled it out of my backpack and unrolled it for her. She was amazed and she loved it too.

I said to her, "This isn't really MY painting. Sophie gave it to me, but I believe it belongs to God. You know it is a picture of Abram, the father of all Jews, Muslims, and Christians. I think you should have it for your auction for the Awaken Clinic and School in Afghanistan which is coming up in April."

Bibi said, "She gave it to YOU. You can't give it away."

I said, "I think Sophie gave it to me to fulfill God's purposes, not for me to possess it. And I think it should be in your fundraising auction."

"Are you sure?" she asked.

I said I was. Then, she said. "The men are in charge of the auction. I'll have to ask them, and let you know.

Later in the week, she called me and said the men organizing the Awaken Auction had agreed to accept the painting. When I got the call, I took the painting to her husband's office. Dr. Bahrami was all in on this project and was also successfully calling on people in the community to raise funds for Cornerstone. Many of the members on his team were people he had recruited. I was glad to have this matter off my plate and move on to other things, or so I thought.

When the date for the Awaken Auction came, my wife and I bought tickets and went to see how the auction would go. Hopefully, the painting would sell for a great price. The Afghani food was always delicious, and we got in line and loaded our plates. As we were eating dinner, my wife Linda nudged me and asked: "What are you doing on the program? Is there something you didn't tell me? It says here: Program—Jim Needham."

I looked at it and exclaimed: "I don't know. I better ask Bibi what my name is doing there." So I found Bibi and asked: "What is my name doing there? Am I the program?"

"Oh," she said, "I forgot to ask, but I thought you wouldn't mind telling the story of the painting before they sold it. You won't mind, will you?"

And of course, when the time came, they introduced me—and I stood up, went to the podium, and told the story God had given me about the painting of Abram just before they began the auction. I told the story of Sophie Jabali's picture of Abram and how she had forced me to bring it home with me.

When it came to auctioning the painting off, I sat down and watched what would happen. To my surprise, the bidding began at $400 and quickly escalated to $1,650. It was as if God had given Bibi and Saber and the Clinic and School for the disadvantaged in Afghanistan, halfway around the world, a big gift, and it was because of Sophie's generosity.

I am at peace now that the painting has been used to glorify God. I think that was what it was meant to do. I also have a story I can tell about what God did for me, and how He helped me to understand that "Everything is NOT ABOUT ME! I'm SURE of that. I bet you know that to be true about you, too.

Our trip to Israel, along with God's gift of Sophie Jabali's painting of Abram, was a strange and incredible journey for me like many others, I have lived through in the seventy-nine years since my birth in 1944 in New Albany, Indiana. I was to live in seven places before going to college, nine places while in college, one place in Canada, two places in Kentucky, five places in Indianapolis, and three places in Muncie. After graduating from Indiana State, I was to work at WTHI-TV/AMFM for nine months, at the University of Guelph for seven months, at Eastern Kentucky University for two years and eight months, at the CBS Affiliate WISH-TV in Indianapolis for four years, manage the TV Station—

WIPB-TV in Muncie for seventeen years, and teach Social Responsibility and Media Criticism for seventeen years at Ball State University.

The only honors I received were for being the top Academic Advisor of the Year among the 55 Departments at Ball State in 2001, and being voted the TCOM Teacher of the Year by our 1,200 undergraduates and a majority of our faculty in 2010, as I retired after thirty-four years at Ball State University.

In 2011, we bought seven condominiums for student rentals that we kept until 2016 when they were sold. Following two major insurance claims and our sale of the condos, Linda and I both retired for good. As landlords, we served ninety-one student renters, and had a very successful time in the student rental business.

What I know is that, in spite of my mischievous spirit, God has been leading me all the way. Many times, I am sure I disappointed my parents, and ultimately myself, but I am equally sure that our heavenly Father was never surprised, nor was He put off by my bad behavior. He knew, better than I did, that in time, I would come to see that trusting in Him was the best, the only way to be truly happy, and that I would make that choice when I did, in the parking lot at Channel 8 in 1975.

I will never be able to adequately thank all the people I have encountered who have prayed for me again and again. And I know that their prayers have been answered because of God's love and His grace, not because I have been a good person or done great things or deserved what He has given me so freely.

Chapter 32

Mother, Wife, Boss
(My Gift from God)

Before we finish, I want to go back to my wonderful, loving wife—mother of our children, and partner, Linda. In 1980, Linda, bored with being a stay-at-home mom, and with our youngest going off to school, decided she would like to work again, but she did not want to teach after her first encounter with the classroom in the midsixties.

With Brian in Kindergarten and no one at home, she was looking for an outlet for her creativity, energy, leadership skills, and intellect. We had three rental houses at that point and Grandma decided to go into real estate at the urging of our realtor and friend, Bill Ables. Bill convinced Linda that if she had a license, he could give her referral fees for feeding him prospects who bought or sold houses, from those referrals. In the process, with encouragement from Joe Allardt and Mike Lunsford, Linda became a Real Estate Salesperson and later a Real Estate Broker.

Linda was licensed in August 1981, and after four months, she sold and closed her first house sale. That means she got paid! She was ecstatic, though unsure if she would ever sell another house. As a result, the check for $1,000 sat on the table on the soup Tureen for six weeks before she finally deposited it. She said, "I'm afraid I will never sell another house."

Spurred on by our agreement to build a large 25' by 25' game-room addition she could use as her home office if she saved up half of the cost, she sold a number of houses in the first six months of the next year, and by summer, we were planning our addition. One year later, we had built it, put in a Franklin Wood Stove, her office, and red McDonald's tile, and she and Mindy, our new dog, moved in.

In 1992, after living in the Queensbury House for twenty-five years, we built our new home on Riviera Lane in Woodland Trails, and created our "Retirement Ranch" with all our rooms on the ground floor. It is actually larger than the traditional two-story house we left in Halteman Village in Muncie.

Thirty-four years after becoming a Realtor and leading the Muncie Board of Realtors in production for many of her last twenty years, and after mentoring our son, Steve as her officemate for four years, Linda retired as Coldwell Banker Lunsford's top producer and handed off her remaining clients and client contacts to our son, Steve.

In her career, she served as President of the Muncie Board of Realtors, went to state and national meetings, served as Office Manager for Coldwell Banker Lunsford for a time, learned everything she could and was awarded many honors for her success as the top residential realtor in closed sales in Muncie, Indiana, again and again.

She retired on December 31, 2014. And our son, Steve took over her office at Coldwell-Banker Lunsford in Muncie. We are both thrilled about his success and that he is the go-to person to whom she can refer former clients who continue to call her occasionally, and even now, years later remind us that customers' memories and good will last a very long time.

We are grateful to God for what we have done and what He has made possible for us to do and after our condo sales, Linda and I have been active members of Rotary and community volunteers ever since.

In the process of my retiring, I was pulled out of retirement once more to help finish a quest I set out on thirteen years ago. Walt and Annette Kowalski had dinner with us sometime in 2008 in a little Russian restaurant in Reston, Virginia. The question they asked, started me on a journey to find out how we could help convince the Smithsonian Museums, one of the great repositories of culture, art, and science in America, to recognize Bob Ross as the great artist and teacher of art he is and has become over the years since beginning his modest classes all across America in the early 1980s. Our rationale was if the Smithsonian could recognize *The French Chef*, they most certainly should recognize the American painter, Bob Ross. After all, Bob's TV ratings were higher than Julia Childs, and more people watch Bob every day throughout the world than ever watched *The French Chef*. The biggest difference is Hollywood made a movie about Julia Childs.

Certainly, as we have reviewed the available evidence and competition, Bob Ross has taught more people to paint, and more viewers have watched Bob and been entertained and inspired to paint or just listen to, relax, and watch Bob paint, than any other painter in history.

However, when you see the vistas of the earth—the mountains, the Grand Canyon, the forests, rivers, waterfalls, and oceans, the incredible cloud formations and sunrises and sunsets, you have to say that God is the master painter of them all.

For us humans, Bob has set a high standard, and tens of millions have followed him and continue to mirror his humility and sense of wonder at what can be captured with a little imagination, a small number of paints, a palette knife, a few brushes and a good instructor who encourages you, stroke by stroke, and helps you focus on your creative imagination and what is true, noble, right, lovely, pure, and admirable in what you have put on your canvas. Bob teaches us to recognize our happy accidents, not mistakes.

While that sounds presumptuous, it is not. When you check out Amazon Prime, Bob's YouTube channel, Twitch, Vudu, and many other streaming venues, it is quickly apparent that statement is truly modest. There is no other painter like Bob with the following or history of people engaging with him as their teacher, TV-mentor, and compelling example.

In the intervening years, I have contacted the Smithsonian directly, worked through every contact I could imagine, and worked through all those in Muncie who had an interest or were willing to pursue a connection to this great national treasure, all to no avail. Then, in a surprise move, after all those efforts turned out to be without success, the Smithsonian contacted the Bob Ross Company and Joan Kowalski, its President and asked for a meeting. As late as 2020, in the midst of the Covid emergency, the BBC added a Bob Ross Channel—BBC4 as a special programming option to help calm the pandemic's paranoia and fear of dying in the United Kingdom. And it was effective. Who else has that testimony to Bob's positivity and calming demeanor and magnetic, and transformational message? It is patently obvious to the most casual observer: Bob Ross is more than just a painter with a "mighty brush" and a burgeoning dose of optimism.

To all those who put their hand in and made the contacts and the calls, and wrote letters that seemed to be ignored, I must say here: "Thank you!" While we do not know who finally brought this to the Smithsonian's attention, I can confirm here that they "got the message," and they made the decision to create a permanent exhibit to honor Bob Ross and what he has accomplished and what he continues to accomplish in the world of Art where he lives on. In that world, Bob will always be fifty-two. He developed Lymphoma and passed away on July 4, 1995, after creating 403 unique TV paintings. Bob is a very special friend who we will always cherish and honor.

As they say, the rest is history. Initially, the Smithsonian asked for a few of Bob's paintings. Joan Kowalski, the President of Bob Ross Inc., forwarded the paintings and memorabilia to the Smithsonian and at some point, in the future, a Bob Ross exhibit will find a home there at the Nation's most prestigious collection of our culture. Later, the Smithsonian asked for artifacts and were given those. They even decided in 2020 to release a story saying the museum had accepted a number of Bob Ross's paintings and was planning something that would recognize his gift and prominence in the world. So the good news is this: the exhibit will happen. When is something only the Smithsonian knows. But when it is ready, they will make it known for all the world to see.

Finally in 2018, Minnetrista, the Museum of Art, Business, Culture and Industry for East Central Indiana, and Bob Ross Inc.—the company owning the Bob Ross franchise— came together and committed to creating a permanent Bob Ross Exhibit in Muncie: "The Bob Ross Experience." It was dedicated on Bob's birthday, October 29, 2020, and fully opened to the world on October 29, 2021 on what would have been Bob's seventy-ninth birthday.

And why not? Bob did all of his television series in Muncie, Indiana at WIPB-TV, and he lived here for a time while he was doing those series. WIPB was responsible for successfully marketing *The Joy of Painting* to PBS stations all across America, ending up with over 350 of the 360 PBS stations in the US carrying the programs on a repeating basis, and now on YouTube and other streaming venues throughout most of the world.

Subsequently, Robert G. LaFrance, Director and Chief Curator of the Owsley Museum of Art and Design on the Ball State campus, and others at Ball State urged Minnetrista to consider this local focus, and the community has now embraced the idea and is looking forward to a long line of interested viewers from all over the world who are already seeking out the place where Bob Ross hung out and brought his programs to life. It has already become apparent as we struggle to accommodate the requests to paint in the very place that Bob created many of the paintings that endure as part of his 31 series of shows. It is fun to see the reservations pile in and fill up as the new Bob Ross painting Workshop schedules are unveiled at Minnetrista's BOB ROSS EXPERIENCE on the Minnetrista Campus in Muncie.

In addition to its many exhibits, Minnetrista regularly presents Certified Ross Instructors conducting workshops where these talented teachers take interested students through the process of creating their own version of a Bob Ross painting at the former studio of WIPB-TV in the L.L. Ball House on Minnetrista Boulevard in Muncie. Those classes are already booked up for the coming months, and demand continues to be intense. We are thrilled to be able to offer this incredible experience in the very place where Bob created many of his paintings and expose Bob's fans to excellent painters who teach the Bob Ross method. As word of this opportunity continues to be publicized, we expect continuing demand for years to come. If you're interested in a class, log in to "Minnetrista.net" for more information.

As I write this, we are comfortable that Bob Ross' series are viewable in at least 27 different countries over YouTube and in dozens more over private streaming networks and through downloads that are recorded and played by viewers all over the world. Suffice it to say, Bob and his *Joy of Painting*, have traveled farther than he ever imagined and have blessed all the people who watch, whether they paint with him or merely enjoy his presence, his soothing voice, or positive outlook.

What does that mean? For me, it means the quest for a "Smithsonian connection" is over. It is an honor to have been a part of seeing that recognition as it is coming into focus. I am pleased and proud of what Bob Ross and Walt, Annette, and Joan Kowalski have accomplished and can now spend a little time sharing with you some of the exciting adventures that God has led me on through something Pastor Lloyd Ogilvie labeled: *A Life Full of Surprises*.

In our Sunday School Class—studying the Gospel in Richmond, Kentucky, in 1970 when I was EKU's TV Producer, we were studying Pastor Ogilvie's book, *A Life Full of Surprises*. One particular notion came from studying that book and has stuck with me through the years. "Wouldn't it be great if the thing you most wanted to do with your life was what God wanted you to do? If you knew that, would anything in the world dissuade you from pursuing that goal?"

"No, of course not!" you intrepidly shout. "But who could know? How could I know that?"

Our class' conclusion was that "If God is God and is omnipotent (all-powerful), omniscient (all-knowing), omnipresent as Jesus says He is (always with us and within us once we ask him to be Lord of our lives and show us how to live), and if Jesus is Sovereign as Paul told the Athenians in Acts 17:26, then our God—the God we serve and worship can mold our desires to do what He created us to be passionate about. I believe that! Do you? If God is Sovereign, how could we NOT believe that?

I personally love that idea and believe He has done that for many of us, even someone who wasn't a good son or didn't adhere to the rules for a long time, like me. If He can do that for me, God can do that for everyone who asks God to be present in his or her life.

Convinced God is sovereign in our lives, when I left WIPB in December 1992, I called all of my staff together and read Paul's speech to the Athenians from Acts 17:16–34. I told my staff that I was certain that as surely as God brought me to WIPB-TV on May 25, 1976, He was moving me out in December 1992.

I thanked them for all of their help and support and for their energy and expertise and for working together as a team to accomplish all the things we had accomplished: growing the station to be one of the top small stations in the United States, producing and distributing *The Joy of Painting* to stations all across America in all fifty states and Japan, Korea, and many other countries, building the new Ball Building and WIPB-TV studios that opened in 1988 on Ball State's campus, and putting together the best team ever for a station to produce local community programs and engage the community.

Then I told them that in 1978, I had been asked by my Ball State Supervisor, Oliver Bumb, to choose between being Tenured and being Ball State Professional Staff, and I had chosen Tenured. While I did that, not expecting ever to use it, when December 1992 came and it became clear that my WIPB-TV Board would not accept my recommendations for resolving some financial issues we had, I was choosing to exercise my status as "Tenured" and be transferred to the TCOM Department to begin teaching there in January 1993. Though I had only taught one TCOM law class at Ball State for the spring semester in 1992 as a volunteer, with TCOM short a professor to teach Law, my teaching was well-received by the students and Department Chair and because of that volunteer effort on my part and the success I had experienced, the TCOM faculty had already overwhelmingly approved my transfer to TCOM by a vote of 13-1. Better yet, the University had already graciously transferred my salary line to TCOM, and I would begin teaching the second week of January. Wasn't that truly God going before me?

Truthfully, I had never planned to teach in College. In fact, when I left Eastern Kentucky University, I said "I will never work at a University TV operation again. It's too political." However, God has a way of helping us "eat our words." In Proverbs 19:21, Solomon writes "Many are the plans in a person's heart, but it is the Lord's purpose that prevails." And that's exactly what has happened in my life.

In this case, in 1972 in Kentucky, I said "never," and in 1992, God said, "How about NOW?" What could I say? It turned out to be a very good fit. I managed WIPB for

17 years, and then I retired after twenty-seven wonderful years in Broadcasting and taught the very business I had so enjoyed.

Then, overnight, I transferred to the Ball State faculty position that was created for me as Assistant Professor of TCOM and taught for seventeen years. During my years as a teacher (as Linda liked to chide me), I was "Linda's 'wife,'" so she could do Real Estate twelve or more hours a day, come home whenever she could and find dinner hot and sitting on the table and ready for her to sit down and eat. Incidentally, in many ways, those were her most productive years in Real Estate.

I have to admit. As I write this, Linda has been fully retired since 2014, and thankfully, she has done the cooking since then. I am now confident she was definitely employing what we in the advertising business, would label "puffery" to encourage me to keep cooking while she was selling. She is so much better and more creative as a chef than I ever dreamed of being, and she encouraged me to believe.

So for my last seventeen years as a tenured Assistant Professor, I fed her and graded papers at home, and stopped going to the "command performances" I attended as General Manager, Community Leader, and member of numerous boards and causes, where a big part of my job as GM for WIPB was to show up and engage with the community.

I have left much of that behind, especially the numerous times I chaired fund drives for various organizations, and our son Steve is now "up to his ears in 'Alligators,'" the way I was for so many years. Kirsten and Brian are also engaged in their communities, helping meet the needs of the cities where they find themselves. I never told them to follow the example Linda and I set, but they all have, and we are so very proud of each one of them as they contribute significantly to the quality of life where they live.

As I write this, Linda and I, are in our late seventies, and have stepped out of the limelight and are doing things in our retirement we never dreamed of doing when we were in our fifties and sixties. We are traveling like never before and are enjoying visiting with our children and grandchildren, whenever possible. Regardless of our efforts, Jim Croce's *Time in a Bottle* lyrics are on target: "There never seems to be enough time to do the things you want to do, once you (retire and) find them."

I believe that is part of a full life and how God meant it to be. Our dear children: Kirsten, Steve, and Brian—you are busy and contributing to your families and communities because you want life in your communities to be as rich and rewarding as possible for your families and everyone else, and that demands engagement on your parts. Like yourselves, your children's activities: sports, friends, schooling, leisure, and worship—all command contributions, and occasionally funding, but more than that, they demand a certain amount of focused time and attention for them to be meaningful in the lives of your children. I know I'm not saying anything you aren't already committed to.

Chapter 33

How God Prepared
Me for Teaching

Going back for a moment to 1993, my move to teaching, definitely turned out for the best. During the year I began teaching, a head-hunter tracked me down and asked me to apply for a job managing the South Carolina Network in Columbia. It was a big job and a great compliment to me for him to seek me out. I told him I would consider it.

When I talked it over with Linda, she said, "Well, if you take the job, I'll come with you. You should do what you think you want to do and what is best for our family. But if I leave Muncie and move with you, I start my Real Estate Career all over, and the income I had last year, disappears as I start working with all new clients. But I will go with you if you decide you must move on, in your career. I know it's a good opportunity."

Then I asked her one more time in a different way: "What do you really think about my taking that job?"

And she gave me what I really wanted: the unvarnished truth. "Actually," she said with a wry smile, "I like you better the way you are now."

That settled it! With extended family in Muncie, my mother and father visiting regularly, and Linda's mother and the children's Slavin grandparents still in town, I decided I did not want to move. I loved living near extended family— something I had never had until I moved to Muncie. So I made the final call and told him: "Take my name off your list, Ron. I'm no longer in the market for another job." And it worked out beautifully. I'm so glad I listened to Linda and to my heart and stayed in Muncie. I believe that is where God wanted me to be.

The teaching at Ball State was another surprise for which God had prepared me. When my parents started the Utila Methodist Community College in 1983, I began regularly going down to Honduras and shooting video and observing what they were doing. Next, I began taking work teams from our church to Utila and led three teams over a period of twelve years. To encourage our church support- ing their ministry, I also took over as Chair for Missions at High Street Methodist Church and served in that capacity for twelve years.

As far as preparation for my teaching, in 1988, four years prior to my transfer from WIPB to the TCOM Depart- ment and full-time teaching, our pastor at High Street Meth- odist Church in Muncie, Lamar Imes, button-holed me and asked me to take on the teaching of the Wesley Class— the older adult and elderly class for ages sixty-five and up. I was forty-four years old and had never taught a class. I talked with him at length, about it and decided that, though it represented a challenge with eighty people meeting in the Chapel, I would give it a shot.

Pastor Imes asked if I would teach it for two years, and I agreed. When we started, we had eighty persons. Over the years, as people moved to be near adult children or passed away, my class dwindled to thirteen, and we merged with the Epworth Class and moved to Fellowship Hall. There, we initially had fifty-five persons, but over time, the Wes- ley/Epworth class dwindled to thirteen again, and I asked to retire after twenty-six years and release our classroom (Fellowship Hall) for a larger class.

The irony in all this: I never taught a Ball State class of more than eighty-two students, and I had never taken a class in college teaching except for one postgraduate class at Eastern Kentucky University in 1970, where I was in the process of producing a number of instructional programs for on-campus use.

Nonetheless, beginning in 1988, week after week, I taught High Street Methodist's seniors' class for forty to fifty minutes each week, and I discovered I loved teaching (as my parents had), and that 80 students, all of which collectively knew more than I did, encouraged me. I liked it. Doing this challenged me to prepare, to outline where I was going each week, to research and learn more about the God I served, and to be open to the Holy Spirit leading me to sometimes teach something I had not planned on.

Often, my elderly High Street students would ask for a copy of what I had been teaching, only to have me say: "Well, I didn't actually plan to teach that, so my notes won't reflect what I gave you this morning. I'm glad you found it helpful, but God gave me today's lesson as I was speaking, and I'm not exactly sure why, except that someone needed to hear it." And sometimes, someone would come up and say exactly that. And I would smile and say, "Thank God! I didn't plan that—God did!"

As crazy as that sounds, I had that happen many times. When I asked pastors about that phenomenon, they would counsel me: "Yes, that happens to me sometimes as well. It's always a surprise, but then, I really do ask God to show me what to say each time I get up to speak, and when He does, sometimes it surprises me too. Just give thanks, and go on and know that God is using you to do His work."

Four years after I started teaching the Wesley Class at High Street in the spring of 1992, I was walking down the hallway in the Ball Building where the station we had planned and built between 1984 and 1988 had moved in September 1988. As I walked along the curving path that meanders through that beautiful new classroom/studio building, I overheard a couple TCOM students complaining that they could not graduate in May as they had expected that year, because they would not be able to take the Law Class in the spring 1992 Semester. I went into my office, sat down, and thought about what I had just heard, and then because of my sometimes reckless curiosity, I walked over to the TCOM Chairman's office and volunteered to teach that class for the Spring semester. I wondered what it would be like, and WIPB was having a great year. I was relaxed as I offered my services for free.

As the Administrative Assistant to the GM at WISH-TV for four years and as the General Manager of WIPB-TV, I had been tutored for almost twenty years by two top FCC law firms who were on retainer, and were headquartered in Washington, DC: Covington & Burling for Channel 8 and Schwartz, Woods and Miller for WIPB. I had the experience and insider knowledge about the business and the legal requirements and challenges that often occur, and I was able to teach the Ball State TCOM class by studying the book and working from my experiences in the broadcasting business. Those two students and others needing the law class in the spring of 1992, graduated on time, and I was proud of what I had done and what I had discovered: I liked teaching college.

I was also happy I had explored teaching and was able to help out that way, even though I did the teaching without pay. In that way, my willingness to step in and take on that challenge to help people I didn't know, benefited me just as it had when I agreed to step in at Channel 8 in Indy and host the 6:00 PM *Teleconference* show every week for a year and the earlier *Religion in the News* program that I hosted for two years, both without pay. *Religion in the News* opened the door for me to do *Teleconference*, and the *Teleconference* program opened the door for me to get the job at WIPB-TV. Donating my time allowed God to use those venues for His purposes, as you can now see, and as I can see too, looking back over the years.

On the other hand, when the TCOM Department surveyed my class, their survey documented that the students really liked my teaching, and frankly, I loved the challenge too. It was meant by God, in my opinion, to open my eyes to that option for me only six months later. What a surprise—for ME!'

Pastor Ogilvie asks: "What would keep such a God who knows you, formed you in your mother's womb, and "numbered all of your days before one of them came to be" (Psalm 139:16)—what would prevent a loving God from blessing you with the knowledge and courage and dream in your heart of doing something for Him that you were born to do? Would anything prevent such a loving and omniscient Father and Creator from guiding you to do *the very things that He created you for* and endowed you with the talent to do?"

Your answer is surely like mine when you think about all the qualifiers I list above:

The answer is "NOTHING would keep God from helping me find that dream and realizing it!"

So my adventure continued. When I say that, I am reminded of our good friend, Virginia Ball who, in 2004, was dying of a stroke herself after forty-eight years as the wife of Edmund F. Ball. Four years earlier in 2000, Ed had a massive stroke and succumbed after three days. As very good friends, we were part of that passage, and I spent an hour with him, the day before he died.

After Ed had a stroke and died in 2000, Virginia continued to live in their house, across the street from Emens Auditorium on the Ball State campus. Ed and Virginia had lived there since their marriage in the 1950s, and Linda and I had been there many times.

In 2004, Virginia had gone to the tiny island of Little Cayman, just south of Cuba, where Ed and Virginia belonged to the Southern Cross Club (a private vacation resort) and had built a small 1200 square foot house there to test construction materials, later to be used to build the Ball Corporation Corporate Headquarters building in downtown Muncie—now the Fisher Building. It was also a great place to SCUBA dive, something Ed loved to do, and Virginia loved to snorkel there. What a fantastic, private place to enjoy the ocean for both of them.

Since Ball Corporation's move to Colorado in 1999, that Muncie building has become the Fisher Campus for the Muncie Area IVY Tech Administrative Offices and some of its classrooms and is sided with the very composite concrete and stone slabs that the Balls were testing on Little Cayman in the "test house." I'm sure the house is still there and as fit as ever, just as the former Ball Corporation building still stands and remains in great shape in Muncie. It really was great building material, and when we saw their small house there, it looked brand new, even after twenty-five years of sitting in the sun and weathering Caribbean storms.

We were only on Little Cayman with Ed and Virginia once in 1992, and then, only for a few hours—long enough to have breakfast and see their "test house." Then they took off, and Linda and I had a truly private and unbelievable second honeymoon there on the beach, looking out 50 feet onto the south side of Little Cayman, meeting other guests from all over the world for one, very private, incredibly romantic week. I really think the Ball's knew they wouldn't be able to stay. But that's okay. It was a gift to us.

However, twelve years later, in 2004, Virginia was back on Little Cayman with Richie Myers and Susan Harmon, a married couple who were long-time friends of the Balls and had travelled extensively with them to SCUBA dive all over the world.

Linda and I did that only twice: once for my first dive trip to Cozumel in 1990 following the PBS meeting in Dallas, where Richie Meyer was the GM. On the 1990 trip, our newly minted Open-Water diver son, Brian accompanied us, and Ed and Virginia and several of the Ball Grandchildren, and Susan Harman and Richie Meyer and their grandchildren filled up a dive-boat for four days of fun in the sun and "getting wet, as SCUBA divers call "diving."

Back to our 1992 trip to Little Cayman. After meeting us on Little Cayman where Ed picked us up at the dirt air-strip there and had breakfast with us, Ed told us we should enjoy ourselves at the Southern Cross Club, but he and Virginia were flying back to Florida where they had an important meeting that had come up suddenly, and they had to leave. We did have a marvelous time there but were sorry when the Balls loaded their twin engine plane and took off.

So, twelve years later in 2004, Virginia was there in Little Cayman with Richie and Susan, and after a great three or four days, Richie and Susan were off SCUBA diving. Virginia got up her last day on the island and didn't feel well, and she asked the couple they had met the night before for dinner (non-SCUBA divers), to accompany her back to Grand Cayman where doctors could make sense of Virginia's symptoms.

When she arrived in Grand Cayman and Richie and Susan returned to the Southern Cross Club from SCUBA diving, they learned of Virginia's illness and immediately called her on Grand Cayman to find out what was going on. They could not fly to Grand Cayman because Susan and Richie had been SCUBA diving that morning, and they could not fly again for twenty-four hours because of the danger of having an air-embolism from nitrogen in their blood, following that morning's dives.

When Susan got Virginia on the phone, she asked Virginia how she was. Virginia shared the symptoms with

Susan, and they both concluded she might have had a stroke. Obviously, they did not know how serious it was.

But Virginia was very smart and loved God and trusted in God, and she had attended Baylor University, a Christian University in central Texas where she had been raised a Baptist. And this was Virginia's answer to Susan's question of "How are you doing?"

Virginia: "I'm doing alright, Susan. I'll be okay. I'm on my next great adventure." And she hung up.

Virginia died of a massive stroke two days later in Florida where she had been flown for further evaluation. I loved Virginia Ball. We all loved her. After Ed died, on a number of occasions, she invited me to visit her in the late afternoon to talk with her and share my poetry, and for her to share her poetry with me. That is where I learned her favorite flower was the Hyacinth. And it has been my favorite ever since. It doesn't last long, but its fragrance fills the room where it sits, and it reminds me of her and our long afternoon talks. Because I was teaching, I had little trouble scheduling time with her. It was a blessing for me and a blessing for her. We both thrived on those kinds of conversations. I will always remember her and Ed as two of our very special friends.

When I first met Ed, he was seventy, just a few years short of where I am as I write this. He and Virginia lived a full life which included for him, flying as often as possible for many decades, active duty in the Army in World War II, Leadership in the Ball Corporation his parents and uncles had created, SCUBA diving, various adventures, piloting his planes, family, community involvement, and support for the "least of these" through all kinds of philanthropy and community projects. Ed and Virginia were dear friends and community leaders in every sense of the word. During World War II, Ed was tapped to be a Staff Officer for General Mark Clark when the US Army invaded Anzio in Italy, and he survived that and came back to lead Ball Brothers to diversify and go into the aluminum can business that, along with

Aerospace now, has been the dominant line of business for many decades.

Theirs was an exciting life. In their seventies, Ed and Virginia participated in the Cross-Australian Air-Race where they flew across the five-thousand-mile wide continent and raced from Perth to Sidney by "deadreckoning" it without the benefit of a compass. Their airplane's instruments covered, they "eye-balled" the direction of the sun and moon and took off for the other end of the Australian continent. They slept under the wings at night, got up the next morning, and took off on the next leg of the race. Later, Ed chronicled their adventure for the *Saturday Evening Post*.

When we went to Australia 10 years later, after he had passed eighty years old, both Ed and Virginia helped to bankroll the WIPB-TV expedition with our promise that they could accompany our production team. They did go as our special guests, but they also carried gear and materials, and helped us produce the documentary that later was sold in thirty countries around the world, and also to all the libraries in Australia. There's more to this story, but my reason for including it here is to illustrate that Virginia knew exactly what she was saying when she said, "I'm on my next great adventure."

When I get to the end of my life, I am hoping I will be willing to say in faith: "God will take care of me," and that I too, am on "my next great adventure"…going to meet my Lord Jesus, face-to-face. Psalm 139:15–16 tells us that "when You [God] were putting me together there [in my mother's womb] Your eyes saw my body even before it was formed. You planned how many days I would live. You wrote down the number of them in Your book before I had lived through even one of them."

Chapter 34

Some Final Stories That Must Be Shared

First, Nag's head. But I'll tell you frankly, I've saved the best for last.

Linda and I regularly go to Hilton Head to vacation and have been doing that since we bought Marriott Time Shares there at Marriott's Grande Ocean Resort right on the beach on the southeast side of the island in 1994. The beach is fantastic—at least one hundred yards deep, with pure, smooth sand, and we have three weeks we have traded in to Marriott regularly to go there and to other Marriott properties all over the world and on vacations to France, Germany, Italy, Holland, Austria, Poland, Denmark, Norway, Australia, England, Ireland, Scotland, Canada, Mexico, Panama, The Caymans, the Caribbean, Bonaire, China, Spain, Portugal, and all fifty states.

So some years ago, Linda and I were finishing up our stay at Grande Ocean on Hilton Head in South Carolina, and our German Rotary son, Jockel Pfannschmidt called us from Nag's Head to ask if we could drop by on our way home. Jockel and his family from Vilseck, Germany, were vacationing there on one of the barrier islands, off the coast of North Carolina, and he invited us to join them there for dinner the day we left Hilton Head.

It sounded easy and good to me, so I said, "Of course we'll meet you in Nag's Head. It's on our way home to Muncie." Well, of course, it WAS, in a way. I quickly made reservations in Raleigh, North Carolina, and tucked that away for our return trip home.

That's how our Nag's Head story began. God's fingerprints are all over it.

Jockel had stayed in touch and knew we were vacationing at the same time in one of our Time-Share Condo's at Marriott's Grande Ocean Resort in Hilton Head, South Carolina. I suspect his family had planned their vacation in such a way that we could connect, if it was convenient, just before they returned home to Germany and we returned home to Muncie.

So when Jockel called to ask if we could stop by and have dinner with his parents and sister and her family who were all gathered there on Nag's Head and finishing up their week of vacation together, I thought we should take advantage of the opportunity. In my mind, it would be great to reacquaint ourselves with his family and to introduce us to his sister, Uli and her husband and kids, and to see his parents, Klaus and Helga. Linda wasn't around when Jockel called, and I said, "Yes, of course we can come." That started the ball rolling.

When we packed up that Friday night before we left for home, I told Linda we were going to take a side trip to go by and see Jockel and his family on Nag's Head, and that we would be staying the night in Raleigh, North Carolina, instead of our usual stop in Knoxville. We would still be home the second night, I told her, so nothing more was said.

The next morning, knowing we wanted as much time as we could have with Jockel and his family, we checked out early and headed north along the South Carolina coast. I thought it would be fun to drive along the coast because we had never done that before, and it was a beautiful day. After a few hours, we transitioned into North Carolina and stopped for lunch in one of the many beach towns along the way. It was quaint and beautiful. Linda casually asked how much father, and since it was before smartphones, I pulled out the map and looked at it. I was surprised a bit, and commented, "Only a few more hours."

"Really?" she asked, "How far do we still have to go?"

I carefully calculated it, and turned to her, chagrined and said, "Well, it's a bit farther than I thought. It's still two hundred miles away.

Then she asked the great question she always asks, "Did you think about how far it was before you said we would join them?"

And I said, "No, I just thought we'd like to be there, so I told them we were coming." That didn't go over well. Her next comment or statement is one I've suffered through more than a few times over the years. "Why don't you dip your tongue in your brain before you speak, next time you are asked a question like that?"

There really isn't an answer to that question, so I just drove on up the highway. No use in making an argument for something I had not done. I thought seeing Jockel was a good idea, and I made the decision. Maybe it will be different next time. Maybe?

In any event, we continued to drive up the coast, and finally arrived at about 4:30 PM in time for a nice outside dinner overlooking the beach, and a visit. It was wonderful to see Jockel's parents again and to meet Uli and Robin, Uli Pfannschmidt Ayers' friend. As it turned out, the kids weren't with them. In any event, after an hour and a half, we said our goodbyes, and got on the road. It was still sunny and a nice evening for a drive. We headed out for Raleigh, never having been there before. It was going to be a beautiful evening.

After driving for about two hours, I was becoming annoyed that a woman was tailgating me on a divided highway, about one-car length behind me. I don't like it when people do that, but since the highway went through small towns occasionally, I finally decided to get in front of a truck at a stop light, and then go slowly enough that the woman would have to pass me and get on her way and stop tailgating me.

When I did that, it worked, and she smiled and waved at me as she passed me coming out of that town. I was happy she was no longer tailgating me, but as she passed, I saw that she was an older woman, probably in her late seventies (our age as I write this), and she was alone.

This woman's car also had an Illinois license plate and was an older model sedan, and I wondered what she was doing, driving alone for hours, going west on US 64, toward Raleigh. I pondered that for a little while, all the time thinking about whether she was more comfortable following an Indiana car than some of the others. I also thought about my mother, who was about the same age, maybe a little older, and how she might have done that, if she had been uncomfortable, driving alone across a very wide state.

Finally, I decided she could follow behind me again. It really wasn't hurting anything, and it would most likely be safe. So what the heck. I'd let her do that if it made her feel better. I pulled in front of her again, waving as we went by, and let her begin to tailgate me again. That went on for another hour, as the dusk began to settle in. We had been driving "together" for about three hours when all of a sudden, in the middle of nowhere, she pulled over to the side of the road and stopped.

There were woods on both sides of the road, and no houses in sight. I wondered why she was stopping, and I kept thinking about her as she disappeared from my rearview mirror over the last hill. What had caused this older woman, in the middle of nowhere, to pull over and stop, I wondered? Was something wrong? I didn't know. I kept thinking about it, and then I started praying for her.

Soon enough, we reached the Interstate, and we took the cloverleaf to the right and were sailing along on the divided highway at seventy miles per hour. My mind and my heart were with the old woman in the old sedan. Something felt terribly wrong.

After about twenty minutes more, I started to pull off on the second cloverleaf we came to and began to turn around. Linda asked me, "What are you doing? It's almost dark. Why are you turning around?"

And I told her about the old woman. "What old woman?" she stammered. "Well," I began. "There is an old woman in an old sedan back there, who just pulled off to the side and stopped."

"What old woman?" she demanded! "I didn't see any-one. What are you talking about?"

And I told her the story.

Linda interrupted, "How do you know it isn't just some-one trying to set us up to rob us or something?"

I said, "I don't know that, but I just feel like God is telling me something's wrong, and I have to go back and find out."

"You're crazy," she said, shaking her head. "We'll get back there, and she'll be gone. We don't know what's going on back there. How far back was it?"

"It was about twenty minutes back to the other road we were on and another twenty minutes south on that road… maybe forty minutes to get back to where she pulled off," I said quietly as we pulled back onto the super-highway and started speeding back. "This will take a little bit. I appreciate your trusting me in this."

Linda said nothing. She just looked straight ahead. I know I've been there before, but I was certain something was wrong. All through my life, I have been drawn to people in trouble, and I have always jumped in, often not knowing what I'm jumping into. But when I sense the need or the dis-tress, I have to find out. So we were driving East toward US

64. After a frantic fifteen minutes, we found our turn-off, and headed South. Surely it wouldn't be too long now.

As we went over hill after hill, Linda finally said, "See, there's no one there. She isn't there anymore. She's gone. It's going to be midnight because of this detour. See, it's already 10:30, and we've lost all the miles we just drove. This is crazy."

My response was soft and persistent. "I'm sure she's still there...just over one more hill." And I kept driving. I also kept praying what I had started praying as soon as we turned around: "Lord, if this is from you, let it be important. Otherwise, Linda will never forgive me for being such a fool. But if it is from you, let her still be there." And all of a sudden, over the next hill, there, on the other side of the road, sat the old sedan with the dome light on, no flashers, and the old woman in the driver's seat. "There she is," I said too loudly. There she is. She's still in her car, and she hasn't moved."

I did a U-turn, and drove up behind her. I looked around and carefully got out of the car, locked our doors, and told Linda that if we had a problem, she was to drive off and get help. But of course, when I walked up to the woman's car, she just looked up at me. I said loudly, "I'm the man you were following for the past few hours. Do you remember me?"

She nodded.

I continued, "What happened? Why did you stop?"

She lowered her window slightly and shyly, said, "Well, I didn't stop. The car just stopped, and I can't seem to start it again."

I said, "Would it be all right if I got in and tried it. Sometimes you can pump it a little and the engine will catch. Can I do that for you?" And she unlocked the door and slid over on the bench seat, and waited. I got in the car, turned the key, pumped the accelerator a couple of times, and clicked the ignition. The starter whined, but no ignition. The engine did not start. I tried it again. Nothing!

Then I looked at the dashboard, and the fuel gauge read: "Empty." I said quietly, It looks like you may be out of gas. Why don't we turn on your emergency flashers like this (and I pushed the flasher button on her dash), and turn off the dome light, and lock your car. I will go to the nearest gas station we passed a few minutes ago, get a can and fill it with gas and be back in a jiffy and see if we can get you started. Would that be okay with you?"

And she nodded, and said, "Yes, thank you."

I eased out of the car, returned to our car, and got in. We drove to the gas station, bought a red gasoline container, filled it with two gallons of gas, and drove back to where her car sat by the road and pulled up behind her. I got out and emptied the gas can into her gas tank. Then I got into her car, pumped it a couple of times, and it started right up. She smiled and said, "Thank you.'

I sat there for a minute and then asked her to follow us to the gas station in the next town where I would fill it up for her so she could continue her journey. She said she would. So I turned off her flashers, and returned to our car. I pulled out around her, and she followed us as she said she would.

When we got to the next town, I drove into the gas station where we had gotten the gas can and pulled up alongside the pumps where we would fill her car, and also fill our car. We were one car ahead of her, and her car was right behind ours.

I said, "How will you be paying for this?"

And she said, "Just a minute." And she looked in her wallet. She had three one-dollar bills.

I said, "Do you have a credit card?"

She said she didn't think so, but she did have a check. So she went to her trunk, opened it, and took out her purse. That seemed strange too. There was no luggage in her trunk—just her large purse. She took out her checkbook from her purse. It was a "starter checkbook" with no name or address on it. I wondered how she was driving across the country with no cash, no luggage, and no credit card. I said, "Don't worry about it. We'll get you filled up in a minute. Then she started writing a check out for $15.00 to me, while we continued talking.

"Where will you be staying tonight," I asked. "Do you know someone here in town?"

She said she would find a place to stay, and that we should not worry. I asked if she had ever been in this town before, and she said she had not. I thought about the empty trunk and lack of luggage. Then I noticed the two empty cereal boxes on the floor of the back seat and scattered pieces of cereal on the floor.

Something did not feel right. I said, "I'm having a problem with this pump. Just a minute," and I went over to where Linda was waiting and whispered to her, "Something is not right with this woman. Call the police! Call the police!" I exaggeratedly mouthed the words: "Something's wrong!" And Linda went inside to call.

So I continued to talk with the woman, and slow-walk the gas pumping. I pumped a little and talked a little. The woman seemed happy and said she was "going home" (her words). And she was glad to be on the road. When I asked her where she had stayed the night before, she was vague and did not have an answer.

I knew there had to be more to this situation than we knew. So I just kept her talking and slow-walking the gas pump. In less than five minutes, a police car pulled up across the lot and a male and female officer approached. I introduced myself and said we had helped this woman get her car to the service station. I stopped pumping gas and went inside.

About 10 minutes later, the male officer came in to update us and send us on our way. He said they had checked out her license plate and discovered the woman was a runaway from a nursing center in Virginia and had been driving all day since escaping. Her son was the medical director for the center, and as she said, "He doesn't have any time for me, so I decided I would go home." She told us she just took her keys, went out into the lot, took her car, and drove away, undiscovered until tonight.

The officer said she would be housed in the city that night, and someone would arrive to take her home the next morning. Authorities had talked with her son, and he was very glad to find out where she was and that she was alright. She had no business driving away like that, and they had all been searching for her.

Linda and I got back in the car, looked at each other, and never said another word about it. But when I got home, I told my Sunday School class about it, and my mother, sitting in the front row, asked, "What happened to her? Did she get back alright?"

I said, "Mom, I don't know. I think we did the right thing, and the police officers said they would be sure that she would be returned to her family and that her car would be taken back to Virginia. What more could we have done?"

And my mother said, "Well, you could have made sure she had a decent place to stay that night." And my mother was right, and I still don't know if we did the right thing, but I like to think we did what God wanted us to do. And we are grateful we went back to find her after all.

What do you do when that kind of thing rears its head? I don't know any more today than I knew then. I picked up on something irregular, and helping the woman was the result. Was it God's Holy Spirit nudging me to get involved? I believe it was. Would I do it again? "Yes, without question." As I drove along the road that night, the directive from God was clear: "Go back and see what's wrong!" I am so glad we did.

Now, when I say "I think we should do something," Linda may roll her eyes, but she doesn't question me. She knows she doesn't always know everything that's going on, but she knows she can trust that I believe I am hearing from

God that I should do something, and she supports my willingness to be guided by love and my own kind of "intuition." I think it's more accurate to say that in events like these, I find myself "being led by God's Holy Spirit." I think that's a more accurate description of what happened that night.

I know we both believe we are meant to be a blessing when we can, even if, sometimes, it inconveniences us. However, being inconvenienced is not the measure of whether we should or should not get involved.

As you now know, I have never been a perfect son, or father or person, but because of the sacrifice Jesus made on the Cross for you and me, I have no doubt that through His grace and love, I will see Him face-to-face at the appointed time. I earnestly hope to see you too when you arrive—not because you are good but because you have decided to trust that Jesus is the Son of God, and He loves you. If you believe that, I will see you again in heaven.

You could not have read this book without recognizing that I have been a disobedient, creative, crafty, sneaky, person more than my share of the time, and every time I would think that I have totally failed God, He seems to have stepped in and said, "Jim, you just haven't learned yet. I still love you. Choose my ways, and your path will be better than you could ever make it on your own."

As I am now seventy-nine in the fall of 2023, and much of the world is over the COVID-19 Pandemic and its Variants, it is my hope that I will have a few more years to "try to get it right." I know that like the Apostle Paul writes to those who are searching in Romans, I will fail to always do the right thing, always *say* the right thing, even *think* the right thing, but I also know Jesus promises to never leave me or forsake me, and I am sure He is promising you He will do the same for you. And me, I know that He keeps His promises. I'm the one who struggles with promises, no matter how hard I try. Thank God for His grace which He says is sufficient. I'll never be perfect on this earth, but I'll keep trying.

In John 14–17, John records Jesus' final talk and prayer with the Disciples in the Upper Room in Jerusalem, the night before Jesus was betrayed, taken into custody by the Temple Guards, and crucified. This is what Jesus prays with the Disciples on this last night Jesus spends with them: "Father, the hour has come. Glorify your Son, that your Son may glorify You. 2 For You granted him authority over all people that He might give eternal life to all You have given him. 3 Now this is eternal life: that they know You, the only true God, and Jesus Christ, whom You have sent. 4 I have brought You glory on earth by finishing the work You gave Me to do. 5 And now, Father, glorify Me in Your presence with the glory I had with You before the world began."

My children and grandchildren and you readers I am just meeting: "I point you to Jesus' words above because in my seventy-nine years, I have come to believe and to know that Jesus is truly the Son of God, and that what He shared with His disciples and with us, through them, is true."

In Jesus' next words in that Last Supper, Jesus is actually praying for the Disciples and also for you and me by saying, as Jesus prays to God, the Father, (Chapter 17:20) "My prayer is not for them (His disciples) alone. I pray also for *those who will believe in Me through their message* (Jesus is talking here about YOU and ME) 21 that all of them may be one, Father, just as You are in Me and I am in you. May they also be in Us so that the world may believe that You have sent Me."

As you read this, I hope you know that you and I are part of the "vast cloud of witnesses" described in Hebrews 11 who have come to believe in Jesus through the faithfulness and sacrifices of Jesus' disciples over the ages, and your parents and grandparents and others who formed this country, believing that God was guiding them and opening doors for them, the same way you now can see that God has systematically opened doors for Grandma and me.

The price of believing Jesus is not always easy or free. Ten of the twelve disciples were killed for what they believed. Judas committed suicide after trying to return the thirty pieces of silver the Chief Priest had paid him to betray Jesus, John was exiled to the island of Patmos by Emperor Domitian after which John, the last remaining Apostle, completed 1 John, 2 John, and 3 John and Revelation before he died of old age in his nineties and was buried in Ephesus.

I am fascinated and revel in the thought that, someday, we will know all of these things and even see John and Jesus, face-to-face. I also know by faith and many specific instances where God has intervened in my affairs, that God is real here and now and that He loves you and each one of us, and somehow, makes it possible for us to know Him when we ask Him to come into our heart and to help us decide to trust Him with our lives and our futures. When we ask Him to come into our hearts and take control of our lives like I did in 1975, I KNOW that He is capable of doing that and also that He will follow through to be the One who is never far from you and is in you, the same way He was in the Disciples and also, over the years, has been in me. While you may learn that over time, I know that personally from the many experiences that are way beyond what I have shared with you here in this book.

Asking Jesus to take charge of my life is what I did in the parking lot at WISH-TV after seeing Bob Davenport. That's the day the world's worries slid off of my shoulders for good, remember? That's the day I recommitted my life to Jesus Christ and put Him in charge of ordering my ways, and the day that changed every aspect of my life...the day that ultimately sent me to Muncie, to Grandma Linda, to your Mom or Dad and Uncle or Aunt, the day that transformed my life from headaches to celebrations, almost without end.

Does it mean that all my troubles and worries and challenges in my life were over? Not in the least. It means that through each and every one of those "bumps in my road,"

God, His son Jesus, and the Holy Spirit have been with me, mediating what happens, and helping me to deal with what confronts me. As long as I choose Trust in God over fear, I can live my life through faith, not despair, and through the Joy that knows that depending on the Triune God who created everything, and even has a plan for me, I will ultimately not be disappointed by whatever happens.

That is where I am today, just having survived some major surgery in March 2022. I've already addressed this earlier, and what happened amazes even me, but it is another strong example of how God goes before us. You can count on God to go before you as well when you put Jesus in charge of your life. You probably didn't know this, but every time Bob Ross and I sat down to eat, and that was many times, Bob would ask: "Aren't you going to pray, Jim?" And I would bow my head and ask God to bless Bob and the "Joy of Painting!" And as we can all clearly see now, God did bless the fire and passion and dedication that He had set in Bob's heart that is now warming so much of the world in so many countries and in millions of hearts everywhere.

I have to admit it: I doubted a lot, over the years, as I came to a more complete trust in God. That is what I thought I did when I was thirteen, and sixteen, and twenty-one and thirty-one, and I am sure that each time I asked Jesus to come into my heart, I had a deeper understanding of just Who God is, and also a deeper commitment to wanting Him to invade my being and make me more like what He must have had in mind when I was created.

I don't believe in chance, and I don't believe in superstition. Friday the thirteenth means nothing to me except that many people around me worry about it and what will happen that day. I just shake my head and trust in God. See Proverbs 16:33, and if you believe that, as I do, you'll never bet on anything again.

Chapter 35

Burglarized—God or Fear?

When I was still in Indianapolis, in 1975, my girlfriend, Bonnie, had her house burglarized. When we drove up the driveway to her house, we could see something was all wrong: the doors were all open and kicked out.

Burglars had kicked every single doorjamb out, and we were aghast and frightened. The next-door neighbors came running toward us as we drove up the long driveway and stopped us from going in. They said they had seen that the doors were kicked out and called the police when they arrived home. Minutes later, the police arrived. The last thing they wanted us to discover were burglars who were still there.

After the police checked the house out, Bonnie and I went in and saw the mess: all the cabinets emptied, the drawers overturned on the beds and all that was in the closets, thrown on the floor. Every single outside door had been kicked out so that if the burglars had been discovered while they were still in the house, they could easily escape. We were shaking as we walked through the debris because there was such a palpable sense of evil there, throughout. It caused us to shudder and wonder why someone would do such an awful thing. Trust me, you can "sense" evil in that kind of event. It made my hair stand up on the back of my neck. What a mess!

Two weeks later, Bonnie's mother and father had put their home back together and had the doors repaired. I walked into the kitchen, wondering what it would be like. It was bright and cheery again, and the fog of evil—the sense of violation that had been everywhere the night Bonnie and I returned from our date, was gone. I wondered what had transformed their house back to a home of peace and security, and then I saw it.

Everything seemed to be back in order, but it was more than that. Bonnie's mother, Jean, had posted a hand-lettered sign in the window overlooking the back yard which read: "To be afraid is to choose to believe in evil more than in God." I liked it when I saw it, and I have always remembered it because it was comforting then, and I know it is always true.

If we truly believe that God is sovereign and works together for our good in everything we encounter, then we need not be afraid. Linda has a favorite saying: "God never wastes anything." I believe that. I hope you believe it too, because it can apply to your life, moment by moment if you decide, if you choose to trust Him as Grandma and I do.

I don't know where this fits in, but throughout my life, God has had His hand on me many times, before I even got to a point where I knew I needed His help. When I first came to WIPB-TV, I was in my second year at the station when my Ball State University supervisor, Oliver Bumb, asked me which I wanted to be: Tenured or Professional Staff. I said, "What's the difference?"

Vice President Bumb told me that Tenured was more secure, but that Professional Staff would allow me to have a higher salary and more vacation time. I checked the box for "Tenured" and never thought about it again. To become tenured at Ball State, one had to raise a lot of money through writing Grants and being funded and/ or publish research papers on my discipline. I never expected to do either.

While I never did publish any research papers, I did write many successful, large grant applications (sometimes, over three hundred pages), and raised almost $500,000 per year for each year I was a General Manager. But I was still surprised when I was notified in a letter in 1982 that I had received Tenure from Ball State University and that I would thereafter be categorized as a Tenured Employee. This didn't seem to make any other difference that I noticed (at least not then), and I went on with my work.

Lots of other things were happening. We were growing the station. By the time I got the Tenure letter, we had expanded our programming exponentially, we had started our televised auction, Telesale, and were bringing in over $100,000 per year in that. We had also added a half-dozen more positions because we were able to pay their salaries, and we had begun to replace outdated equipment, all the while growing in our programming offerings, including an unknown painter, Bob Ross. Little did we know where that would take us.

Fast forward to 1992 when we had been in the new station for four years and made it our home. We had grown from 4,600 square feet in an old house to almost 18,000 square feet and two deluxe studios, and we had built it on Ball State's campus. We were living and working out of the nicest Public Television Station facilities in Indiana that we had built between 1984 and September 30, 1988, when we moved in. It was wonderful. From the beginning of my tenure to 1982, I had also testified in Congress for the Public Broadcasting System and Corporation for Public Broadcasting and written a successful grant for $540,000 to purchase and install a brand-new transmitter and bought 1.3 million dollars' worth of new equipment for our new building. Everything seemed to be going well. We also had grown from our original staff of ten persons including me, to thirty-two full-time and eighteen part-time employees. Things were going well.

I want to digress a moment to tell you about why it is so important to be early. When we went to Washington, DC, in 1986 to discuss our grant proposal, we met with the head of the Government Agency that oversaw station facilities grants, and when we arrived, we were ten minutes early. When the Director's Secretary saw that along with me, there were two Assistants from Indiana Senator's offices, she announced their names, and the director called out for us to come in early. We were introduced and then, after chatting casually with them for a few minutes, the Director turned to me and said, "I can see you think you need a lot of new equipment, but we don't give grants for $740,000 to anyone. Why do you think you need that much to move into your station?" And in about one minute, I covered the fact that we operated out of a 100-year-old house, that our community had never had a real station, and that we were the only station in town, and were doing a great job of serv-ing our community. Because of that, the Speaker of the House in Indiana who was from Muncie had managed to build this new building on Ball State's campus, and we had the matching dollars that we had saved from our auctions so that we could have new cameras, lights, switchers, and tape recorders and be able to do the kinds of things that other stations had been doing for the past 20 years. "We need a chance to be a full-service station," I said.

The Director of the Public Telecommunications Facilities Program (PTFP) rocked back in his chair and smiled. "You really believe that, don't you? Well, I've looked your grant over, and there's no way I can give you more than $500,000, at the most. We'll see how it all shakes out." There it was: my "elevator pitch" in less than a minute, at most.

At about that time, the two representatives from our Congressmen's offices came in, and it was exactly 10:00 AM, the time we were supposed to be walking in the door.

I was never asked another question about the grant during the meeting which continued for about ten minutes, but I felt good when we left.

I felt even better when, two months later, we received a letter telling us we were receiving $540,000 for our equipment—enough to do everything we had hoped for. What a great surprise and incredible incentive to be early for every meeting. When you're early, everyone is relaxed, cordial, and able to ask you questions they have already considered. What a welcome surprise and an unforgettable lesson. Always be early! That happened in the fall of 1986. We moved into our new station in September 1988 with all of our new equipment. We were very grateful and proud of what we had accomplished together.

Chapter 36

A Hobby in My Spare Time, After All That

When I was about forty, I decided that I should try to run a marathon. That is 26.2 miles without stopping. I just wanted to see if I could make myself run that far. So I started training. Some of our best friends were doing crazy things, and I decided that my "crazy thing" would be to see if I could run a marathon. One of my best friends at the time was Ted Fullhart, and he had run several. So I started running with Ted.

One of the things I remember about practicing was that when Cousin Sarah Slavin and her nineteen-year-old son, Hale Schramm, were visiting us during that time, Hale was in great shape then, and we ran together, and ran about seven miles at a 6:30 pace. He ran ahead of me the entire way. I will never forget Hale and his mother and sister. They will always be a part of our family.

As I write this in 2023, Hale is now in his fifties and, tragically, can no longer run like he did with me. Thanks for encouraging me in my running, Hale. I never made it to Boston, like we talked about. I don't know when this will be published, but there were many people who encouraged me along the way. Hale, you were one of the early ones to do so. To you I will always be grateful!

I managed WIPB-TV until I was forty-nine, so this was the period in my early forties when I was running almost daily. Sometimes, I would run from our home in Halteman Village out to the I-69 interchange and back on a long run, in preparation for the full marathon distance of 26.2 miles, and Grandma Linda would meet me halfway and trade my empty water bottles for full ones. She really worked hard to support what I wanted to do with my goal.

Later, I ran five marathons: my first marathon was the First ever Muncie Marathon, October 20, 1985. We started at the Walnut Street Bridge just north of Muncie Central High School, then to the downtown YMCA, then out to and around the Muncie Prairie Creek Reservoir—and finishing in 5:43:45 and the last one to finish; the second was the second Muncie Marathon, when I finished in 4:00:00 even. I received a prize for being the last runner for the first ever Muncie Marathon and received "The Slow Runner's Handbook." For my second outing, I got the award for "The Most Improved." That I cut my time by 1:43:45—an astounding time for my second race, wasn't hard since I had run so poorly in the first race.

In the first race, I had been sick for two weeks before the marathon, so I decided I would have to run a half-mile and walk a half-mile if I had any chance of finishing the course. So when the SAG wagon (a Red Cross Emergency Vehicle to pick up injured runners) pulled up beside me at the corner of Jackson and Walnut, after the first half-mile and asked if I needed a lift, I told them I would be doing this all day, and that they needn't worry. I would finish the race, but at my own run/walk pace. And I did!

Ultimately, the SAG wagon pulled away from me about four miles before the end of the race, and I was running alone, and discovered the orange peels on the pavement at the twenty-two-mile marker, but no one working the last water stop. I was so mad that I resolved I WOULD darn well finish the race, regardless of how much my legs and feet hurt, and I did more running per mile in the last four miles than in each of the first twenty-two.

When I got to the finish line, Linda was not there. She had told me the truth— she didn't want to see me "kill myself," so she wasn't coming, and she was as good as her word. Fortunately, Sunny Spurgeon, Julie Etchison, and Julie Skinner were there to cheer me on, and they each gave me a big hug after I crossed the finish line. What an encouraging, welcoming committee.

Linda was there for me the second year and each year thereafter when I finished three Muncie Marathons. My third marathon was the Indianapolis Marathon which was the trial marathon for the Pan-American Games in Indianapolis where we started at Fort Benjamin Harrison in the northeast corner of Marion County, and after doing a loop out into the country toward Pendleton, we turned and ran past the Fort and onto Kessler Boulevard, west to Meridian, and South on Meridian to 16th Street where we turned West and finished on the IUPUI track. We were all beat, having run into an eight-knot headwind for the last six miles since turning onto Meridian Street at Kessler, in Broad Ripple.

We were all stunned too, as we sat on the rubberized surface and moaned about the poor times we had. As we stoked up on apples and bananas, I recognized I had finished that race at 4:00:00, not fast enough to qualify for Boston. What a disappointment!

As I crossed Thirty-Eighth Street that day going south on Meridian, I knew I could qualify for the Boston Marathon if I just ran 8:00 minute miles for each of the last four miles, but shortly after I stopped to go to the bathroom in a port-a-john, my quads cramped up and I had to walk the rest of the way. Everyone else had the same experience because when we turned south on Meridian, we ran into an eight-knot headwind, and running at about eight knots, we were dehydrated by the sixteen-knot breeze and didn't realize it until our bodies were so dehydrated that our legs all cramped up.

Once that happened, it was too late to drink water to rehydrate the muscle tissue and we had to walk.

Unfortunately, tired and dehydrated, we weren't able to realize it on the fly, and while we were angry with our bodies, there was nothing we could do to remedy our slow times.

George Branam and Jose Ponzi, both experienced marathoners and doctors who might have guessed what was happening, missed the cues and didn't figure it out until we were sitting on the track at IUPUI and the race was over. Jim Kirkwood, a local running enthusiast and running columnist for the *Muncie Star* also ran with us that day, but no one realized what was happening as we ran.

This is one of the miscellaneous things one learns when you are running the actual marathon. None of us ever anticipated this, though we had all run marathons before. How true of other life circumstances. My fourth marathon was another Muncie Marathon where, for the first time, our son, Brian, rode his bike along with me to help me qualify for Boston. While we tried for a 3:30 qualifying finish time, I did not make it.

I wish that could have happened, but it did not. I was running really well—about a 6:30/mile pace, when, out of nowhere, ten miles into the race, I developed a terrible ache in my chest and left arm as I ran. I was afraid I had been pushing too hard, that I had strained my heart. How would I know? It was the fastest I had ever run the first ten miles of a marathon, but I did not want to scare Brian, so I just told him I had to slow down. (I was scared for both of us. I DID have to slow down) At that point, I had been averaging less than 7:00/ mile, and I felt fine, except the pain was very intense and made me wonder if I was having a heart attack. It was on my left shoulder and down my arm, so I started walking.

Brian slowed down and urged me on, but I didn't tell Brian in order to shield him from the fear I was experiencing. I didn't know what to do, but I had visions of having a heart attack right there on the road, and I decided I had to walk and see if the pain would subside. Eventually, that happened, but I had truly been scared by this novel pain that had never happened before on any of my runs, and when I started running again, I was tentative and had lost too much time to finish in the 3:30 time I had so hoped for. I know Brian was disappointed too. But I didn't want to really scare him the way I was scared. So I told him I was just too tired to keep running at that pace. I actually WAS too tired but finished at the disappointing time of 4:00 even.

I went to the doctor the next day, and we talked it through and decided that what I had done was to hunch my left shoulder as I ran, and actually cause my left shoulder muscle to cramp. Then, when I walked, it relaxed, and the pain disappeared. I wish I had not done that, but that's the truth. I admitted that to Brian later, but it was hard to say that I lied to him, even though I had what I thought was a good reason.

My last marathon was the best. I was supposed to run the WMEE Marathon in Fort Wayne that weekend. I had been preparing and tapering and was ready to run and registered. I thought I was all prepared until Steve asked if we had it on our calendars to chaperone his Northside Prom. We did not have the Prom on our calendar until he asked, but Grandma and I immediately decided to chaperone, and I delayed my marathon to another time. The next week, I ran the Indianapolis Mini-marathon at 13.1 miles and had my best Mini-Marathon time ever. Remember, I had been training for the 26-mile race, and I finished the 13.1 miles in 1:35:00. I think I was 14th in my Age Range for that race, the best I ever did.

The next marathon venue I could register for was the Sunburst Marathon in South Bend, and I was ready for that one. As I had done before, I had developed a routine so I could get a good night's sleep the night before, and so I drove to South Bend and checked into my motel to go to bed early and get up at 4:00 a.m. to eat some apples and bananas and some cereal and go back to bed for an hour before heading out to the starting line.

I went to bed at about 10:00 p.m. but couldn't go to sleep because I kept remembering that I was only about 4 miles from my aunt Wini's house and sensed that I just had to call her and tell her I was in town. Maybe I could see her after the race, I thought. The still small voice of God, I believe, kept prompting me to call her, so finally, in an act of submission to that nagging voice, I sat up, lifted the phone, and called her number. She answered cheerfully, asked why I was calling, and I told her I was close by.

Then my aunt Wini floored me by asking if I wanted to speak to my mom and dad. I was shocked because they had wanted to see me run the WMEE marathon and I had wanted them to see me run a marathon, and when that was cancelled, I had to call them and let them know they would not get to see me run.

Unbeknownst to me, my parents had been in Kalamazoo to visit my cousin Bobby Needham, my Uncle Will's only son, and had stopped for the night in Mishawaka at my Aunt Wini's so dad and mom could see his sister, Wini Needham. My parents had no plans for the next day, so they asked what I was doing. I told them, and they said they'd get out and stake out a place along the course somewhere and greet me as I ran by. They did meet me at about the seventeen-mile mark and traded me a banana for my soaked Gore-Tex jacket which I had worn for the first 2 ½ hours. When I put down my hands to give them the jacket, water just poured out of my sleeves where, in the steady rain, it had collected at my elbows, without my ever realizing it.

I had been running in a light rain, in sixty degrees, and while I wasn't cold, I was very wet from sweating, and the rain on my face. When I crossed the finish line on the fifty-yard line in Touch-Down Jesus Stadium at Notre Dame, there at the finish line were my mom and dad and Linda and

Kirsten and Steve and Brian, all waiting for me. It was my best finish ever at 3:43:45.

Shortly after that, going in to work at WIPB-TV, one night in the dark, I stepped on a small, round dime-sized pebble, rolled my left knee out, and "POP"—tore my left Lateral Meniscus which culminated in surgery seven months later, and left me in rehab for months, never to run long distances again. I'm glad I ran five marathons but sorry I never got to go to Boston and run that storied race. However, I did get to see the Boston Course when I was there in 1978 for a Manager's Seminar in the Harvard Graduate School for Management and I dropped runners off at the starting line in Hopkinton, Massachusetts. What a marathon course!

Chapter 37

Leaving WIPB-TV for Good

Then, in 1992, when it was growing more difficult to fund our operations because the times were changing, the University began demanding that we carry all PBS programs that were offered to us, regardless of the "raw" nature of the scripts. I refused, and my EICTV Board to which I reported for operations, supported my decisions and my responsibility as GM to make those decisions. The University was unhappy with that outcome. And shortly thereafter, ordered me to amend my budget to include a set-aside of $50,000 per year for a new equipment reserve fund.

I researched our situation with other station managers in the system and with industry turn-around experts I knew who were very successful, and they all agreed that my recommendation to lay off six of the thirty-two full-time persons then on our payroll and hire them or someone else back for peak work times as free-lance workers to fill in for those busy times, was a well-reasoned solution to the University demand that we increase our escrow funding. I did not like this option, but that was the only reasonable way of addressing the problem that I could devise and continue our heathy operations. Laying those employees off would have accomplished that objective.

Ball State and my EICTV Board's response was to reject my recommendation, and said I would have to find another way to reserve those funds and amend the station's proposed budget.

That was the first time in my seventeen years as General Manager that the University and Board literally balked at my recommendations. I had done many things successfully, and they had never pushed back on me like this. We had two meetings where they literally stone-walled me, and I decided they needed to hire someone they would trust. I told them that.

So as I met with Associate Provost, Tom Kaluzynski, who had informed me of the Board's refusal to accept my recommendation, I invoked my Tenure status and said that if the Board would not take my recommendation, which was thoroughly researched, then I would like to be transferred to another position at the University. "Oh," I added; "and I can do that because I'm tenured."

I said I had been tenured since 1982, and I wanted to be transferred to the TCOM Department and begin teaching there. I had taught the semester before—the spring semester of 1992, to fill in for an absence of a Law Professor, and the students loved me, and I found out, I loved teaching. "I'd like to be transferred to TCOM and begin teaching. I know they need another professor." Dr. Kaluzynski was surprised at my request, left the room, and returned with the Board's response.

"Well," Kaluzynski commented, "we'll have to contact the TCOM Department and see if they will vote to add you to their faculty."

The vote happened later that week, the TCOM Faculty voted me in 13-1, and I was told to move into my TCOM office by January 3. I would begin teaching in the TCOM Department for the Spring Semester, 1993, and I would be teaching Law. I was re-titled as "Assistant Professor," a title I was to keep until I retired in 2010. Along the way, I became the Primary Advisor for our 1,200 TCOM students, the primary guide for most of them as they were introduced to TCOM, and the Assistant Chair to Steve Bell and later, Nancy Carlson. What a surprise to me! I am sure; however, what transpired did not surprise God. He had made sure along the way that I would be ready.

After I had met with my board and turned in my resignation, I called a meeting of all my staff in the small studio. I had not briefed any of them about what was going to happen. When I explained what I had decided to do, most were startled that I had resigned. I did not explain everything, but I did thank them for their service, for working with me to build one of the best small stations in the United States, and for helping us to build the new station, do the TV documentary: *Australia's Art of the Dreamtime* in Australia, produce all the *Joy of Painting* programs, the thousands of hours of on-air pledging, and Annual Telesale campaigns, and all the other great community engagement programs we had done over the years.

I finished by sharing *Acts* 17:26 with them and my conviction about why I was leaving the station. In that verse, the Apostle Paul tells the Greeks in Athens that God, our Lord "determines the exact times and places that people should live." I continued: "I am sure God brought me to Channel 49 from WISH-TV in Indianapolis in 1976, and I am just as sure that He is moving me out of here for His own purposes. I hope everything goes well for the station I love, and for each of you. I will miss you all, and I will continue to support you and pray for you. But beginning in January, I will be an Assistant Professor in TCOM and will begin teaching and no longer be associated with the station."

They were in shock; some were crying. They did not say much. They just listened. My time at WIPB-TV, Channel 49 was over. What I could see clearly was that the station that Linda Slavin had helped to put on the air with her sorority sisters, community leaders, and *Sesame Street* advocates, was about to be turned over to the University to redirect it as the University saw fit. Two years later, in 1994, the University converted the EICTV Board of Directors to which I had reported for seventeen of the station's most productive years, from a Board with responsibility for supporting and directing the management to purely an "advisory" capacity, and several years later, Ball State disbanded the board altogether. I was not surprised to learn that had happened.

The University was committed to making the station more student-centered and no longer focusing on the community and its programming needs. That is beginning to turn around as I write this in 2023 because the University is finding without more ownership on the part of the community, WIPB cannot command the level of community support it needs to flourish, and that it enjoyed in earlier days. In late 2020, the University decided to rename WIPB-TV as "Ball State PBS" as it entered its fiftieth year of operations. That telegraphs, more than anything, the direction the University intends to take Muncie's PBS station. Let's hope that is best for the community and the University. I was brought to Muncie to make WIPB-TV a station rich in community programming. I had done that, but in December 1992, the needs and desires for WIPB by the station's licensee had changed. It was time for me to leave.

Chapter 38

Other Children Who
Have Chosen Us

There are several other stories I want to share that deal with the other children that have become a significant part of our lives. This includes in order: in 1994, Joachim Pfannschmidt of Vilseck, Germany; in 1995, Michael Madsen of Copenhagen, Denmark; in 2003, Tinku Sangini Bhatt Greenstreet of Denver, Colorado; in 2007, Diane of northern California; in 2010, Hyejin Kim of Incheon, Korea; and in 2015, Josh Rush of Muncie. All of them are important extensions of our family, and persons some of you have met or heard about. All of them have played a role in our family, and we have played a role in each of their lives. We have decided that to a great degree, "family is made up of those we love," not just those who were birthed by us. I think our six additional "kids" would agree with that.

Joachim (Jockel) came to us in April 1994 as a Rotary Exchange student. We came to love Jockel in the two months he lived with us, and subsequently, have maintained our relationship with this professional French Horn performer from that day forward through this year when he and his family were planning to return to the United States for his nephew's wedding in West Virginia. Because of Covid-19, that visit did not happen. Maybe it will occur next year. We have to hope so, or else we'll go back to Germany to see them again. Their girls, Anna and Marie, are growing so fast, and we can help them as they study their English lessons.

We helped bring Jockel and his 10-member Bavarian Brass back to the United States in 2000, and were in Jockel and Anne's wedding at Pommersfelden, Bavaria in Germany in 2007, and have been with him a dozen times since he first lived with us, both in Europe and in America. Jockel and Anne have two beautiful daughters, and we can't wait to see them again.

Michael Madson was our second Rotary Exchange student and came to live with us in November 1995 from Denmark. We went to meet his parents and visit him in 1996 and returned in 2008 for his wedding in Copenhagen at Gladaxe Church, an eight-hundred-year-old brick-and-stone church in a city of at least that age. It was incredible and his sister, Birte, took us on an unforgettable tour of Copenhagen the next day, and to the airport on Monday for our two-day immersion in Danish family life, their wonderful wedding, and the day following, we had a thorough tour of one of the great cities of Europe—Copenhagen—with Michael's sister, Birte as our local guide. It was mind-numbing and awesome!

The day of the wedding, I lost a crown on my tooth, and Dr. Birte Madsen, DDS, glued it back on in time to make it to the church on time. What an adventure! Talk about a miracle. God was there, just when I needed a miracle. Birte was like an angel. Maybe she was. She died of Cancer two years later. We sat with the family at the wedding and toasted them at their reception. Michael and Anja now have three boys.

Tinku is our "daughter" from Minneapolis, Minnesota with Hindu parents who emigrated to the US from India, and was a TCOM major who graduated in 2002. I was Tinku's Advisor, and after meeting her, she became the personal trainer for Linda and me until she graduated and moved to Indianapolis where she added her Master's Degree in Physical Fitness and Exercise Science from IUPUI. Several years later, Tinku moved to Denver, and subsequently, invited us to participate in her Hindu/Christian wedding in the Denver Botanical Garden. It was a fascinating afternoon: a Hindu/ Christian wedding—something I never even imagined was possible. It was beautiful and honored her parents' Hindu traditions and all the Christian brothers and sisters who participated in that unforgettable place. Before she moved to Denver, Tinku had become a Christian, and when she arrived in Denver, she met and married a wonderful Software Salesman, Rustin Greenstreet, from Wisconsin. We still enjoy their friendship and their two beautiful daughters.

Diane was a foreign exchange student who came to Ball State to study journalism and ended up studying TCOM. She was bright and energetic and studied hard and not only studied TCOM (Radio and TV at Ball State) but also the violin. She was an excellent student and won our hearts when we celebrated her twenty-first birthday with her and introduced her to the culture of the Midwest and Muncie, Indiana. She had never been here before and was far away from her parents, as were most of the other children who have landed here from another country and needed and wanted additional mentoring and guidance. She arrived just as her first semester was beginning, and I helped her get the classes she needed. Our next-door neighbor helped her get the violin lessons she wanted and to play in the Ball State Symphony. We really enjoyed her time here as a student.

Diane gravitated to us because of what she was learning about the people and culture of midwestern America. When she graduated from Ball State, she moved on to another midwestern university to earn an additional degree in marketing with help from our letters of recommendation. Diane will always be special to us.

Finally, in a surprise to us, having learned that we had other "children of another mother," as we often called our German and Danish Rotary sons, she asked if we would be her "American parents." Of course, we said "Yes," and Diane has been a part of our extended family ever since. Along the way, she decided to accept Jesus as her savior after attending church with her boyfriend, and we even got to attend her baptism as a newly born Christian. She is married now and enjoying her life in America where she is happy and working to discover her own American dream—whatever that will be.

In 2010, as I retired from Ball State, I immediately shipped off to South Korea to teach Media Criticism at the University of Incheon for six weeks. Hyejin Kim was to be my next surprise. She was a University of Incheon Campus Tour Guide, and somehow, had learned I was coming. As I wandered across the campus—in and out of various buildings on my first day there, I showed up at the Campus Observatory where a young dark-haired student addressed me by name as I walked in the door and asked if she could talk to me.

"Of course," I said. "How did you know my name?" Hyejin said she had discovered I was coming to campus from Ball State University in Muncie, Indiana to teach Media Criticism, and she wanted to be in my class. She had not been able to register because of a scheduling conflict, but if I would grant her special permission to enroll, she said, she would be permitted to be in my class anyway. "It would really help my English," she argued.

I admired her planning, her diligence, and her spirited request, and after chatting with her for a few minutes, I told her I would see what I could do. Later that day, I had worked out the details and had her enrolled in my class when June Young Choi, my Administrative Contact, and the University made an exception and admitted her to my American Media Criticism section.

She already had made plans to attend Ball State in the Fall of 2010, and I agreed being in my class in Incheon, would benefit her and be easy to accommodate.

Hyejin Kim's English was already very good which helped the class. Heyjin's presence in my Incheon class, presented no problems, and when she arrived in America, she was an outstanding student as well. We loved having her over to our house, as she fit right into our culture without any problems.

As soon as Heyjin got to Muncie, she went to church with us. Along the way, she asked if she could go by the Baptist Church where in Korea, she was the keyboard player for their local worship band. When we got to the back door of Muncie's downtown Baptist church, there were people meeting just inside, and when we knocked, they opened the door to talk with us. Hyejin immediately asked if they had a worship band. When they told her they did but were trying to find a keyboard player, we all laughed. Hyejin volunteered on the spot and played in Muncie's downtown First Baptist Church worship band until she returned to Korea a year later.

What a surprise for us, but not for Hyejin or the Holy Spirit. Hyejin made a lot of friends quickly and won our hearts. In Korea, she had heard the stories about our other "children" who called us "mom and dad" and when she was here in Muncie, she asked if we would also be her "American Parents." We said "Yes." She remembers our birthdays and holidays faithfully. She is a delight, and we have just finished visiting with her and her very new husband, Jaehoon Lee. They were married in Korea in November 2022 and, as a final stop, came to visit us and introduce Jaehoon to us on the last leg of their honeymoon through Hawaii to the US and back to Korea. What a privilege we have to be a part of their lives and celebrate with them in this way.

Finally, Joshua Myles Rush of Muncie has become nearly a constant presence in our lives. In God's perfect timing, Josh became my Mentee in July 2015, having been accepted at the University of Saint Francis, Fort Wayne where Josh hoped to play college football. He had a partial scholarship awaiting his enrollment, but the additional funds needed never materialized, and Josh enrolled in IVY Tech Community College in Muncie, instead. After clearing our Mentee/Mentor relationship with Josh's mother, Calandra Hill, I started meeting with Josh regularly and working with him to help him negotiate College—something none of his siblings or family had ever completed successfully.

Linda and I were going to First Presbyterian Church of Muncie then, and our Pastor there, J.D. Georlett, knowing my background as the TCOM Advisor at Ball State, strongly encouraged me to mentor Josh. Mary and Cornelius Dollison had introduced me to Josh at a Whitely Neighborhood Clean-up Day our church was doing, and at lunch that day, I sat across from Mary Dollison and, Josh sat down next to me.

Mary Dollison is someone I have known for many years as the founder of Motivate Our Minds, a preschool and after-school enrichment program, and she broached the idea that Josh was going to college, and no one from his family had ever done so. So being forthright as she always is, she asked if I could have lunch with Josh and give him some tips on how to succeed in school. I agreed and met with his mother two weeks later at the Minnetrista Farmers' Market where she wanted to check me out. Calandra talked with me briefly and afterward, gave me permission to help Josh as much as possible and became Josh's mentor. That was over eight years ago… Wow! How time flies.

In May 2020, Josh received his BA in TCOM from Ball State University with a 2.92 GPA—higher than mine was as an undergraduate at Indiana State University. I am still Josh's mentor. He is now through Army Basic Training at Fort Jackson in South Carolina, and in the Indiana National Guard and, since graduation, has had various jobs as he prepares for graduate school in Florida using his Guard scholarship, his university assistantship, and a part-time job at Florida International University. In graduate school, Josh plans on majoring in Public Policy and Foreign Relations. He is a skilled linguist and fluent in English and French and dreams of one day, serving in the US Embassy in France. I hope Josh is offered that opportunity at the right time in his future to fulfill a long-kept dream. Only God knows if that is the right place for Josh, and someday, Josh will find out.

Josh has a clear vision of what he wants to do, and a deep conviction that Jesus is leading him through his life. With his gifts and great personality, I am sure he will succeed in whatever he does after graduate school, his next goal.

GRANDCHILDREN: Each of you we count as grandchildren (NINE in all) has played a very special role in our lives. Addison Housand, Steve Slavin, Aubrey Housand, Ben Slavin, Arianna Slavin, and Elliott Slavin. In addition, we have recently added Sofia Stefani and Nathan Stefani with Brian's marriage to Jennifer Stefani in October 2017, and in 2019, Caroline Hammonds joined us when Kirsten married Eric Hammonds. We are grateful for every one of you and especially those of you who prompted us to write this recounting of "my life before I met Grandma." Maybe that should be a "subtitle"?

Chapter 39

Other Life Lessons and
What I Truly Believe

When I thought about this book, what resonated with me the most was that I wanted you each to know what I think my life lessons have been, and how I have come to have such a strong conviction that God is real, and that He has walked with me through the good times and the bad.

I know this: Jesus is in charge of my life, and He has rescued me and blessed me so many times that I don't want to draw a breath without him being in charge. I don't know how much more time I have, but I want to spend what I have, loving Him, loving you, and all He loves and being an example of someone who trusts Him more than anyone else. If I do that, I will feel satisfied that I have done what He created me to do and, on His terms, I have been a "good and faithful servant." That's what I want most of all, and that will be enough.

You may not have encountered Him the way I have at so many different points in my life and circumstances. But when we went off the road in Colorado on our only trip out west, driving a Van we borrowed from Denny and Sandi Baron, with our whole family on board, asleep, and someone shouted, "You're not driving anymore!" I still thank God somebody else was awake and grabbed the wheel and kept us on the road.

You never saw that. You were all asleep, and I was driving; I never saw it either, but I remember it like yesterday. I had gone to sleep driving, trying to let the rest of you sleep, and I woke up just as the tires left the road. I owe God a lot for that move. And you owe Him a lot too. Your parents were in that Mini-Van along with Grandma and me. And we all survived because we did not crash that morning at 5:00 AM. I was embarrassed and grateful, but I never drove through the night again with my family. I admit it. Doing so that night was foolish and something I will never repeat. That's a lesson you will never want to learn either. So learn it from ME, here.

Earlier in my life, when working in Canada, I remember my tires going off the road a number of times while I was commuting 600 miles each way back and forth from Guelph, Ontario, Canada to Terre Haute, Indiana, where my first wife, Judy, was finishing up her Indiana State Bachelor's Degree in Music Education. And as I drove, time and again, the noise of my tires going off the road onto the gravel each time woke me up. Thank God I'm a "light sleeper" and I awoke each time I dozed off or I wouldn't be writing this book. God saved me for this!

I would become "Coffeed Out" ... too much coffee, and the caffeine was no longer keeping me awake. On that twelve-hour road trip from Guelph, Ontario, to Terre Haute, Indiana, after a long week at work, it was just hard to stay awake. When that happened, God saved my life a number of times, and I learned to stop and eat, because the coffee would only keep me awake so long. A twelve-hour drive alone after a long two weeks of working, was very difficult and really, kind of crazy. Why did God save me from going off the road so many times? I don't know, but I remember those scary episodes, and I'm only sure of this: "He had more for me to do with my life than die on Canada's "Super-

highway 401" as they called that four-lane monotonous con-
nector from Toronto to Detroit. For fully 186 miles each trip,
this black ribbon in the gathering dusk, wound straight along
the north shore of Lake Erie from Guelph to Windsor, with
little to keep me awake.

Much earlier in my life, when I was six and playing keep
away with my brother and his older friends in Stone Lake,
Indiana, near Goshen, in my exuberance to be the person
who got the stick the older boys and my brother were "keeping away from me" as the younger little brother, with my
dogged determination, I ran off the end of the pier and dove
right at the stick they had thrown into the deep water. After I
grabbed the stick in my hand, I almost lost my life too. I DID
go after the stick and got it, but when I got it, I realized I was
in the lake, way over my head. I didn't know how to swim,
but I had the stick. That was youthful exuberance, not wisdom. They all thought it was funny. It was NOT!

I started drifting down and knew I was in trouble. I was
six years old, and I remembered what my dad said about
paddling with my hands. I let go of the stick and started
pushing down with my hands and kicking with my feet and
pretty soon, my head was above the water again. Scared by
this brush with the unknown and coughing up water, I lost
the game and survived. And I promised myself I would learn
to swim! I didn't play keep-away anymore that day. But I
was motivated, and I did learn to swim later, when I had the
chance in a pool.

I never forgot Stone Lake and the beautiful and frightening view of the green water and the mossy plants and
going down into the deep toward the foreboding bottom and
realizing I had to go back up, somehow to survive. It scared
me a lot and it sharpened my resolve.

When I turned fifteen, I applied for and earned my WSI
(Water Safety Instructor's Badge) and life-guarded for three
summers at the Dolton Pool. I actually pulled two children
from the water who were drowning, only to be yelled at

by their mothers who were busy smoking cigarettes in the snack bar and not watching their children who were in over their heads.

My big regret as a lifeguard was using Baby Oil to tan instead of sunscreen. We learned that if we only used Baby Oil, after we got a really bad burn three or four times each summer, our skin didn't hurt any more, and I would be a nice chocolate brown. I loved it, and I loved my job and once worked 84 hours in one week. I was tuckered out. I really pushed the envelope. I bet you have too, sometimes. That's not always a good idea.

Only later, when I was forty years old, did I discover I had precancerous lesions all over my face and had to burn them off with Fluorouracil Cream that I put on for twenty-one straight days; then put on a vinegar wash for seven days. When I finished the treatment, I had a complete face-peal of all the skin on my face from the top of my lip to my hairline. What an incredibly painful experience. My facial skin was very sensitive. When that happened, Kirsten saw me turn into a giant blister-faced person, and she stopped sunbathing without a wide-brimmed hat.

I also had Asthma during my time as a Lifeguard and only later learned that eating 5 or 6 double-decker bread, peanut butter and jelly sandwiches, as I did while my mother was working full time, caused me to have a rattling in my chest when I breathed that would later keep me from going to Vietnam. When I volunteered to enlist in the Air Force for Vietnam, after finishing my bachelor's degrees, the Air Force rejected me because my doctor said I had had Bronchial Asthma as a child.

Actually, I had a very serious case of Gluten Sensitivity that I discovered when I was seventy and volunteering for "100 Men Who Cook" in Muncie. It was a fundraiser, and I asked Cindy Slavin, my sister-in-law, who is Celiac and highly allergic to Gluten, what she most wanted to eat that she hadn't eaten for years.

Cindy looked up and told me without batting an eye: "Chocolate Chip Cookies. I haven't had one of those for twenty years." So I went to work creating a gluten-free cookie recipe, and as I did that, I decided to skip all gluten for two weeks to see if it would have any effect on me.

Wow! Was I surprised! I was seventy at the time and from my teen years until then, I had lived on antihistamines every day to avoid the allergy symptoms I always experienced if I didn't take them daily. What a surprise when all of my allergy symptoms vanished. What a gift. What a surprise. I wasn't supposed to go to Vietnam. But no one knew at that time or talked about Gluten sensitivity or Celiac disease. If they had, I would have been flying over the rice patties instead of attending Graduate School.

As a teen, our family doctor, Dr. Weidner had listened to my chest and the wheezing and gave me little yellow pills with a red hourglass on them that took the wheezing away. After that, over many decades, I took Contac until it didn't work anymore, then Allerest, then Loratadine, then Sudafed, and finally graduated to prescription Allegra to fight the rasping throughout my life until I turned 70. Think of it: 55 years of antihistamines because I had been misdiagnosed. What I discovered at that age, while cooking for the Muncie "100 Men Who Cook" benefit was that if I would stop eating bread with gluten in it, all of the symptoms of my allergies would disappear. I only have two allergies left: raw onions and raw cucumbers. But they only make me sick to my stomach. Since I now know that, I don't eat those two foods, and my allergies and wheezing are gone.

What a surprise for me at seventy! If I did not eat Gluten, I did not have wheezing, and I did not have the runny noses and tearing eyes that came when I ate Gluten and lived on antihistamines. What a blessing that I did not have to go to war and was able to go on to graduate school and get my Bachelor of Science in Speech (Theater) and Psychology, and my Master's Degree in Radio-TV and Psychology, though I never defended my research in Psychology and only finished the coursework. My supervising professor told me I had to re-do my research because I did not prove my null hypothesis (what I thought would happen in my research). I said I had already completed my Radio-TV Masters, and that would have to do.

I wasn't staying in school another 8 months to finish my Psychology Masters. I had already been in college six years. What I learned in all those Psychology classes did help me a lot, however. As grandma says, "God never wastes anything!" At the time, I had no way of knowing I would one day become the Primary Advisor (Departmental Academic Problem Solver) for 1,200 TCOM Students along with serving as a Professor at Ball State University for seventeen years. It must have given me a lot of background for the counseling I did because in 2001, I was named the top Academic Advisor of all the fifty-five departments at Ball State University for that year. I am proud of that and enjoyed my time at Ball State, along with the three classes per semester that I taught. I also served as Assistant Chair of the TCOM Department for about 5 of those years, working alternately with Steve Bell for a couple of years, and Nancy Carlson, for three years—both Chairpersons for short periods and alternately, appointing me to assist them.

Another time, when we were in Dolton, Illinois, when I was ten and we were living on 144th street, a friend and I had dug out caves in the sandy prairie across from our house, even though we had been warned not to do that. The mixture of clay and sandy soil made it easy to dig down and create a space underground where we could hide out and where we had gotten together several times.

I always believed I could manage the situation when I decided to ignore the rules. It was fun to do what we wanted to do and also to have our own private space to play in. But it was also dangerous. One day, however, when I had been down there by myself, I was crawling out of the tunnel at one of the two entrances, when all of a sudden, HRUMPH! the ceiling collapsed on my legs. Fortunately, I had just gotten to the entrance shaft, and I was barely able to pull my legs out from under the weight of the earth that had fallen on me. I never did tell my brother or my father or my mother about that, and we never went back. Thank God my friend was not there that day. When I told my brother about that, just before he died last year, he chided me because he too knew digging caves in that soft soil was very dangerous and that my father had told me not to do that. He said I was lucky. God was watching over me. But what I did was truly very foolish. You're beginning to see that God saved my life again and again. It wasn't luck at all.

If my friend or I had been in the center of that cave in, I would not be writing this. We never did dig the cave out again. My parents and brother never knew. But I remember it all, and I am still claustrophobic because of that experience. God saved me then. I remember thinking that at the time. And I was grateful, and even knowing that, I have been afraid my whole life of closed spaces like caves because of that dreadful experience when I once again, disobeyed my dad.

It was a very bad idea to dig in that sandy soil, only a block away from the Chicago & Eastern Illinois Railroad Switching Yard where they "humped" the freight cars on a high ridge and the railroad cars came crashing down the slope and made the ground shake when the two railroad cars and the tons of steel they weighed, connected their couplers. I still remember feeling the ground shake every time that happened and the loud noise that accompanied it.

And then there is the time when we were in the San Juan Mountains with Young Life, and we were in places where we were in real jeopardy and climbing with no ropes and no railings, and just free climbing up the area above the tree line with Steve and later with Brian. We were all at risk and yet, with God's help, we never had a serious problem.

To take everything up there above the tree line to 12,000 feet from our base camp at 9,600 feet, we had to sacrifice a lot of personal gear so we could carry meals for everyone, or "Fly poles" or the Fly itself—a big round piece of canvas with a hole in the center. It was about 40 feet across and used three segmented poles to hold the center ring—about a foot wide—that we would suspend about ten feet above the center of the Fly.

We did that by staking the Fly down about a foot off the ground, because above the tree line, it gets down to freezing every night, and if you don't do that, our "Fly," which served as our shelter, would be wet underneath from our collective breathing during the night under the Fly, and when we would wake up, a wet Fly would necessitate hours of waiting for it to dry before we could pack it up and move on. So we took the Fly instead of a tent. And when we got up each morning, the Fly was dry and so were all who slept under it. The moisture in your breath, goes up and out the center hole in the Fly while you sleep, and your sleeping bags and the Fly are dry as a bone when you awaken in the crisp, crisp (read that "frigid") air.

We would strike the Fly immediately, eat our one eight ounce mug of breakfast, roll up the fly and we were on our way in an hour. The worst part of camping at 12,000 feet is bathroom breaks in the middle of the night. While there are no wild animals up there, it is thirty-two degrees or less if you happen to wake up, and while everyone else is sleeping and the sky is the most beautiful blue-black and you can see forever and the stars are right in front of you, you won't find your way to the latrine without a light, and then, if you need to sit down, the rocks are VERY cold.

So we all learned to use the latrine before going to bed, and not to drink water after dinner. (Just sayin'.) I personally know how cold and beautiful the night sky is at 3:00 AM above the tree line. You don't personally have to try it out to believe me. But ask Steve or Brian and they will testify to the truth of that statement. We had the time of our lives, however, and I wouldn't trade those trips for anything. I was just glad that I only went to the San Juan Mountains' Second Timer's Camps twice. Kirs never did get to go. I think she went to Windy Gap in North Carolina, instead, as an assistant wrangler for the horses and a head wrangler named Patrick. But that's another story.

On my trip with Brian, we were also required to repel from a seventy-foot cliff using a carabiner around our waist and upper thighs, and go over the edge and let ourselves down, hand-over-hand. Letting ourselves down was no big deal. Going over the edge WAS! For me, it was the scariest thing I have ever done. When all but three of us had repelled over the edge, with my son Brian being the first to go, I was the only guy left with two other girl campers. I decided I couldn't be last, so I said a prayer, and asked God to take me to heaven if I died doing this, and I told Him I could not let Brian's dad embarrass him.

First, I sat there and watched over a dozen others go over the edge. Nobody screamed as they fell to their deaths. That should have calmed my heart. It didn't! My heart was pounding very hard, and the Camp Guides told me to turn around and hug the mountain to help relax. I did that, and you know what? It worked. Then, when it was my turn (third from the last), and I turned around and crawled to the precipice, they clicked the belaying rope onto my carabiner belts, and made me turn around backwards. Yes, I had to BACK OFF the cliff backward!

I prayed, "God, hold me in the palm of Your hand. I can't do this!" And then I heard my guides say, "Okay, now grip the rope, start sliding backwards and gently let your feet hang over the edge." As I did this, I felt my feet waiving in the wind and said one final prayer.

All of a sudden, my knees cleared the rock, and my feet and knees were out of sight, hanging there, over the edge, and I was not dying or falling.

I was just hanging there, and I started letting myself down the rope. It was so easy. Why had I been afraid? Sounds like many other real-life experiences where you're scared to death to decide, doesn't it? On the ground, they all started cheering, and I let myself down. Did I want to do that again? "No!" But I did it. I repelled. I didn't embarrass Brian (or at least he never said a word), and I made it to the ground and am here to recount this story. I'm almost embarrassed to tell it, but like all the stories in this book, it's true, and there's a moral: Most of the things you fear the most, never happen to you. And you can do more than you think you can, if you believe in God and ask for His help. That's my modus operandi. It works pretty well. And I believe God likes us to ask for His help. In fact, I know that is true. GOD says it over and over in his book... I'm sure He means it. Talking with God is called "prayer." Use it or lose it! If you don't use it, you may forget prayer is the easiest and best option. Trust me on this one, or trust God. He's definitely more reliable, and He's always available.

At one other time, near the end of that trip, the last night after we had gone back down from the tree line about 11,000 feet, it was raining, and at dinner that night, our Young Life leaders told us we were going to spend the night outside, under the stars (read that—rain clouds) and we were not happy about that. It was raining pretty hard, and Brian and I were laying in the Fly on our sleeping bags, dry and not eager to move out into the weather. Finally, Brian asked me if we really had to do this. I told him, that we did, and we'd be alright. We'd stick together, and we would be warm enough to be alright all night and not to worry. Then he asked, "Is there anything we can do to not go out there in this rain?"

And I said, "Well, the only thing I know to do is to pray really hard to God and ask Him to open the clouds and pour down on us so hard that the leaders will change their minds." So we began to pray, really pray in earnest. Ten minutes passed. Then twenty minutes passed, and about a half hour later, a leader came by and told us, "It's raining too hard to go out without any cover. We're going to cancel this part of the trip tonight. You're just going to have to miss this."

And Brian looked at me, and I looked at Brian, and I said, "We need to thank God for hearing our prayer and thank Him that we're sleeping in here tonight." And that's exactly what we did.

Intellectually, and experientially as I have already testified, I know God is always with me. I know what God said through the Prophet Isaiah 41:10–15, and what Jesus said (Matthew 28:20) when He told His disciples, "Lo, I am with you always, even to the ends of the earth"— but sometimes, in the heat of the moment—when life comes at me fast, I get a chance to really trust Him, and afterward, I know for sure that He is with me, because I sense His presence and His gentle and firm hands, all about me. I bet that has happened in your life too. If it has, maybe someday, you'll tell your children about that, or maybe, if we have the chance, you'll talk with me about it. I hope so.

Many of you have seen the poem of the person walking along the ocean beach with Jesus, reviewing the life of a person as they walk toward the gates of heaven. And the person says to Jesus, "Why was it that in my darkest hours, when troubles were all around and overwhelming me, as I look back over the path I have walked with You, there are places where I see only one set of footsteps in the sand. You said You would never leave me or forsake me."

And Jesus answers, "Oh, my child. I have always loved you, and I will never leave you. In your most difficult moments, when you see only one set of footprints in the sand, it was then that I carried you."

I believe Jesus has carried me many times. How about you?

And when Brian and I went to Colorado on our first trip to Young Life's Frontier Ranch, we rode horses, climbed Long's Peak, and went river rafting. We were all in the raft one day, and I got "Popped out" into the water—like spring-ing off of a diving board. It was very sudden! Yeow! Frigid—so COLD! I wasn't holding on tightly enough—the water was snowmelt and VERY cold.

I quickly swam to the side to get out, but the banks were undercut so I struggled to pull myself out. When I finally did, the raft was a hundred yards ahead of me because that part of the river was a rapids, and the raft kept moving. So I climbed up on the train tracks that ran alongside the river and began running to catch up with the raft. All of a sudden, the people in the raft and Brian in particular, were yelling at me, waving their arms—GOING CRAZY, but I couldn't hear them—I could see them yelling, and they were all pointing at me and behind me. And when I turned to look, a locomo-tive was bearing down on me, not one hundred yards away. Because of the rapids, I had never heard it. The train never could have stopped, but I jumped off the tracks, and let the train go by, and then had to catch up again. The raft had kept moving, but I was safe. Why was I safe there? Then? Only because God spared me. Thank God, AGAIN!

You have your stories. I'm sure you do, but I am sure of this. I have never walked alone. And because I have given my life to Jesus, He has given it back to me over and over in such a glorious fashion that I cannot take credit for what we have or what I have lived through, and I cannot imag-ine what it would be like to live without Him beside me and inside me.

If you are living that way too, then you know what I'm referring to. If you're not yet there, I want you to know Jesus loves you and has loved you since before you were formed in your mother's womb. How do I know that? He said so in Psalm 139:14–18.

Chapter 40

Just a Few More Stories

Well, we're getting close to the end of the book. I haven't run out of stories, but Grandma told me I had to limit this to one hundred pages or so. I know! I'm pushing it… but here goes… there's just a few more stories to check out…and then we're done… if you want to be.

In 2009, when I was still teaching summer school, I was teaching a class in Social Responsibility. All TCOM professors were asked if they would like to take their class to hear Gideon Yu, the former Vice President of Yahoo, and former Chief Financial Officer (CFO) for YouTube, who was coming to Ball State University's Indianapolis campus in downtown Indianapolis. I volunteered that we would go, and all twenty of us in my summer class showed up at the event on West Washington Street at a presentation room which probably seated one hundred people. There were only thirty of us present—my class, two older adults who turned out to be Gideon's parents, and several other Ball State students interested in hearing what Gideon had to say.

Gideon Yu is currently a co-owner of the San Francisco 49ers NFL football team, but when we saw him, he had just resigned from Google where he had been retained by Google following the Google purchase of YouTube by their company. Here is his story.

I met Gideon fourteen years ago when he was thirty-five years old and had just retired to move back to the Midwest from California where he had been heavily involved in high tech companies. His final stop was to be hired away from Yahoo where he had been for four and a half years, and to go to YouTube in 2006. The owners were two entrepreneurs who had created the company several years earlier and, disgusted because customers were suing them and were threatening to destroy the company the two owners, twenty-nine years old and twenty-seven years old, had worked so hard to create, the owners decided they would rather sell YouTube. That was Gideon's first job, the first month he was at YouTube.

So they hired Gideon Yu to market their company, and asked him to get at least one billion dollars for it. He was challenged and flabbergasted they were asking so much for a company that had yet to turn a profit. Nonetheless, Gideon Yu started shopping the company around in Silicon Valley and found an interested buyer in Google.

Here is the back story on this. Gideon was a brilliant student who earned his Bachelor's degree from Stanford University in Engineering and Engineering Management and his MBA from the Harvard Business School, two of the top universities in America. Along the way, Gideon worked for Disney, Credit Suisse, Facebook, Hilton Hotels, and finally, Yahoo!

After successfully helping grow Yahoo, Gideon was hired away from Yahoo, to be CFO (Chief Financial Officer) for YouTube. He had already made a fortune, but he was interested in this brand-new platform. When he got to YouTube, he found two very angry owners who were in the middle of a season where they were fending off lawsuits and felt their company might be destroyed if they didn't sell. So the twenty-nine-year-old and twenty-seven-year-old owners told Gideon as his first piece of business to find someone who would buy the fledgling company for one billion dollars or more. Where do you begin with this kind of demand? Ultimately, Gideon figured it out, and the bid went for more than they expected: actually 1.65 billion dollars. From there, Google retained Gideon Yu, and he finally retired in 2009.

Talking about the negotiation, Gideon said in his presentation, he was afraid he was asking too much, and didn't sleep a wink for the week the negotiations went on. It finally peaked with Google giving their final offer, after Gideon had asked for over two billion dollars. Gideon said he barely slept until Google made its decision.

After the sale, Gideon learned that, in their due diligence, Google had carefully researched what the dynamics were of newly evolving streaming platforms. Google quickly discovered that new versions of this technology platform usually lasted only eighteen months. Google already had a video streaming service that ranked seventh in popularity, but in their research, Google had learned that only the top two versions or iterations of a new platform, manage the transition to the next level. And they also knew Google only had about seven months left in the eighteen-month cycle to acquire the leader in streaming if they were going to have time to understand it, improve it, and rebrand it as Google YouTube dba (doing business as) YouTube. That's exactly why Google paid so much for YouTube and jumped at the chance to acquire it, even though the platform they bought was only good for another seven months.

Since Google had 16 billion dollars in cash sitting on the sidelines, and Google's video streaming service only ranked seventh place, Google knew they needed to buy position, and YouTube was the number one video streaming service in existence.

When Gideon got the 1.65 billion dollar offer, the owners of YouTube said, "Sell it!" And Gideon did. To start the streaming service, the two owners had borrowed heavily from "angel investors" who had put in funds to help pay for all the start-up costs, so when YouTube was sold, the Angel

Investors AND owners would both earn a huge return on their investment.

The sale of YouTube was obviously going to be successful for the two entrepreneurs, and when they were paid for their share of the original investment costs, the two owners each departed with several hundred million dollars. I don't remember the exact number, but both could have retired based on what they made from the sale. The Angel Investors got the rest.

What did Google get? Google acquired the most popular and successful video streaming service at that time, and today what you see when you log into YouTube is "Google" YouTube. Google still owns the service, but it's still called YouTube. Why would you want to confuse the users? So Google kept "YouTube" as the name and added this service to their portfolio. You're really logging into Google's platform, even though YouTube has gone through a number of updates and improvements since Gideon, acting for YouTube, facilitated the sale of the YouTube company to Google.

I don't know what Gideon was paid for doing that, but his many different experiences enabled him to retire at thirty-five and do what he always wanted to do. I asked him at his presentation to our class at the Indianapolis Center for Ball State, what he would do now that he was retired at thirty-five years of age. He said, "First, I'd like to see my two-year-old son grow up. And I'd also like to teach high school math in Kokomo, Indiana, close to my parents who are in the back of the room and are pastoring a church there."

Some time has passed, and Gideon Yu has managed to stay busy. He is now heavily involved Philanthropically at his Stanford Alma Mater and other enterprises.

My students who accompanied me on this optional field trip received a very rare treat: a visit with a visionary genius who succeeded way beyond most of our wildest dreams. It was a treat for me too. I'm sure, with his background, Gideon

Yu has also received a lot of prayers for his success. Indeed, he has been blessed beyond what I could ever imagine. The admonition from the Bible says that "From those to whom much is given, much will be required." Gideon is obviously giving back to his community, to his alma mater, and to his family.

Chapter 41

Other Strange and
Unforgettable Experiences

Many other strange things have happened to me, where I have been a participant or a witness to greatness.

Our Winter Olympics adventure is something else that was unforgettable. It all started out in August 1992 when our best friends, Doug and Jackie Bakken (Doug is Norwegian), invited us to join them and their family on a trip to the Winter Olympics in Lillehammer, Norway in February 1994. We asked what we had to do, and they said, "You need to write the Winter Olympics Committee a check for $2,200 and fill out an application for the Winter Olympics. You want to request the Opening Ceremony, and checkmark the venues you are interested in seeing. You'll probably want to go to the ones we are all thinking of, but you can branch out if you like. You may or may not get the events you ask for. They say that in the application."

So not realizing we would be changing jobs in the meantime, we wrote the check in August 1992, never dreaming that by 1994, I would have changed jobs and that all the while, we would not know which events we would even be going to. But it sounded like a great adventure, and we decided we wanted to go with the six Bakkens whom we were going to accompany to this land north of the Arctic Circle.

We all bought Red, White, and Blue Parkas, extra warm pants, long underwear, socks, stocking caps, and heavy-weight gloves. And Doug's wife, Jackie knitted us all American Flag motif wool neck-warmers. We were prepared to be covered from head to toe. In fact, in the newspapers, as we neared our departure date, it was rumored that it might get down as low as zero degrees, so we went prepared to layer up as necessary.

Once we got there, we realized it was SERIOUSLY cold. In fact, it was zero or below every day we were there, and it got down once to -17. We never counted on it being that cold, but because we layered up and walked two miles down to the shuttle bus each morning with our passes in our jackets, we never really got cold. The other thing that was magical was that because it never got warm enough to melt, everything was pristine and white. The snow was not dirty, the ice sculptures that were created never began to melt, the paths and streets were white with frozen snow, and the venues were perfect throughout the 14 days we were there. We also had an American cook who spoke English, and for $100 per day for all of us, she shopped for us, cooked for us, and cleaned up for us every day we were there. If you figure that out, we had breakfast and dinner each day for $12.50 each, way less than we would have had to pay for any restaurant in Lillehammer.

Honestly, we were spoiled. And when it came to the Opening Ceremony, we were in line with our $150 tickets, and people were offering us $600 per ticket, but none of us would sell, and neither would anyone else. We had a great time, slept well, and got to go to different venues all over the Olympic area. We did see the Ski Jumping, Pairs Skating, the Ice-Skating Practice Sessions where Tanya Harding and Nancy Kerrigan were warming up with everyone who competed (and we snuck home early the day of the ice-skating finals to watch them on TV in our long underwear, snacking by the TV and not having to take the bus home late at night when it was all over). It was wonderful, and the ice sculptures in Hamar when we saw them, had not melted at all and were incredibly ornate and beautiful. Wow! We saw the Luge, the Downhill, and Ski-jumping, and lots of Ice Hockey. Why Ice Hockey? Because Ice Hockey was in the heated Ice Hockey Arena—a comfortable slice of heaven for all smart enough to sit there for a game or two. The Ice Hockey arena was the only place that was warm and inside.

The Opening Ceremony was unbelievable. We arrived at 1:00 PM that day, had lunch at a wonderful restaurant and had Reindeer Steaks. Then we got in line and were in the stadium by 3:00 PM when the pre-Opening Show began with a performance by Sissel KyrkjebØ. What an enchanting singer and performer. When she finished, the master of ceremonies, Thor Hyerdahl who wrote *The Voyage of the Kon Tiki, The Voyage of the Ra,* and *Fatu Hiva*, came out and MC'd the entire show. At nearly 4:00 PM when the show was to begin (10:00 AM EST in the USA), the King of Norway came riding in on a sleigh driven by 8 beautiful reindeer, but they appeared to be miniature Norwegian Reindeer. We did not know, but Norwegian Reindeer are really small. They stopped right in front of us, where the King got out and climbed the four steps to his luxurious Throne, about forty feet to our left from where he was to watch the show.

We had been standing since 3:00 PM, and thought it was ridiculous that we had been charged so much for these "standing seats" where we could not sit, but when we saw where our location was in relation to where the King was sitting, we began to feel really smug and thought we had "incredibly good seats" after all. The only challenge for us all was that the Porta-Potties were not warmed, and it was below zero. If you didn't have to sit down, it was fine. If you did, it was very, very cold indeed. But we made it through.

The opening show was incredible with cross-country skiers skiing uphill and down on the mammoth ski jump, and some performers opening up hidden holes in the ice floor and coming up out of passages beneath the floor of the ice arena. The openings appeared in the ice at the bottom of the jump, and the skiers climbed right out in front of us. These were invisible ports in the ice on the flat, circular landing space which was about fifty feet in front of us.

It was just amazing. And to top it off, as they were playing and singing the Norwegian National Anthem, two paratroopers parachuted from a plane way up in the sky. The lights had just come on as the parachutists circled down to the landing area. As they drew closer, we finally realized they had a Norwegian Flag between them and were going to land right in front of us and right in front of the King. These truly were TERRIFIC standing seats, weren't they?

As the paratroopers came into view and were in the lights, all of a sudden, we realized it was snowing because the strong lights made each snowflake glisten like a little crystal, and there were millions of them. Finally, the sound system, even in this open area arena, was perfect—absolutely perfect. It could not have been better. As we expected, this Opening Ceremony was the highlight of the fourteen days. Although we attended many exciting events and competitions, made it to many venues, indoors and out, and had fabulous food and company, this was the best show ever! We will always be grateful to Doug and Jackie for arranging this incredible adventure and inviting us to join them. We decided we could never attend another winter Olympics because there is no way it could measure up to the miraculous time and experiences, we had with the Bakken family in Norway. Thank you, Bakkens.

On another unique occasion, we attended the 2013 Masters Golf Championship in Augusta, Georgia. Our friends, George and Linda Branam had an employee who annually purchased ten Tournament tickets to the Masters every year for for decades, and they offered to sell George four tickets at their cost for the Masters. George asked Linda and me and the Bakkens to join them, and we agreed to go in our minivan and take turns using the tickets, inside the Masters venue, four of us at a time, to go inside the Masters grounds and see the tournament.

It gets better. As we drove into the Masters parking area, one of the volunteers directing traffic noticed our Handicapped sticker and stopped us. He asked if anyone had problems walking. George used two canes at the time, and we showed them to him, and he said, "You all need to drive up to Handicapped parking, right across from the gate. They will direct you.

When we arrived, it was no more than one hundred feet from our car to the front gate. What a blessing. The tickets normally go for hundreds of dollars for a single day if you participate in the ticket lottery as our Chiropractor did. When he went to watch a practice day, he was selected by lottery, and he paid $1,300 for one ticket for that one practice day. He didn't even get to see any of the tournament. We ended up paying $125 for each ticket, and our four tickets were each good for the entire week from Monday through the final Sunday Round. What a bargain! However, we were cautioned to be sure and follow the rules. "What rules?" we asked.

Before the ticket owners agreed to sell us the tickets for this one Masters Tournament, they said they had to meet with us and get our assurances that we would be respectful of the Masters rules for behavior—no shouting, no pictures when someone is on the tee or green, no littering, and being respectful of others throughout. If we misbehaved and we were ejected, the officials would take away our tickets, and the friends selling us their tickets would not get those tickets back the next year. We actually saw that happen once, and it was just as they said.

I was watching Tiger Woods tee off on the first tee, and as Tiger teed off, this little ten-year-old boy, shouted out, "IN THE HOLE!" really loudly. In less than thirty seconds, two officials were at the boy's side and he and his mother were quietly being ushered toward the gate. That was the only tragedy we saw, but it was unforgettable and underlined what our Donor Family had warned us about.

We couldn't believe it, but it all happened very fast. Everybody turned to watch, and we realized the cautions we had received had a severe penalty attached. Our friends weren't kidding.

Later, we were sitting in the bleachers on the sixteenth green, watching PGA players playing the hole, two at a time, and a member of Augusta was sitting beside us, talking about Augusta. "How much do you think it costs to belong here," he asked. We guessed $100,000 per year, and one of us said $50,000 per year. And he laughed and said, "It seems like it would be worth it, but. No!" he said. "All you need is to 'be invited.' The Masters Tournament income pays for everything, including members' green fees, their membership, and their tickets to the event. All you need is to "be invited to membership" by someone who is a member." It blew us away.

Anyhow, we had a great time. When we got there, we bought official Masters Chairs, and put them at the Eighteenth Green so we could see the final pairing on Sunday and watch the winning putt in person. And we left our jackets and cameras there on our chairs, and as it was at the Olympics, no one moved or took any of our belongings.

Lots of people did that, and there were Hospitality Employees everywhere picking up any little bit of litter. The course was immaculate, and the grounds were spotless. All the bushes and trees were trimmed, and the greens and fairways were in fabulous shape. Also, the lunch was very inexpensive. The Pimento Cheese sandwiches which are so famous were only two dollars each, and chips and Cokes were a dollar each. It was a wonderful experience. And we found out that if you don't buy Masters gear at the Masters you don't have it because it is never sold online—only to those who get to go to the Masters. So we bought souvenirs and headed home. It was another great Bucket List adventure.

Chapter 42

An Out-of-This-World Adventure

Earlier in our marriage, while Kirs and Steve and Brian were still at home, we were invited to go to Australia in 1988 where our WIPB-TV team had traveled in 1987 to film my last TV documentary on Australian Aboriginal Rock Art. It was called *Australia's Art of the Dreamtime: Quinkin Country*. Our vacation was a wonderful two-week trip that included a stay at Jowalbinna (Aboriginal for "Dingo's ear"). Jowalbinna was Percy Trezise's Station (ranch) where he had twenty-five square miles of property he purchased which had a lot of the Aboriginal Art on it. So we stayed there for three days and saw some of the rock art, some of which is thousands of years old.

We were awakened every morning at 5:15 by the Kookaburra's, the (Australian Kingfishers) that do sound like they are laughing.

But waking up to their "laugh" is no laughing matter. Anyhow, we had great fun there, good food, and hot showers from the creek that ran through the camp. To take a hot shower, we had to light a wood fire under a fifty-five-gallon drum, put a hose in the river to draw up the water, and then the hot water would go up the hose into the shower heads and we had a warm shower. Kirs and Grandma had an interesting time keeping the shower curtains from blowing away and took turns showering and holding the curtains. But we had fun and an experience we would never forget. I think it was our best vacation ever.

From Percy's Station, we drove south through Surfers' Paradise, and then on to Port Macquarie where we attended the United Meeting Church where all the protestant church members meet weekly. When the Pastor asked for visitors who had come the farthest, we won the prize and had to stand up and introduce ourselves.

We told them we were from Indiana in the United States and said we hoped to see Koala's, but that none had been sighted. After church, a local Rotary member who oversaw the only Koala Hospital in the world, came up to us and said she was on her way to check on the Koala's at the hospital and asked if we would like to come along. We did, and we checked that box off. We got to spend an hour there with them. It was really fun.

Then we went on to Brisbane, the state capital of Queensland, Australia, where World Expo 88 was being held for six months. We just happened to be there at the right time. There, we were able to see for the first time on display, pictures and samples of the Terra Cotta Soldiers that had been discovered in Xi'an, China. What a bonus and a good sample of God's humor. He is always way ahead of us. We did get to go to China in 2018 and go to the excavations at Xi'an, and they were fabulous. There's much too much to tell about that and so many other trips Grandma and I have taken since our three children left home. But suffice it to say, our trip to China was a once-in-a-lifetime experience. We are so glad we went then, before Covid-19.

Last, we drove down to Sydney, went to the Opera House in Sydney Harbor and watched the first ever experience of seeing a Symphony in the Round. The entire chamber was paneled with Eucalyptus wood, and it had terrific acoustics. We sat behind the orchestra in the three rows of seats, directly facing the Conductor, and the Conductor led the entire ninety-minute performance with no sheet music. It was incredible. From there, we went to our hotel in the King's Cross section of Sydney. Kirs and Steve could tell you stories about their foray into that section of the city, later that evening, some, I suspect, we've never even heard. Little did we know until they came back, wide-eyed and ready to go to bed, that it was a pretty tawdry place. The next day, we all went to the Government Hall where our Documentary, *Australia's Art of the Dreamtime,* was to be premiered. The Premier we had planned in 1987, that we had traveled to Sydney for, from halfway around the world, did not happen. We were "pre-empted" by time and events that could not be foreseen.

The day before in Sydney, when we were in the Opera House, Australia's Prime Minister had announced that all parents of middle-school children would have to pay a fee for the first time to send their children to school. Subsequently, the day of our documentary premier, Sydney had the largest peacetime demonstration ever in the Government sector, and our building had guards all around it and the doors were chained shut. We were able to talk our way in through the back doors, but the expected attendance of the news reporters never materialized and only those from Australia who had participated in the making of the documentary were in attendance. We got almost zero publicity, and that fact made it very difficult to sell the documentary in Australia.

Ultimately, we did sell our documentary to all of the libraries in Australia, but none of the Australian TV networks would buy it because it was not one of their productions, and they had not partnered with us. So instead of selling it throughout Australia, we had to settle for selling it in 36 countries around the world and premiering it on half of the PBS stations in the US that received permission to broadcast it. The documentary on Aboriginal Art was given critical acclaim, but it did not generate the $100,000 we hoped for so that we could do another documentary. We had raised and spent almost $80,000. But our sales receipts were only $20,000. We had quite an adventure producing the documentary in the three weeks spent among the escarpments of the Cape York Peninsula of northeastern Australia with our 13-member team in September 1987, the year before. But while the experience was unique and notable and recognized as a success, it was the last documentary I ever did. What a memory.

Chapter 43

So How Does God Grow Faith in Him in Me?

When I recommitted my life to Jesus and put Him in charge on October 15, 1975, I was continuing to learn how to be a Christian where I would try all the time to do what Jesus would want me to do. That meant for me, I needed to grow in my faith. I knew I needed help.

Corrie TenBoom had been on my TV show in Indianapolis, and shortly after that, Jeanette Clift, the woman who played Corrie in *The Hiding Place* was in town for the film premier of Corrie's life story. Jeanette Clift had been cast in the part of Corrie, even though Jeanette was not a believer. When I learned that, something seemed odd to me.

Jeanette was agnostic—not sure Jesus was the only Son of God as He claimed. Because I had hosted Corrie on my TV show, I was invited to have dinner with Jeanette in early December before the Indianapolis premiere, and as we talked, I asked Jeanette how it had been for her, working with Corrie. She said Corrie was remarkable and as the filming moved forward in the year it took to create the extensive non-fiction story of Corrie's life, *The Hiding Place*, Jeanette found herself being drawn to what Corrie believed.

Ultimately, Jeanette decided she too wanted to trust God and put her life in His hands.

I asked Jeanette how she grew her faith—what was the secret—did Corrie give her advice? And she laughed and said shyly, "She was so helpful: when I asked Corrie the same question, Corrie's answer was for me to read Romans 10:17 and do what it says. You know what it says, don't you?" And without waiting for an answer, Jeanette continued, "Read God's words, and your faith will increase."

When you read His word (the Bible) and trust that God is speaking to you through those words, just ask Him to show you what He has for you that day, and He WILL show you," Jeanette continued. "Do that one day at a time, and your faith will grow—you'll learn all you need to know. I know that because that's what He did for me. He'll transform your life, one day at a time."

"God is always faithful," she reminded me. I listened to Jeanette, and decided I needed to read through the Bible for the very first time. Corrie had tutored Jeanette for the last year, and I knew I needed to be tutored too. I didn't really know what the Bible said about a lot of things, and I was eager to find out what God had for me.

Along the way which took me over a year, I came across the admonition to give a tithe of everything I earned, and I decided to do that. My first wife, Judy and I had never tithed, and we had always been in debt. My father always said you needed to have some debt so you would be sure to be motivated to go to work each day and earn a living.

As I read the Bible, I decided always being in debt wasn't the way I wanted to live my life—that God had something better in mind for me. So after that conversation with Jeanette, I wrote in my checkbook inside the check register where I would see it every time I wrote a check, these words: "Out of Debt in '76" and I prayed to God and asked Him to make it come true. I knew I couldn't afford to get out of debt in my present circumstances, but I never doubted that God could show me how if I was faithful to my promise to Him. It was December 1975. My life was changing.

I had never been without debt in my life since I started college, and I was ready to get rid of it. Believe it or not, being in debt is a heavy burden, and each month, it feels heavier. Only later, as my life unfolded in miraculous ways— the TV program as it continued, the conversation with my General Manager, my application to Ball State and WIPB, and the program about "I've found it...You can too" that my prospective employer saw and approved of...all of this came together in early May with a new job and salary!

By the time I got to December 1976, all my debt was paid off except for the new car I was driving, and I was "free" from the terror of the credit card bills that had piled up. I had been able to pay them all off! What a relief. What an answer to prayer. What a "Life full of surprises" I had experienced that year!

I was living beneath my means, and able to save and spend money without worrying if I could pay it off each month. And I decided I would pay my bills completely every month and not leverage the credit card debt by only paying the minimum payment. Frankly, that is one of the things that got me in trouble in the first place. No more! I made my decision: I would write my check to the church each month at the beginning of the month for ten percent of what I would be paid, and I would take God at His word: trust that He would provide and not let me down. And He did, big time! I discovered God is trustworthy, even in this. I was happy, and I was gradually and systematically climbing out of debt. What a journey. What a valuable lesson. What a wonderful, faithful Heavenly Father. Wow!

Chapter 44

My Family's Encounter
with God and Prayer

I will never forget in 1956 when my father had his first bout with Sciatica. Sciatica is the word used to label the sensations of *pain*, *numbness*, and or *weakness* felt in the leg that originates from the lower back and transitions through the buttocks and down the back of the leg. My dad was working at Sherwin Williams, and all of a sudden one day, he could not get out of bed. His back pain was so severe, he couldn't even walk into the bathroom. I remember him crawling into the bathroom from the bedroom so he could go to the toilet, and how he moaned when he crawled! It was awful, and he couldn't go to work. I don't remember all the circumstances, but I know we were worried we wouldn't be able to pay our bills. Medical care wasn't like it is today, and we were all worried. He wasn't himself, and he just laid in bed, day after day. It lasted about a month until one of his friends suggested he see a Chiropractor. We had never even heard of a Doctor of Chiropractic, and my parents were skeptical. But we finally called the Offices of the Palmer Method Chiropractic Center in Harvey, Illinois, and one of the doctors said he could make a house call using a folding Treatment Table.

On the day the doctor was coming, my mother and dad asked us all, as a family, to come into the bedroom after my dad's weeks in bed and get down on our knees around his bed and together, pray that God would somehow make my father better. We prayed to God that the chiropractor could help in some way so my dad could go back to work again. I remember crying. I was twelve, my sisters were four and eight, and my brother was fourteen. We had never done this before. Nonetheless, we all got down on our knees and prayed for my father and that God would somehow miraculously heal him. We didn't even know what to pray for, but most of all, we prayed that my dad would get better. I guess we were really asking God for a miracle, though we didn't think of it that way. We just hoped something good would come from the doctor's visit. We didn't have long to wait.

The next thing we knew, the chiropractor was knocking on our front screen door. He had a brown, padded cube the size of a small portable refrigerator, maybe eighteen inches square, that he carried into the front room. He was a kindly man and quietly introduced himself. He sat down and talked with my mother for a few minutes as we all watched from the doorway. Then, he carefully moved the coffee table aside and set up his portable table. It unfolded and made a bed about eighteen inches wide by eighteen inches high, by five feet long, and then he went into the bedroom to talk with my father. We were all watching to see what he would do, and we were praying that maybe this man would be the answer to our prayers.

After my father talked with the Chiropractor, the Doctor asked him to come into the living room where he had set up the portable table. My dad said he couldn't walk because the pain was too sharp. So he crawled from his bedroom next to the living room and made it to the side of the Doctor's "portable table." The Chiropractor then asked my dad to pull himself up on this narrow table, and my dad did his best with the doctor—lifting him into position. Finally, my father was there on his stomach. As we watched, the Doctor touched my father's back with his fingers, beginning at his neck and moving gently down my dad's bare back. My dad moaned again and again, at each touch. Sometimes, he whimpered in pain. Then the doctor twisted my father's back a couple of times, twisted his head, and my father groaned again. He groaned again and again—the pain was so sharp, we winced! We watched and cried through our hope.

As we watched, the doctor touched my father again and again, noting where the pain was worst. The Doctor said, "I think we can help you, Fred. Just relax as much as you can." Then the Doctor began to manipulate my father's legs and arms and lean down on him. Usually, my father would groan. And after doing this maybe twenty times, the doctor, asked, "How does that feel, Fred?"

And my dad groaned: "I think it's a little bit better." The Chiropractor went through the same process again, focusing on where in my dad's back, the pain was greatest. Finally, he took my father's legs and holding them, from the ankles, he jerked them slightly. I think we heard a pop. He did it again, and then he moved to my dad's head and did the same with his arms. Again, there was a little pop. He then asked my dad if he felt a little better.

Slowly but surely, as he repeated this process, in the next twenty minutes, my father was groaning less and breathing better.

After that, he said to my father. "I would like to see you in my office again next Monday. I thought, "Did the doctor say what I thought he said?"

And then the doctor said to my father, "Please get some sleep, start eating better, and I'll see you next Monday, early in the afternoon.

Then the Chiropractor asked, "Fred, can you make it back into your bedroom?"

"I don't know," my dad barely whispered. "I don't know if I can walk or not."

The Chiropractor answered with assurance: "Fred, I'm going to help you walk back into your bedroom. You're going to be able to do that alright, and I'm going to put my arm around you and help you, and although you may feel some pain, I think you may be pleasantly surprised at what has just happened."

And then, the doctor helped my father sit up for the first time in a month and swing his legs over the side of the portable table. For a few moments, my father just sat there, upright for the first time in what seemed like forever, and ever so slowly, he leaned forward and put his arms around the Chiropractor's neck. The next thing we saw was my father, ever so gingerly, standing up. We were crying. I can still see him standing there for the first time in so long. And the Chiropractor said slowly and quietly, "Are you okay, Fred?" And my father nodded.

And with the help of the doctor, he haltingly walked back into his bedroom, and the tears fell down our cheeks as we thanked God for the miracle we had just seen. Don't ever tell me God doesn't answer prayers. How would we even know to call a Doctor of Chiropractic we had never even heard of and ask him to come and help our dad to walk when we had all seen him crawl to the bathroom again and again, and saw each other's pain, and his grimace and groans as he tried to get back and forth? Why am I crying as I write this to you? Only because I know it is true, and I will always remember and always thank God that I saw what He did for us that day. Miracles happen every day, and our job is to recognize them and call them what they are...the hand of God in our everyday affairs.

Even as I edit this for the last time and read the words, I cry. The memory is so vivid! I will never forget that moment and that breakthrough in my faith walk—God does heal!

From then on, I have always known that God can heal, and that He hears and answers prayers, though not always as quickly as He answered this one or in the way we expect.

Don't ever doubt that God does answer prayers, in His way, in His time. He hears you when you pray, and when you decide to trust Him.

I have never forgotten this. And I can tell by the tears that have stained my pants today as I sit at the computer, and that are just as real now as they were then, that seeing this miracle changed me. I think it changed each of us. Thanks be to God. My dad lived another forty-three years, most of them good, healthy years, and he and my mother were able to become missionaries twenty-six years later in their late sixties, and go to Utila, Honduras as healthy missionaries to fight the battle of the school board that wouldn't speak to them and kept them waiting three months. With their faith that God sent them to Utila, my parents fought the battle with the minister who met them at the plane and told them, "Go home! We don't need you or want you!"

With their faith, they fought the battle with Mr. Duncan, their contractor on Utila. When they had purchased the land near the soccer field, that spring, when they went home to raise more operating funds, they gave Mr. Duncan $5,000 and the plans for the school so while they were gone, he would spend that money pouring concrete for the in-ground cistern under the school and the concrete foundation for the school building.

When they returned to the island after the summer, they were jolted as they discovered that Brad Duncan had "invested" their money in a "sure-thing" gambling scheme and lost it all trying to double the $5,000 US dollars in a "get rich quick scheme. When they arrived, Mr. Duncan admitted he had no money and no in-ground cistern or first-floor foundation poured at all. In fact, he had nothing but an apology for losing their $5,000.

But my parents would not give up on the dream God had given them. My parents had to start saving from their meager retirement funds again and begin all over, this time without Brad Duncan. What a painful, difficult lesson.

We only heard about Brad Duncan secondhand. I cannot imagine how frustrating and disappointing it must have been to hear it for the first time from this person they had befriended and trusted to create the concrete foundation for the school—only to find that no work on the school had begun, and the money was gone.

But they did not give up. Neither did my dad give up after a month of crawling back and forth to the bathroom. Praise God for their faith and their faithfulness. My dad did get well, though he went to Chiropractors the rest of his life, about once every other week. By doing that, he was able to live virtually pain-free, and tell others about the value of having an "Adjustment" regularly to get rid of the Sciatic pain and be able to work and live a relatively healthy life, in spite of the pinched nerve in his crooked back that caused that pain.

You've already read about the success of Utila Methodist Community College. Ultimately, the school was a big success, and as my parents would say if they were writing this: "To God be the Glory for the things HE has done!"

One other story from Utila, and we'll move on. I recruited and organized three High Street Mission trips to Honduras and the island of Utila. During the last one when we finished building the on-campus Teacher's Residence, we were trying to secure the small residence and put a door on it so no one on that poor island would steal the plumbing and the wiring we had just installed before the next work team came. We were warned by the islanders that things we installed would likely disappear if we left the building unlocked, so there was concern and we were doing what we could to get the house enclosed and secure. But there were serious problems, and we didn't know how to solve them. Let me explain.

When we arrived on the island to build the one-story Teacher's Residence, we only had the 12-inch diameter PVC pipes in the ground full of concrete which we had buried in the ground and filled with concrete the summer before. They were installed to elevate the one-level platform about 6 feet above ground so the moving air would keep it as cool as possible. There was always a breeze, but to keep the house dry, one had to build it on the 12-feet long PVC stilts we had buried six feet down in the dirt. Collectively, they were heavier than the house, and they would help it to withstand hurricane winds which it would see over its lifetime. On those concrete-filled pipes, we would build our 1,000 square foot, stick-built house, and it would help us subsidize the salary of the Principal who would live on the school property and provide on-site security for our school building by her presence there.

On our 2000 summer mission trip, at the end, not needing all the PVC we had purchased from the local lumber yard, we gave back the leftover 12 PVC pipes to the lumber yard that sold them to us, and they said they would try to sell them before we returned. When we got back in June 2001, they had not sold even one of them, so they gave us a $400 credit and ordered a solid Mahogany front door, which we needed to lock up the house. Since the door and the lock would cost us $600, we paid the $200 difference, and the door was ordered immediately.

The lumber company there on the island promised they could have the solid Mahogany door produced and back to us in two weeks so that we could lock up the house and protect all the interior furnishings we installed while we were there. That would allow us to have peace of mind when we flew out at 6 AM on the final Saturday of our two-week visit, and the house would not be stripped before the next mission team arrived from Louisiana at six that evening. It is amazing what people will steal when they know that no one is around to observe them. The islanders are very poor, and electrical and plumbing materials are very expensive for people that have very low incomes and great needs. And because it is very small, everyone knows what everyone else is doing.

So we prayed, and we prayed, and we prayed. One of the Board members told me not to press the lumber company owner too hard as he was related to the criminal elements on the island. They told me to just keep nudging him by visiting each day and asking how it was coming. Before long, we were in the second week, the door had not arrived, and there seemed to be little progress.

"Oh, it should be here in a day or two," the Lumbar Company Manager would say. And I would thank him and ask him to call and see if he could get them to speed up the delivery so we would get the door in time. I had been going to see him every day he was open since the middle of the first week when we made the deal, and he said he would have it by that Friday. Friday came and went, and no door came over on the Ferry. Saturday passed—no door. Sunday, he wasn't open. Monday—no word yet. He said he was encouraged it would arrive on Tuesday. But Tuesday came and went—no door. On Wednesday, he said they had run into a problem, and he wasn't sure the door would be finished in time.

Late that Wednesday afternoon, I was sitting on the front porch of the Mission House where all of the men were staying and where all of our Mission Team meals were served. I had run out of options and was depressed because of the roadblock we had encountered and did not know how to overcome. It was almost dinner time, and I found myself sitting alone on the front porch, facing the six-foot high concrete wall that surrounded the Utila Mission House, my eyes closed, rocking slowly by myself and praying.

I didn't even know what to pray for. I was broken! Utila Methodist Church volunteers were making dinner inside, our team members were relaxing and chatting about the day, and I was sitting there, all alone, rocking and praying with my eyes shut, and hands folded, saying over and over again, "Jesus, Jesus, Jesus! Jesus, Jesus, Jesus!" I was praying and trying to figure out in my own mind how to get the door back from the mainland in time for us to take off on Saturday and leave the Teacher's Residence secure.

All of a sudden, the large metal gate of the Mission House enclosure, clanged open. In shock, I opened my eyes and looked up. A man I had never seen before, belted out, "Jim! Jim Needham?" This tall, square-shouldered man leading the small group of Americans walked in, smiling and boldly approached me.

I was startled but answered, "Yes, I'm Jim Needham. Who are you?"

And he laughed loudly and said, "Didn't mean to scare you. I'm Tal, Tal Lanius from Baton Rouge, Louisiana. We're here early! Glad to meet you. How are you doing?"

And I blurted out the sordid truth! "I'm terrible! The lumber yard hasn't gotten us the door from the mainland like they promised, and we won't be able to lock up the Teacher's Residence before we leave this Saturday…" I stopped talking, just beginning to realize what was happening. "What are you doing here? It's only Wednesday!"

They were all gathering around and introducing themselves. Some of them laughed when I said, "Terrible!"

Not Tal!

So Tal asked, "What is so terrible? What's the situation with the door?"

I told him, and he turned to one of his team members and said, "What are you doing tomorrow."

The fellow next to Tal had been listening in, and he said, "Me and Al are going over to LaCeiba on the 6:00 AM Ferry in the morning, and we're not coming back until we have that door in our hands. We have nothing better to do, and it sounds like that's what we would love to do. Right?"

"The fellow next to him said, "Sure thing. Love to do that. Count me in." And right then, right now, my "Jesus" prayer was answered. I just shook my head.

The door would be brought back on Friday at noon, we would take off Saturday morning at six, safe and knowing the Teacher's Residence was secure along with its electrical and plumbing installations. And the Teacher's Residence would be completed before Tal and his team finished up their work the next week.

We were all surprised, as you would have been. I had never met Tal Lanius, a friendly, God-fearing dentist from Louisiana, but he knew my parents, had brought work teams before, and was an answer to a prayer that we would never have known we could pray. But then, God is omniscient— He knows everything. Why was I surprised?

For reasons unknown, the Baton Rouge work team all changed their tickets two weeks earlier and decided to come to the island three days early. They never did give us the reason for that, but they came early, they were there, we celebrated and thanked God for his provision and for solving this "unsolvable" problem, and went home happy, confident that God, not only was in this, but was able and willing to answer our prayers, even when we didn't know what to ask for. Truly, we learned, God is sovereign in all our affairs. Sometimes, we just have to be jolted into that reality by surprises only God can stage, like he did that day.

The reason Mission trips are so powerful for those who volunteer to help this way, is that on every single one I have been on, something happens, and the only solution is to pray and ask God to help us do whatever we encounter that cannot be done. Then, as we keep moving forward, praying and trusting in Him, something occurs that is not expected or often, impossible, and the situation is resolved and glorifies Him.

That has happened on every mission trip I have ever been on. So while this was unexpected, what happened was part of the rhythm of a mission trip where God is lifted up, praised, and an active participant. Thank you, God, for this "small miracle" that we were all allowed to witness and praise You for. It was just what we needed and right on time. No one who was on that trip missed the majesty of that moment or would ever forget what You did that day.

Chapter 45

Life After Life—You're Kidding, of Course?

One other event, back in the fall of 1974, is impossible to forget! I was busy working at WISH-TV and had added an Assistant Community Affairs Director, Hallie Crombaugh, to our staff. She was the Indianapolis Head Start Coordinator, and we were happy to have her on board. We were sitting in our office one morning, watching an interview on our morning show, *Indy Today,* and hosts Wally and Natalie Bruner were talking with a guest about near-death experiences.

Raymond Moody was a medical doctor who had been studying near-death experiences, and he had just published his first book, *Life After Life.* As I watched, I began to laugh and scoff at what he was saying. I remarked to Hallie that his stories were really bogus, not grounded in reality at all. I said I thought he had just made them up to sell his book.

After a few minutes of this, Hallie commented quietly to me. "I don't think they're bogus or made up. That happened to me when I was fifteen and having kidney surgery. I died on the table, and it took the surgical team twenty minutes to get my heart started again. So I know that happens! My future husband was out in the hall and later in the hospital chapel praying for me, and I was hovering above the operation and the doctors and nurses working on me and watching what they were doing and listening to their conversation.

Hallie continued: "When I told them what they were talking about and what they were doing later, after I had been revived, one of them said, 'You couldn't know that. That's when we were trying to bring you back.'"

So Hallie concluded, "If you think Dr. Moody is bogus, go down and talk to him. I know that happens, sometimes." I left the office and went down to the studio and watched him finish the interview on the set. When I talked with him afterward, I became convinced that what Dr. Moody reported is what he had experienced with his patients. He was authentic. Why had I never heard of this before?

From that day to this, I believe near-death experiences are happening all the time, and most people won't reveal them for fear they will be mocked or made fun of, or that people won't believe them. I suppose when you look at the way I first reacted, I can see why people won't talk about this very personal, intimate experience that they themselves, aren't sure happened or they aren't comfortable revealing.

This is why I have recommended several books below, that focus on what God is allowing us to witness. If you go to YouTube, you will find many testimonies of people who have had these experiences and lived to tell about them. I have met several of them myself and am convinced from their accounts that what they describe as happening to them, really happened. They were really in heaven, if only for a few moments.

Hallie Crombaugh was the first person I ever talked with about this. Raymond Moody was the second. Don Piper of *90 Minutes in Heaven* was the third. Dr. Mary Neal was the fourth, in her book *To Heaven and Back: A Doctor's Extraordinary Account of Her Death, Heaven, Angels, and Life Again*. Many more books are just as compelling. My most recent read is John Burke's *Imagine Heaven: Near-Death Experiences, Gods Promises, and the Exhilarating Future*

That Awaits You. The most riveting book I've read about near-death experiences was made into a popular movie: *Heaven Is for Real*, written by *Pastor* Todd Burpo. His son, Colton Burpo, had his near-death experience when he was three years and nine months old. And the media has interviewed him numerous times over Colton's last nineteen years. He continues to appear on YouTube videos and is now twenty-three years old. His interviews are amazing. Finally, there's Dr. Chauncey Crandall's *Raising the Dead: A Doctor Encounters the Miraculous.*

Just a note: Todd Burpo's book is better than the movie, which doesn't quite mirror the accuracy of the book. So I would start by reading *Heaven Is for Real* by Todd Burpo.

And so it goes.

Most of these testimonies are now available as YouTube interviews and are incredibly compelling. If you really have doubts that God is real and alive, watch and listen to their interviews, what they say, and how they say it. In my mind, that leaves little room for doubt that God is allowing these glimpses for His reasons to prepare us for what is coming next. Many scholars believe Paul's reference in 2 Corinthians 12 where Paul claimed he knew a person who, fourteen years before, was caught up to the third heaven is a reference to Paul's own experience. The Bible does not tell us that, but it sounds to me similar to the near-death experiences that are now ubiquitous on YouTube; and for those who have them, they cannot be refuted, once they have been experienced.

Chapter 46

The Incredible Woman Who Had Ninety-Nine Kids— What Could I Learn?

One other incident happened right before Linda and I were married. I was coming back from a PBS meeting in Arizona and our plane was twenty-first in line for take-off from O'Hare in Chicago. The Captain made the announcement, telling us it would probably be about an hour before our turn to take off came, and knowing that in those kinds of situations, people either chat with each other about nothing, or they sometimes talk about real issues, I decided to try a little experiment...

Our plane was an older commuter jet with only one seat on each side of the aisle, and perhaps, twenty-six seats overall, so it was really intimate, and everyone was close. Being ever-curious and having an interesting situation with a plane full of potential counselors, I quietly asked, rather randomly, "In about a month, I'm getting married to a widow who has three small children. Does anyone have any great advice for me that would help me be a good dad? I've never been a father before." Everybody laughed! Then the silence closed in again, and I opened my briefcase and began to shuffle papers. After about five minutes, the old woman in the seat just in front of me, loosened her seatbelt and turned partially around. She smiled and said quietly, "Well, I have had 99 children; maybe I could give you a wee bit of advice."

I craned my neck and looked around the seat at her, hoping to not appear disbelieving. She looked to be of normal size, and I said, foolishly, "Well, for ninety-nine children, you look terrific. What's your secret?"

And she laughed out loud. "Oh no!" she said. "You don't understand. I had five of my own, and over the years, we had ninety-four Foster Children. I'm on my way to visit my son who is an architecture professor at Ball State." Then she paused and collected her thoughts.

She continued, "My name is Mona Adams. We quickly learned that lots of rules were not the answer, and that the fewer rules we had, the more likely they were to remember them and the harder it was for them to claim they had 'forgotten' the rules!"

"That makes sense," I agreed. "So how many rules did you have?"

"Just one," she countered. "Just one! And it was this: 'If what you're about to do hurts you or hurts us, then it's wrong and we'll be upset with you for what you did or whatever it was you were thinking about doing."

I said, "Well, that's pretty easy..." and Mona added: "And when that's the ONLY RULE, you can't say you can't remember it. It's simple and to the point: If it hurts them or hurts us, then it's wrong, period! Don't do it."

"So were there any other rules?" I asked.

"No, that was it!" Mona smiled. "But there were other guidelines we kept to, that helped our kids stay in line."

Curious to know what they had figured out, I continued: "What else did you do?"

Mona began again, "You have to know that 'more is caught than taught.' If they don't see you doing what you're asking them to do, they never get it, and they don't know how to evaluate whether it's gonna hurt them or hurt you, so this is critically important: 'you gotta walk the talk.' You have to do what you expect them to do. If you do that, they'll see you leading by example, and it'll sink in."

"Is there anything else, you haven't told me, that will help?" I quizzed her.

"Yes, and this is the hardest part of raising children that you love. You want them to succeed and be happy, but there's a price you have to pay for that to happen: later on, they grow up and you aren't with them, and you may not even be with them nearly as much as earlier, and you won't be there to monitor their behavior or help them out of jams. All they'll have to go on is what they remember from what you've said and the example you've set."

"And at that time, your job is to pray for them and to 'let go and let God do the rest,'" Mona added. "You have to trust that God can take their lives from there, and when you see them, embrace them and tell them you're proud of them and you love them. They will mess up some, as we all have, but in the end, if you do these things, we've seen, when they grow up, they will be more like you than unlike you. And you and they will be grateful to God that you were and are a part of their lives."

I thanked Mona as we began to taxi up the runway. It was an incredible clinic on what to do and what not to do. And I thanked God for putting Mona Adams in the seat just in front of me with a lifetime of experiences to share with a neophyte father like me. I didn't do exactly as she said, but Mona's wisdom has accompanied me throughout the last 45 years, and Linda and I have always tried to lead by example and to love you who are our children, you who are our grandchildren, and "you who have been adopted into our family in our informal way: all of you whom we love and for whom we want the best that life has to offer you."

As you can guess, this also carries over to what we believe and to leading you to be involved in our church life, in our daily prayers dealing with everyday events, difficulties, and triumphs, and before each meal—wherever we are—where in our minds, Jesus is the most important guest at our table. As you've been with us on more than one occasion, you know we pray, regardless of where we are or who is looking on. Our prayers are not for show— your parents will tell you that our prayers are our intimate way of thanking God for all He has given us—which includes you—and for all we have received from God—for every generous gift we have been given.

We hope we have done the right thing, but Mona was correct: The hardest part of being a parent, and Kirs and Eric, Steve and Staci, and Brian and Jennifer—you are all there now, and you who are grandchildren, and the six of you we have mentored and loved as our own, are already standing, or soon will stand on the Podium and be there yourselves—if God blesses you with children—the hardest part IS the third element—"letting go and Letting God do the rest." When you set your children free, you have to trust that they are in God's hands and that He will protect them and guide them because of the knowledge and convictions you have communicated to them through your beliefs, your love, and your consistent example.

Chapter 47

Crutches, Wheelchairs, Canes—Everywhere

When I was sixteen, my family went to Canada on vacation. There is one place we visited that I have never forgotten: the Basilica of St. Anne-de-Beaupre.

This is a moderate-sized basilica located along the St. Lawrence River about 19 miles east of Quebec City, Quebec. When we saw it, only one of the two bell towers had been completed. It was 1960. Years later, I found an updated picture that shows both towers having been completed. When we visited there, what struck me most was the sight that confronted all who enter the Narthex.

There on the walls, reaching to the ceiling, are hundreds of crutches, wheelchairs, canes, and all manner of mechanical devices used by crippled people who have visited there with their infirmities, and left there, healed, leaving their devices behind as silent testimonies to the miracles they were part of.

That still strikes me as a very Holy and special place. When we asked the Nuns why people leave their devices after being healed, they said it was a testimony to the love of God. I can't think of any other reason for them, and I know it so impressed me that as I write this here today, I can still see the crutches and wheelchairs and canes and braces as if I were standing there for the first time. What a loud, compelling testimony that still resonates within me sixty years later. If you have never visited that basilica, it is worth the effort and the trip. Once you see it, what you see there will never leave you. It is truly a Holy place. Does everyone who goes there and prays, receive healing? I don't know. Does it matter? It matters for all those who are healed! And for all who come later and observe the evidence, what does THAT tell us? Some are still being healed. What does that tell us?

Chapter 48

Bible Roulette

Have you ever heard of the game Bible Roulette? I did it with a yellow pages phone directory when I was traveling in Massachusetts and far from home. You know, you open the phone directory, and you pray and say, "Lord, where should I go to church tomorrow?" And then you take the pen in your hand (at least we did when we had paper directory books) and you close your eyes with your Phone Directory Book open to the pages with Churches, and you plunge it down to where it strikes the page. Then you open your eyes and look at the church where you will be going.

That is exactly what I did when I was staying in Waltham, Massachusetts in April 1978 and attending the Harvard University Graduate School's Advanced Management Seminar for new PBS managers, of which I was the youngest. I was thirty-four years old and scared to death because of Harvard's storied history and the way they challenge their students—some of the most highly ranked students in America.

Remember, I went to Indiana State University, a little school of five thousand students when I started. At Harvard, I was definitely thinking "I'm in over my head," or at least I was about to be very seriously challenged and knew I'd have to really focus to be able to take advantage of all the teaching we would receive during the two weeks of intensive classes.

What I did not focus on was that I was not alone—that God was with me, even in this, and the Bible Roulette I played on that first Sunday, following the first week of classes, punctuated what I had learned with this reminder from God: "The Lord, the Sovereign Lord is in charge, Jim. Do you remember? And if you don't, you need to re-learn that again today" (Jeremiah 29:11–13). God allows us to fulfill His purposes. So what happened? It wasn't accidental, was it?

Back to my Roulette! The church I spiked with my ball point pen was the United Methodist Church of Waltham, Massachusetts. It was a very old church, very traditional in its architecture. It was about two miles from where I was staying, and I got up early so I could be on time. I arrived about 8:45 for the 9:00 AM service, and when I got there and parked my rental car, I was amazed to see that all the doors and windows were wide open, and the lights were on. However, no one was there. The parking places were empty, and no one seemed to be there. I sat there in my car for a moment, and then decided to go in anyway.

When I entered the front door, it led directly into the sanctuary, and it was a beautiful, but very old church, with all wooden pews, I'm guessing 150 years old. It seated maybe 250 persons, and had doors exiting to the back, probably to Sunday School rooms or a Fellowship Hall, but no one was there. So I called out: "Hallo! Hallo! [louder] Is anyone here?"

The silence was deafening. I walked down the aisle toward the altar, and was ready to call out again, when an old woman in a suit, stepped into the sanctuary and called out to me from the other side, "Over here... Welcome! Glad to see you. Let me come and meet you. I'm Pastor Jeanette McGlinchy, and you're the first to arrive this morning. How are you?"

I said, "I'm fine. My name is Jim Needham, and I came to go to church, but obviously I got it wrong. I read in the Phone book that your services began at 9:00 AM, but there's no one here. What time is church?"

Pastor McGlinchy had an easy laugh and she cackled as she chortled, "Well, we don't change the time in the phone book every six months, so it's right half the year and wrong half the year. Why don't I get you some coffee and show you our church? Are you from around here?"

I told her what I was doing in town and how I had found her church, and when we walked through the balcony, she told me that very balcony was where their high school class met for Sunday School, but that this week, the teacher was absent, so they wouldn't have a class unless someone showed up to teach it. I swear—that's what she said.

She said she and her late husband who had been assigned to this church for many years before he passed away two years earlier, had always hoped that having a high school class would substitute for a Young Life club in Waltham, but no one seemed to know what Young Life would be like, so it was really hard to get it started. In spite of that, she continued to hope there might one day be a Young Life Club in Waltham. When her husband died, since she was also ordained, the Bishop asked if she wanted to stay on and serve as the pastor. It made the transition easier for her and for her congregation. So that's exactly what she did.

My eyes were opening up to what I had "stumbled" into. You already know, don't you?

I laughed and told Pastor McGlinchy, "Until last year, I had been a Young Life leader in three different High Schools back in Indiana. Would you like me to teach the class today and tell them about Young Life?" The gleam in her eye and smile was all it took to know I was teaching. She and her husband had financially supported Young Life for many years, but they never were able to get someone who knew how, to start a club in town. So while they continued to send money and ask people to help, it never came about.

And then, this stranger from Muncie, Indiana shows up and offers to teach the high school class, and he not only knows about Young Life but was a Young Life leader. What an answer to many, many prayers over how many years? Only Pastor McGlinchy would know that, and I'm sure she never counted.

So I thought to myself, "I'm not here by accident. This is another one of those Divine appointments." And indeed, it was. The second Saturday, after the Harvard Seminar was over, I was invited to stay at the Parsonage since my room stay ended Saturday morning. That night, I went to a Candlepins bowling party and pizza dinner with everyone. The High School class teacher was there, and he invited me to come back the next day—my final day in town—answer questions, and tell more stories about Young Life and what it was like and how they could get it started.

I never followed up with them to see what happened, but I will always be grateful that when I plunged the "'dagger' into the phone book," it struck Pay Dirt! Big-time. It wasn't an accident I wanted to go to church. It wasn't an accident I was an hour early and got the tour of the church with the Pastor. It wasn't an accident she told me about her dream that had never been fulfilled or about her prayers for Young Life, nor was it an accident that the teacher was not there that first week and they didn't have a substitute.

There were too many coincidences for this to be merely a "coincidence!" It was indeed a Divine Appointment. And as you have read elsewhere, I've encountered many of these. God has thrown so many of these "curve balls" at me that I cannot waive them away and say, "Awe, that was only a coincidence." I just can't say that anymore.

I can't help it! God grabs my attention in everything I do. I see His face everywhere. I see His fingerprints. I even hear Him calling my name to do things I can't understand, but I know He is (what the Bible tells me) "The author and perfector of our faith" (Hebrews 12:2) and having read His word from start to finish four times, now working on five, I can testify that again and again, the Holy Spirit calls to my mind whatever it is He wants me to remember at appropriate times, and to the chagrin of those who see me as being preachy sometimes, and overzealous, my excuse is "I only say what He gives me to say."

I believe our job as Christians is to scatter the seeds. God determines if the soil is rocky, or the soil is a thin, well-worn path, or the soil is good soil and that it always is true that the Holy Spirit's job is to harvest the wheat, not mine. My job is to plant the seeds and remember that the Bible tells us that "No one calls Jesus 'Lord,' except the Holy Spirit draws him or her to Him!" (1 Cor. 12:3). It's not my job to count noses of those who choose Jesus—as one of my friends reminds me, "God's got that!"

Chapter 49

You Scream; I Scream—
We All Scream

My third cousin, once removed, Bill, a dentist in town, died at the age of seventy-three. He was a wonderful dentist here in Muncie, and while he never attended my Sunday School Class, his wife was in my Wesley Class at High Street Methodist Church where I taught the elderly for twenty-six years.

After her husband's untimely death, I visited her a number of times to talk and play the card game, Flinch, with her. When I asked what happened to him, she unabashedly told me, "I killed him!" I said, "What? Don't say that. What do you mean?"

And she continued. "As a dentist, he had always been very disciplined. Yet when he retired at sixty-five, he decided he would like to add desert to his evening meals, something he had always avoided for most of his adult life." So every evening, after dinner, he asked his wife to provide him with a cereal bowl of the highest fat vanilla ice cream with chocolate sauce. And she did what he asked.

After a couple of years, she told me, she noticed that he was beginning to forget simple things, and that he occasionally would slur his words. By the time he was sixty-nine, his memory was definitely impaired, and he was needing help getting around. To help him, they got him a wheelchair. By the time he was seventy-one, it was clear that he was suffering from Dementia, and could no longer walk. Bill had to constantly use his wheelchair, and, she told me, "We got a device to lift him off his chair and help him in the bathroom, and all the while, he insisted he have his favorite desert— that dish of vanilla ice cream with chocolate sauce." By the time Bill died at seventy-three, he was totally incapacitated and could no longer speak.

His daughters, shocked by the speed of his decline, asked that the family have an autopsy conducted. When the results came in, they got the surprise of their lives. Bill did not have Alzheimer's or Dementia. He had severe Atherosclerosis of the arteries of his brain and died because the fat and plaque in his brain that accumulated from the rich ice cream, clogging his arteries and killing him. Bill's is a tragic story, but his two daughters wanted to know so they could have a better idea of what to expect in their own lives. Little did they suspect, and little did his wife think that what she was doing in giving him the desert he asked for, was actually killing him. As she sadly admitted later, she never realized what was happening. But knowing this is something for all of us to ponder.

Chapter 50

Spiritual Gifts

Please read 1 Cor. 12 and 1 Cor. 13 for the Biblical explanation of Spiritual Gifts. That's truly the only way to understand what I am talking about in this chapter. The American Heritage College Dictionary defines *Charismatic* as "of or relating to, or being a type of Christianity that emphasizes personal religious experience and divinely inspired powers." By now, you must know that I believe that God does interact with those of us who have asked Jesus to be Lord of our lives, who worship Him, and pray to Him, and expect Him to hear and respond to our prayers. I am definitely one of those persons.

When I first met Linda, she said she was part of a Bible Study. She didn't tell me it was a Charismatic Bible study— just that she was in a women's Bible study. And if she had told me that, I would have been skeptical. I didn't believe in speaking in tongues, and although Paul writes that he spoke in tongues, he said it was not one of the greater gifts. But Linda believed in that empowerment of the Holy Spirit, and honestly, I did not.

I was quickly pointed to this scripture: 1 Cor. 14:27, "If anyone speaks in a tongue, two—or at the most three— should speak, one at a time, and someone must interpret."

It was clear to me immediately that this was something I had never read before or at least that had not registered with me.

To become a part of what Linda was doing, we started attending the Community of Praise services on Thursday evenings at St. Mary's Catholic Church's Community Hall in Muncie. I loved the singing, and the teaching, but I was a bit put off by those who spoke in tongues and also those who interpreted. I did not believe in that, nor had I ever experienced that and never had I been present when that happened.

I was afraid tongues could be a barrier between us, but I never talked with Linda about that. I just prayed about it, and asked God to show me if that was from Him, and how I should respond to that. One night, after months of attending the Community of Praise celebration services, as I was sitting downstairs alone, reading my Bible in the family room in our house on Queensbury, I closed my eyes and prayed that if God was in this—if the gift of tongues was a gift from Him, I asked if He would show me so I could understand Linda and what was happening.

And all of a sudden, I was praying in a language I had never learned, and was lifting my hands up, and thanking God that He was answering my prayer, right then, right there. And the tears began to fall.

I rushed up the stairs, excited at what had just happened, and told Linda. God had given me HIS prayer language, not to abuse it or lord it over others who did not exhibit it, but to understand that it was a gift that only He can give, and that it was real, and I should not be afraid.

Since then, I rarely rise to that level, but I know it is real, and I do not disparage those who have been given that legitimate gift. I think I am more of a teacher than a prayer warrior. But I know God is real in my life, and that in the midst of times when I have no way of knowing what to pray for, and there are still many of these, I sometimes move to

His prayer language and thank Him for His answers, His perspective, and His Peace, and plan for the moment and the way forward. It's a wonderful way to rely wholly on God and His promises.

Recently, a very dear friend sent me a card and asked: "What does FROG stand for?"

I had no idea, but she proceeded to answer that: FROG stands for "Fully Rely on God!"

Do I do that? "Yes! I do!" As often as I get in a jam and know I need His answer to deal with a situation that is unexpected, or to which I have no answer. The rest of the time, I hope I'm praying and thanking God for whatever it is He's placed in front of me—the blessings without number that, too often, I only count in retrospect.

Later that same year, as we were getting into living as a family, we were at Dr. John Klem's house, having a little party after the Thursday evening Community of Praise meeting at the church. As we mingled, John called out for those who needed and wanted prayer, and I raised my hand. The room quieted, and John asked: "What can we pray for you, Jim?"

And I said, "I am in the process of being an instant father to three children I dearly love. Pray that I will be able to be a good father for them, and I will learn and be willing to learn to do what it is they need, to love them in the way God wants me to love them, and to have the wisdom of God as we make decisions and take steps to knit our family together into the family God wants it to be. Help me to know what Wisdom means to God and help me to employ it always to benefit my wife and our family."

The next thing I knew, all those in the room were reaching out and laying their hands on me and on Linda as John began to pray there in John's living room. And they all prayed silently as John prayed aloud for the Lord to give us wisdom. Only our children and God will be able to say if that happened. I believe that God, in His providence, answered that prayer.

My hope and my prayer is that they have seen God's wisdom acted out in our lives, and in the love we continue to give them in every circumstance. And that they may see by our example, the fruit of that prayer, offered as a sacrifice to God on our behalf, so many years ago.

Chapter 51

Dieting—Do We Know
What We're Doing?

When my mother moved to Muncie and to Westminster Village in 2004, I went to give blood as I often did, and the Phlebotomist refused to take my blood. She said my blood pressure was too high at 205/105. I said I had never had this problem before, and I'd wait a few minutes and then take my blood pressure again.

She waited, and my blood pressure was even higher. I said I have never had blood pressure problems before and asked what I should do. She suggested I call my doctor. When I called and talked to his nurse, he called me back in five minutes and said he had already ordered a prescription for me and I should call him after I had it filled and took my first set of pills. That my doctor himself had called me back with these urgent instructions, scared me. I was in trouble.

After we got that settled down, I went to the hospital to get a Cardiolite Stress Test and they told me I had Left Bundle Branch Block or LBBB. They said I should not worry about it, but I wanted to know what was going on, so I scheduled a sixty-four-slice CT scan at the Indianapolis Heart Center on North Meridian. When I had completed the CT scan, the Cardiologist told me the good news. He announced over the

PA system in the lab that I had absolutely zero blockage in my heart, and I had nothing to worry about.

It was then I decided, since I had no blockages, that I would embark on the Atkins Diet which featured high protein and fat, and low carbohydrates. I loved eggs and bacon, both of which were on the diet, and other high-protein foods and different kinds of meat. In 2014, ten years later, an Adult Fitness Center Graduate Student where I regularly exercised in the mornings, came around and asked me to let him check me for Carotid Artery Blockage. I said "Sure, but I have no blockage at all." When he finished, he backed up a little and told me, I think you have 70 percent blockage in your left Carotid Artery. I told him he was wrong and should do it again. And again, he came up with the same reading. He said they would forward their findings to my doctor, and I should go to the hospital and get it checked. The Staff Supervisor came over to me and checked the Ultrasound reading and confirmed it. She agreed I should see my doctor soon to review what they had found.

So I scheduled an Ultrasound test for Carotid Artery Blockage, and began reading about what they were telling me. I read on the Mayo Clinic website that anything over 50 percent blockage qualifies for an Endarterectomy where they open up the artery in your neck and strip out the fat. I didn't want that kind of surgery, so I began to ponder my options. That is when I learned of my friend's surgery that had almost cost him his life and decided I needed another option. The only other option that I could find was to diet and go on a Vegan Diet.

To assist us with our transitioning to a Vegan Diet, we accompanied our vegan friends—the Branams and Pearsons—on a Vegan Cruise where we learned about Dr. Michael Greger and his New York Times Best-selling book *How Not to Die*. Linda and I have been following Greger's Vegan diet since 2016, and in 2019, instead of having 70 percent blockage of both my Carotid Arteries, by December 2019, my Carotid Artery readings showed less than 50 percent blockage in both of my Carotid Arteries. I now do not have to look forward to two Carotid Endarterectomies where they strip the fat out of my Carotid Arteries—a very dangerous operation I do not ever want to have. Thanks be to God for the Vegan diet and a willingness to learn about it, and Linda's willing spirit that urges her to cook our Vegan diet food night after night. We are both healthier, have lost weight, have more energy, and our blood pressure has dropped as well. The "not-so-good news" is that in eating more than a handful of nuts a day as I drive long distances, in June 2022, my doctor alerted me that my annual Carotid Artery Blockage test revealed my assessment had sneaked up to read 50–70 percent blockage (not quite as bad as before but dangerous), and since that reading, I have stopped eating nuts by the handful to keep myself alert and awake as I drive. What that recent reading reveals is that if I rely on something that is not healthy to keep myself awake, I can just as easily add back the blockage to my arteries without knowing the damage I am doing. So now, I am judiciously avoiding eating lots of nuts, even if I think they have a good effect in keeping me awake as I drive. Instead, I stop and walk periodically or rely on celery and hummus or similar foods that are not high in fats to keep me alert. That strategy, along with my continuing Carotid Artery monitoring, has diminished my Carotid Artery blockage to a sub-50 percent reading again in 2023.

My doctor said it was very difficult to transition to a Vegan diet from a "normal" diet where one eats meat and dairy and vegetables and a great variety of things. The "Normal" diet is referenced as the SAD (Standard American Diet) because so many of our illnesses are the result of ingesting the Standard American Diet for many years and literally killing ourselves by what we choose to eat and what we choose to leave out of our diets. When I knew the options were either "change my diet" or "someday have two Endarterectomies," the choice was easy! Remember my cousin Bill and what the SAD diet and the ice cream did for him. That's as SAD as anything I can think of!

Chapter 52

Leading Me Through My Shadow of Death: Cancer

Even as I do what I can to wind up this book, stories come upon me that must be told, so here are the two final stories God has put on my heart. This book is leading me... God is leading me. This continues for me...stories unravel...they must be told, and yours must be told too, your family, your children, your grandchildren, your friends, your brothers and sisters in Christ, those you've never met before, to strangers and associates alike, to all who will listen, to share the Good News that God is with you—that He never leaves you, that He leads you on. That His fingerprints are everywhere if you'll just look for them. So after more than six years now of writing and remembering and revering God, here is one of the last two stories I must tell.

In the Bible, David writes in Psalm 23, "Even though I walk through the Valley of the Shadow of Death, I will fear no evil, for You are with me. Your Rod and your Staff—they comfort me. You prepare a place for me in the presence of my enemies. You anoint my head with oil. My cup runs over. Surely goodness and mercy will follow me all the days of my life, and I will dwell in the House of the Lord, forever."

How does David know this? How do I know this; because I am seeing it, day after day. Night after long night, at the end of a journey; at the beginning of another journey—Your Hand, dear Lord, is always upon me. When I look for You, I find you. When I do not look for You, because of Your hovering presence, I sense You have found me! How can I merit such mercy and love? But it is not on merit, but a gift from You and Your Holy spirit. You go before me and make my ways, smooth, even when they feel so very bumpy!

The Valley of the Shadow of Death... in Israel, on the way down to Jericho, 3,500 feet below Jerusalem, there is a Valley aptly named "The Valley of the Shadow of Death." It is the Wadi Qelt! Why did people fear it? Because it is a very narrow valley, hemmed in by very steep walls that meander downward for eighteen miles and only at midday does the sun touch the floor. So it is mired in shadows from dawn until dusk, and in the shadows, it is a fearful place where people have died and rumors tell passers-by that their very lives may well be in danger if they choose this shorter path to get from Jericho to Jerusalem or from Jerusalem to Jericho. Everyone has heard the tales, and the story of the Good Samaritan, and many fear going by that route when they have to travel between these two cities.

Cancer! The Bane of our existence. One of the most hated words and terrorizing diagnoses you can have in our culture in this day of terrors, surprises, victimizing and cruel circumstances. When wars rage on in far countries and on the very streets of our cities, towns, and farms. Cancer! How can that be a diagnosis for me?

A year ago, a friend who has been a friend for over forty years, called me from his room in the hospital to ask: "Jim, I have Cancer! Can you come and visit me before I go into surgery tomorrow?"

What do you say to that request? How can you say "No?" What do you say when you arrive? How can you look this deadly "beast" in the eyes and snarl and confront

310

it with all your might to encourage and comfort a loved one, a friend, or a stranger who is being strangled by this unwelcome guest? What if it were you on the other end of this dilemma? Where do you go for peace—God's peace?

So my friend, Wayne, called me and said, "Can you come?" And of course, I did. That's what you would hope your friend would do when you call and say, "Something I never thought would happen is knocking at my door. Can you come?" I had to say "Yes! I'll be there shortly!"

And so the odyssey, the magnificent dance began. Not lilting or graceful! Not wanting this for him or me! Not knowing where or how to move about, but willingly, to support, to pray with, to listen, to consider what was happening, and Who was present, but being there with my heart and my ears and my mind open to the scary presence that had somehow entered our lives.

I talked with Wayne into the night and tried to comfort him, reassuring Wayne that "God had this too!" This was something Wayne knew from his years in church and in Bible studies and in conversations with others who had walked with him over the years. But when it's MY CANCER, somehow that's different! It's immediate! It's my life! This is the most real thing I can imagine, and it's here and now! Where do we start?

"God is with us, Wayne!" I assured him. "We know that because we have read His very words, indelibly inscribed on our hearts and minds over years and years of claiming that incredible volley of promises He has waved as a flag over Abram, and Isaac, and Jacob and Israel, and all of the world.

"Some see the flag waving and are caught up in His grandeur and persistent love and history. Some never choose to see God's love, and walk alone, proudly, in a bluff against the vagaries of life, knowing there is a showdown coming, but not knowing what it will be or when. But in their own overconfidence, believing they will 'hunker down' and get to the other side of whatever it is. Because they are 'tough' or 'resolute' or 'resilient' or hardened by life or circumstances that pale beside this one.

So we prayed, asking God to confirm to us His Glory and His might, and His presence, and His confidence that regardless of all of our sins (and they are many), He has gone before us and forgiven us in the sacrifice of Jesus Christ on the Cross of Calvary. God has not done this because we are special, or have earned forgiveness, or infinitely faithful, but because we have decided to recognize that on our own, we can never measure up to the holiness that would earn us the right to stand or kneel, or lie prostrate in the presence of a perfect, Holy, Loving, Grace-filled, Forgiving Creator. No! God says and shows us in manifold ways, that He has loved us before the beginning of the world and throughout eternity if we will only believe in Him and His only son, Jesus. When we claim Him as our Lord and Savior and declare that faith to all who will listen in the unique ways God has provided for us in our gifts, our talents, our foibles, and our missteps where we thank Him countless times for picking us up when we fall down, God forgives us and saves us. That's it! As you've already read, I've done this multiple times.

Micah records that God tells us there and in other Books of the Bible and other ways that when God forgives our sins, because of Jesus' sacrifice on the Cross, ALL our sins—past, present, and future—were washed away, and when we appear before God with Jesus at His right hand as He tells us in Revelation, we will be washed clean of our sins and be "white as snow" in our purity. How can that be? Being there, calling the God of the Universe, "Abba, Father," is the ultimate miracle that by faith, we will see this in His presence when we are with Him face-to-face!

Look at Micah 7:19 where God speaks to us through the Prophet, saying: "*You will again have compassion on us; you will tread our sins underfoot and hurl all our iniquities into the depths of the sea.*"

Why? Because this was God's plan from the beginning.

So Wayne and I pray in his hospital room, thank God for His loving kindness and eternal forgiveness, and claim His healing of our hearts first, our bodies next, and our spirits eternally, and the Peace of God enters the room. I cannot tell you how we knew then, but we knew by faith, that God was in control. What does that mean in a moment of crisis? It means, we don't have to carry the load alone!

We don't have to carry the load! That's what it means. So throughout the twelve months we endured visit after visit to the Cancer Center, to being poked and prodded, radiated, infused, treated in every way, we knew—Wayne knew—he was in God's hands first and the doctors' hands as assigned by God.

One week ago, the doctors reported that for now, Wayne is in remission. There is no observable Cancer in his system or in his body! Praise God with us for that. Is his remission permanent? In God's eyes, it always was! In our eyes and in our hearts, we only have gratitude and an oversupply of hope.

Let me skip to my own Cancer diagnosis now. *"Surely it was for my benefit that I suffered such anguish. In Your love you kept me from the pit of destruction; You have put all my sins behind Your back"* (Isaiah 38:17).

As I read these words, written seven hundred years before the Messiah was born, I remember also David's words in Psalm 139:16, where David writes: "Your eyes saw my unformed body; all the days ordained for me were written in Your book before one of them came to be."

Everything I know informs me that God sees the end from the beginning. And nothing that happens takes God by surprise.

I do not believe He makes us act in any way, but He knows in advance, the choices we will make. And I choose Him out of love and adoration, and out of the context of my moments, days, years, and life adventures... I am created to praise Him eternally, and I choose Him because of Who He is, not because He makes me choose Him. I love You God, and as Rich Mullens wrote in his lyric: "I will always praise You! I will praise You in the morning. I will learn to walk in Your ways. And step by step, You will lead me, and I will follow You all of my days."

Chapter 53

Truth Is Stranger Than Fiction: Where Are You Now, God?

Well, I've told you many stories, and there are many more I have left untold. I love each one of you, and hope and pray for a long and healthy and productive life doing whatever God has created you to do—something that fits your gifts and your passions, and hopefully, that includes leaning on His guidance and love whenever you need it.

Did you know that one of the last things Jesus does before offering the Disciples the bread and the wine of the Last Supper in the Upper Room was to comfort and share with them, for the last time, what they should NOT do and what they should do? In all that happened that night, Jesus was talking about His relationship with them and ultimately, HIS relationship with us—those of us who will choose to know about Him from the disciples' testimony. Very soon after that, Jesus is taken away by the Temple Guards to be tested, cross-examined, whipped, scourged, and crucified as a sacrifice for our sins and the sins of all who will trust in Him.

In fact, that night, before Judas identifies Jesus for the Temple Guards, Jesus even specifically prays for us there in John 17:20–21, where Jesus (praying to God His Father), says, "My prayer is not for them (the disciples) alone. I pray also for those who will believe in Me through their message."

That prayer is for you and me.

Jesus begins His last talk with His disciples before the last supper by saying in John 14: "Do not let your hearts be troubled. Trust in God! Trust also In Me!" That is the secret.

If you want to hear Jesus' last words on earth before He left His disciples, His words are all recorded by John in John's Gospel, chapters 14–17. Finally, Jesus admonishes them all: "Remain in Me and I will remain in you. The one who remains in Me and I in him bears much fruit, for apart from Me, you can do nothing."

Later He says, "No one comes to the Father except through Me" (John 14:6). If you want to be with God now in this life, and in the life to come, Jesus is the one on the other side of the door where you must knock.

You might have seen the picture of Christ standing at the door (see the illustration on the back cover). Remember He says in John's Revelation, the final book in the Bible: "Behold, **I stand at the door and knock.** If anyone hears My voice and opens the door, I will come in to you and dine with you, and you with Me." You'll notice, if you look at that picture—THAT DOOR HAS ONLY ONE HANDLE and it is on YOUR side. You have to open the door to Jesus! It's up to you to open the door of your heart. Just ask Him to come into your heart and help you to trust what you know of Him. He will not disappoint, just as He did not disappoint me when I began to read the Bible and His words like Jeanette Clift suggested. When you ask Him to show you what He is saying, He will do that for you as He did for me.

Having given my life to Jesus several times and giving it to Him anew, each morning, my goal is to keep doing that until I go to be with Him forever in heaven when my days here are completed.

Until then, my heartfelt wish is that you would come to know Jesus and trust Him the way I have learned to trust

Him. I pray for you that your life will be full and filled with the blessings that can only come from God and the Joy that comes from knowing you will be with the people you love and with God and his son Jesus who created you, forever and ever. And finally, I pray that through knowing Jesus, you will discover the mysteries of the beginning of all mankind through to the end and will be filled with God's peace and Joy forever.

That is my wish and my blessing for you—each of you... even now and for your future here on earth.

Addison, Steve, Aubrey, Ben, Arianna, Elliott, Sofia, Caroline, and Nathan. You are all special, and every one of you is unique and made in the image of God. That means simply that love is the most important thing you will ever experience and the most important gift you will ever give anyone.

The central verse in the Bible is the one that summarizes everything that God came to tell you... It is smack dab in the center of the Bible with the same number of books, the same number of Chapters, and the same number of verses in front of and behind this summary statement. Check it out and see if you don't agree. It covers everything.

If you were God, wouldn't you put the verse that summarizes what the entire Bible says, in the very center of your Holy Book? Well, He did that, and I am sure it is not an accident.

Psalm 118:8—read it and live it, and your joy will be complete. And you will *know* God! If you will read Psalm 118:8 and believe it to be true as I do, you will find joy and peace on your journey...what I call my last great adventure: living the life in the Spirit that God has given to each of us.

And for our children of "another mother," as Linda calls you—those for whom we have agreed to be YOUR American parents, mentors, or however you would identify us to your family or your friends (for Jockel and Anne, Michael and Anja, Tinku and Rustin, Diane and your husband, Hyejin and Jaehoon, and Josh)—this IS intended for you—you who have been grafted in, even though not a one of you is our progeny except as a beneficiary of the promise Jesus high-lights in His final talk with the disciples, where He directly prays for you and where I say in this narrative, "You, too, are children of the promise my mother spoke of."

Not one of you is my birth child, and yet every single one of you has won my heart.

May you always walk in the Light as He (Jesus) is in the Light, for in God, there is no darkness at all...

I love you all.

Grandpa Jim

Chapter 54

THE BEST FOR LAST

I said I'd saved the best for last, and here it is: A Dream from God… What a Gift!

This really happened to me on February 23, 2007, about five in the morning.

Here is my Dream of God revealed:

We were all assembled in a large hall, everyone in choir robes.

We were there because God had called us to assemble.

We were all waiting on packages to be delivered like Federal Express Boxes.

Then we got the word, and we made a dash to be there.

Once we got there, we were told that the angel of the Lord was going to announce what was in the box.

We were told to take the message out of the box, and inside, there was a brown cardboard box, that folded together.

When we were told to do so, we pulled the flaps out of the box, and it opened to reveal a book.

In the book, there were only seven things written:

1. While the angel of the Lord was announcing these things, there were professors in the crowd that were

answering the angel's questions that were seemingly, rhetorical. But they would answer out loud anyway. And the angel of the Lord would wait for them, seeming to understand that they had to say their say. The photographer from the newspaper was trying to get photos all the time of the angel of the Lord announcing these revelations, and finally, decided he should get the two professors in the shot, along with the angel of the Lord. And I remember, I was in the left hand side of the shot. The photographer was only interested in taking the picture, not in what the angel was saying.

2. The angel was off to my left, in a choir pew, along with several other rows of pews, and he was standing, announcing his words and our instructions, and one professor was to his right (my left) and the other was in the end of the congregation assembled, and he was sitting to my left (the angel's right) and the two professors were taking turns making comments—answering the angel's rhetorical questions, and I remember thinking, "I know the answers too, but don't we want to hear what the angel has to say and what is in this book we've been waiting for?"

3. Yet the angel was patient, and he waited for the professors to have their say.

4. The contents of the book:

5. There were seven items:
   - First, Love the Lord your God with all your heart, your soul, your mind, and your strength.
   - Second, go on doing what you are doing
   - Third, be sociable—be with people, share my message. Tell them what I have told you.
   - Fourth, keep running the race. Do not give up. Do not quit.

- Fifth, tell others who weren't able to come to the angel's announcement, about this event and what happened.
- Sixth, remember the other words I've given you, and meditate on them.
- Seventh, the poor will always be with you. Do not become discouraged by that, but neither do I tell you to sell all that you have. Give generously, and keep doing what you are doing. The day of my coming is near.

George and Linda weren't there. Linda called to say they weren't able to be at the gathering, and so they didn't get their box. What happened, Linda asked? So I told her. Then I woke up, being amazed at this dream that I had had, and wondering what I should do with what I had dreamed. Why me, why now? What am I to do with this? How will I ever remember it all?

This is frightening and wonderful, all at the same time.

I feel like I am supposed to keep doing what I am doing. This is not a call to retirement. This is a call to action. But to what action? I am challenged, and I await further instructions…

Subsequent to the dream, I woke Linda at 6:00 AM. She rolled over and said, "What is it?"

And I gushed: "I just had a dream! But it wasn't like any dream I have ever had. It was a dream from God, and it was an angel talking with me and lots of other people that were assembled in our church at High Street."

And she said what I was to hear again and again from others as I told them about the dream. She said, "That's not like any dream I've ever had. Why do you think it's from God?"

And I said, "The angel told me to share it with everyone, and frankly, I have to do that. I know it's not like any dream I've ever had either, and I've never had a dream with an angel in it before, and certainly not one telling me what to do with the dream. So I just have to share it with everyone who will listen to me telling them about it. Those were my instructions."

She remarked again, "Well, it's not like any dream I've ever heard of either."

And so it went when I told my pastors, and when I told my Sunday School Class, and when I told my fellow professors at Ball State and my Department Chair, and my friends. They all said basically the same thing. "It's not like any dream I've ever heard of before."

Well, I don't know for sure what the angel was telling me, but this I know:

The dream was from God. The dream was a real angel. I was not afraid, and I am still not afraid to share this dream, and I believe I am doing what God has told me to do for His glory, not for mine.

When you retire, or before if you feel like it, ask your kids or grandchildren if they would like to know what you were doing before you married Grandma or Grandpa. And if they say "Yes," ask them if they would read it if you wrote it down.

If they also say "Yes" to that, then get busy. You have a final assignment that will never be completely absorbed or "graded" in your lifetime. However, it may be the most important and enduring project you undertake...

This labor of love has taken me on a journey I did not expect and that I did not request, but it has been fun and enlightening, even for me, and it will be for you. In the meantime, you will have opportunities to share what you really think about a lot of your life you have never discussed with others—family and friends and sometimes, even acquaintances, and you will be called to testify to what you truly believe about life and the God who made us all.

Becoming an author for your family will be worth the effort for you, and unforgettable for them. And in the end, doing so will bless your children and grandchildren, and also bless you because you will have added the last chapter to a book that they will never read in any other way. May God be with you as you journey through the seasons of your life and share them with love for those you love the most...

My Final Thoughts and My Blessing for You

"Thank you again for being part of our "family" in the broadest sense. Some of you who will read this will know what I mean, and some will only wonder how you were "grafted in" and became a part of our "family." But all of you should know that "family," by our definition, is the circle of persons who have come into our lives that we have decided to love and connect with on a permanent or semi-permanent basis and are those with whom we hope to sustain a long relationship for as many years as we have.

If you are not related in any way and do not even know us, then I hope what I have written here is something that has uplifted you and your life and given you some ideas about how this author has been led to relate to a personal and loving God who knew me from before I was born, and stayed with me through the good times and the bad.

Ultimately, I am convinced this God whom I worship, continues leading me, even as I finish this book and you close the cover for good.

My hope is that in hearing my stories, this narrative has brought you closer to a living relationship with Jesus Christ who is my Savior, my Lord, my God, and my friend, and without whom I would never have made it this far in my personal journey.

May God continue to bless you with instances like the many I have recounted here, where you whirl around and shout, out loud, "Wow! I am seeing the fingerprints of God in this." And that you'll share what you are seeing with those around you—your family, your friends, your colleagues, and particularly, your children.

Doing so will broaden and lengthen the Joy of your life and give you hope in times of sorrow, Joy in place of happiness, and security in the midst of uncertainty about knowing where you will be tomorrow when your life on this earth comes to an end.

Most importantly, continually thank God for all He has given you...your family, your very life, your friends, your gifts, your sunrises and sunsets, this incredible earth on which we live, and the people He has surrounded you with. They are the greatest gifts of all, and yet are the most easily taken for granted and the most abruptly, taken from you.

And finally, thank God for the adventure on which He has taken you from learning to walk, to talk, to eat and ride bikes and to communicate what is in your heart, and share your discoveries with those whom God has surrounded you with when you most needed help and least expected it.

Those are the "Divine Appointments" of which I have written. And they are all true. May you have your own surprises for which there is no other answer than "God is present" and "a present help in time of trouble" (Psalm 46:1).

If you don't remember anything else from this book, remember this: "God Loves you and wants to have a permanent relationship with you. May He bless you in the unique ways He needs to so that as you seek Him, you will find Him, sooner than later.

Trust me: I've learned the hard way AND the easy way: The real joy is in Walking through your life *with* Him...

May the Lord bless and protect you; may the Lord's face radiate with joy because of you; may He be gracious to you, show you His favor, and give you His peace, now and forever more. (Numbers 6: 24–26)

And because of His grace, may we meet again, some-day in His timing, at the feet of Jesus…
Amen!

Epilogue

There are many more stories that could be told, but thanks to Grandma Linda, I was admonished to shorten this, or she promised to urge me not to publish it. That this has reached print in a somewhat longer version is a tribute to her love and forgiveness and willingness to subject you to a few extra pages, after all.

As we arrived at the end of this process, I thought I was done and would have been except for our forty-fifth Anniversary Trip to Hilton Head where sixteen members of our family gathered for a great time together and a party of sorts to celebrate that Linda and I made it together for this extended period. For all who came and those who wanted to but could not, thank you. It was a very special time, made even more so by one singular event.

On Wednesday of that week, our grandson, Ben, and his fiancée, Kaelyn, decided at about ten o'clock that night to go for a final dip in the ocean, with their clothes on. They carefully emptied their pockets and walked gingerly into the surf with its crashing waves—it was warm and inviting. The sun had already set after a day of high eighties, and a dip in the ocean seemed particularly appropriate.

I am sure they exchanged some wonderful words and hugs and kisses like those who are planning to get married, and then they were on the beach again, filling their pockets with their things to go back to the condo where Ben's parents were hosting them and probably wondering where they were. The dilemma came when Kaelyn reached for her phone on the towel where they had carefully placed their things, only to discover her phone was not there.

In the heat of this romantic setting and the crashing surf, she had overlooked her phone and, along with it, in her phone case, her driver's license, credit card, and room key, snug as a bug in a rug. And while she thought she had removed this priceless package from her pocket, she had not. So with the abandonment of young adults, Kaelyn waltzed into the ocean with the man she loved. In short order, they were back on the beach. Oops! Oops! BIG-TIME! They searched the sand and the area around their towel, but the phone was not there.

What to do? Ultimately, they called her father and reported what had happened. He pinged the phone, but they couldn't find it. He said, "I got it," but they couldn't see it or hear it. He said again to no avail, "It's in the ocean." It was in the ocean, but they couldn't locate it. Ultimately, her dad agreed to call the insurance company in the morning and order a new phone so she would have it to work with her two separate schools for her internships in the coming fall and connect with everyone who depended on her to be reach-able by phone and text, her last two busy semesters. When she completed her internships, Kaelyn would graduate in May from Indiana Wesleyan with her degree in Art Therapy.

NOT HAVING a phone would not be an option! No one said anything about this to Grandpa and Grandma. Ben's father was feeling a little under the weather, and they decided to head home early Saturday. But after Friday night's festivities at the Japanese Steakhouse, everyone felt refreshed, and Ben and his folks decided to stay until Sunday and drive the 808 miles home in one day. Saturday morning, they were all on the beach, enjoying the Sun and ocean breeze, and someone mentioned to me that Kaelyn had lost her cell phone Wednesday night on a late-night visit to the ocean and had ordered a new phone so she could reconnect when she got home.

When I heard this, I immediately headed for the beach. When I got there, I asked Kaelyn what happened, and she briefly told me. I asked if she had prayed about it and asked God to show her where it was—admittedly an audacious question, and she had not, so there on the beach, I knelt down on one knee and prayed with her that God would show us where it was and help her to find it. After that, I got up and walked over and took pictures of Ben and his father playing pickleball, and a tall, thin man was wandering our way with a Magnetometer, looking for lost coins, jewelry, and other things that had been dropped in the sand. I ran up to him and asked if he would look for the phone. I told him I'd give him twenty dollars if he found it and returned it to the Marriott Barony Beach, and he said he would. But he quickly added, "I've never found a phone before. If I find it, I'll turn it in. If it's here, and I'm over it, the phone will light up this gizmo like a Christmas Tree. But I've never found one before. I'll be glad to keep looking like I do every three or four days, but I've never found one before. I don't need the money. I live up the way on the beach, and this is just something I do for fun. I found a gold ring this year and also an earring, but that's what I usually find. And that's not often."

Shortly after that, Kaelyn came up to him and asked him if he would keep looking for her... that the phone case also had her driver's license and credit card and room key, and she was turning twenty-one in four days. At that, he said, "Then it's really important that I find it. You can't be twenty-one and not have your driver's license." And they both laughed. His name was Mark, and he continued to look for it.

I went back to Barony Beach, and unknown to me, Mark did keep looking. Not twenty minutes later, he walked over to Kaelyn and dropped the phone in her towel. "Oh, Golly!" she stammered. "You found it." He smiled. Kaelyn didn't know what to say, and they asked if they could pay him. Mark just shrugged his shoulders, noticed their cooler, and said, "No, that's not necessary, but do you have a cold beer in there? That sure sounds good." So they handed Mark a can of beer, and he sat down on the sand and visited with all of them for a few minutes. He said he lived just north of the breakwater on the beach and that this was the largest prize he'd ever found.

Then, all of a sudden, Kaelyn remembered me and our prayer, along with hers earlier and her family's prayers and others in her church family... and she took off running to our condo to tell us the news.

Earlier, after we prayed and talked with them and with Mark, I went back toward the Barony Beach Resort and stopped at the equipment rental and sales desk run by Alisha. She said no one had turned in a phone that week, nor had they ever turned in a phone. I asked if she was a praying person. She said she was not because she had been raised in a Christian Cult community and been taught a lot of things that she now knew were not true, so she didn't pray anymore. But she knew some people who did pray, and she would pass it on.

I told her God knew where the phone was and that forty-five years ago, we had lost my daughter's dental retainer for her teeth in Lake Michigan, and after praying and looking, thirty-five minutes later, my wife had picked it up in the surf, and we had run back to the picnic table and celebrated in the miracle God had given us. The retainer was a mile and a half down the beach. Alisha said she had seen some crazy things too, but she doubted that we would find the phone again if it was lost in the ocean. After talking with Alisha, I immediately went to the front desk and talked with Kaela who was on duty. I told her what had happened and asked if anything had been turned in. I gave her my card, told her the story about the lost retainer forty-five years earlier, and went up to our room.

Interestingly enough, about thirty-five minutes after I had gone down to the beach, someone knocked on our Condo door. When I went to open the door, it was Kaelyn and there, in her hand was the lost phone... Mark had found it with his Magnetometer about twenty minutes earlier, and she had run back to show us and tell us the good news: her phone had been found. Wow! How could that happen?

After two huge downpours on Thursday and Friday evenings, two nights with lots of rain and pounding surf...after seventy-two hours of wondering what had happened to her phone, there it was in her hand!

I went down to the beach and all the kids were sitting around All Y'all's Beach Bar and Grill, talking about the wonderful time they had had. And I walked up to them. "You'll never forget this trip," I said, "partly because it has been so wonderful, but also because forty-five years ago, I lost Kirsten's retainer in Lake Michigan, and thirty-five minutes later, Grandma and I found it in the lake. I lost it. Grandma and I prayed and asked God where it was, and thirty-five minutes later, Linda picked it up out of the surf. God showed us where the retainer was.

Today, you were here when Kaelyn, and I prayed about her phone and credit card and room key and driver's license, and just a few minutes ago, her phone was found by that crazy guy with the Magnetometer, the guy scanning the beach in front of where you guys were sitting. The phone had been there all along. Remember this day. No one at Barony Beach has ever known when a phone that was lost in the ocean was found again.

"This is a gift God has given all of us. When we pray, He hears us, and sometimes, He answers our prayers in ways that astonish us, just like today. And you were here, and you can ask Kirsten or Steve or Brian about the retainer. And forty-five years ago, God answered our prayer so you will KNOW that God answers prayer. You were here, and you will never forget this day or what God has done for Kaelyn and for us."

And I walked away. This story is over. But then again, it will never be over for Addison and Michael and Aubrey and Kaelyn and Ben and their families who will hear the story and wonder about how and why God answered our prayer. A phone is such a little thing unless it's yours. So are the hairs on your head the Bible tells us that God has numbered… (Matt. 10:30). Thanks be to God… what we can all see now, a little more clearly is that the Incredible Journey continues…

Frankly, I have had a wonderful life, and was featured a few years ago at our Civic Theater as Joseph in *It's A Wonderful Life.* I've mentored a number of people over the years, hundreds of students with problems in our Telecommunications Department, new colleagues at Ball State, community contacts, and others who have sought me out. But only once, did I get to mentor an angel. It was a great experience, and night after night, "Clarence" always got everything right. That's more than I can say for myself, but I've been blessed to enjoy it all.

Thank you God for allowing me to complete this journey. And thank *you* for reading my book. It's been my pleasure to share the adventures I've had along the way with Him, and now, here with you.

May God also bless you with adventures you cannot ignore and HAVE to tell others about. The Bible is full of them, and so is YOUR life. Learn to recognize them for what they are and choose to honor God by sharing them with your family, friends, and even with strangers who see what is happening in this incredible adventure with God in your life. It is the best way ever to thank Him and repay him for His favor He has shown you. I firmly believe that honoring God is the highest calling any of us will ever have.

So start looking, and when you do, God will surprise you by granting you His favor in unexpected ways, and like me, you'll begin to look closely at what is happening to you and soon be identifying God's fingerprints are there, in the midst of everything!

About the Author

James R. Needham retired after twenty-seven years of broadcasting and seventeen years of teaching at Ball State University. He began as a production engineer and ended his broadcast career as General Manager of WIPB-TV in Muncie, Indiana.

During his time in broadcasting, Jim worked for WTHI-TV in Terre Haute, Indiana; at Eastern Kentucky University as Television Producer; and as Community Affairs Director and Administrative Assistant to the GM at WISH-TV in Indianapolis.

In 1976, Jim moved to WIPB-TV as General Manager. There, he was responsible for growing the station from ten to thirty-two employees and for bringing Bob Ross and *The Joy of Painting* to Public Broadcasting in 1982–1992. He helped plan and build the new Ball Building, housing the WIPB-TV station on the Ball State University campus and retired from broadcasting in 1993.

Jim then became an Assistant Professor, teaching in Ball State University's Telecommunications Department and serving as its TCOM Departmental Advisor from 1993 until his retirement in 2010.

In his community service and as a Christian, Jim served on the Chamber of Commerce, the Salvation Army, as Young Life Leader, Adult Sunday School teacher, Church Pastor / Parish Chair, Missions Chair, Mission Trip Leader, Emmaus Walk participant, Cancer Patient Advocate, and

Prayer Project convenor. He has chaired numerous community fund-raising events, and is an active member of Rotary International.

Jim married the former Linda Slavin in 1977 and they have three children, nine grandchildren, and six other adults who claim them as Mentors or American Parents and live in Muncie, Germany, Denmark, Korea, Denver, and California.

Jim has Bachelor's and Master's degrees from Indiana State University and is convinced that everything we do shows how we love God and helps us learn to see God's fingerprints everywhere and accept His love through Jesus Christ as the Gift of Grace He is...